HELP. THEM. HEAL.

Teaching You Both How to Heal Your Relationship After Sexual Betrayal

CAROL JUERGENSEN SHEETS, aka *Carol the Coach*, LCSW, CSAT, CCPS-S, CPC-S, PCC

SANO PRESS, LLC
CLAREMONT, CA

1st Edition

Layout, book design and graphic design by Chris Bordey.

ISBN-13: 978-1-956620-01-6

TABLE of CONTENTS

CHAPTER 18: THE THIRD PHASE OF PARTNER BETRAYAL—

Author's Note

~

When I started as a Certified Sexual Addictions Therapist, I felt a bit uneasy about using the labels "sex addicts" or "partners." But as the field has evolved, I have found that sex addicts feel very comfortable with this term since it captures how unmanageable and out of control their life had become as a result of the addiction.

Later the World Health Organization referred to it as Compulsive Sexual Behavior Disorder (CSBD), and I knew that I could reference people with this disorder as having CSBD. That description does not fit the purpose of this book, so I am going to return to my original roots. As I talk directly to your coupleship and to you both individually, I will be referring to the person with CSBD as "the sex addict" and to the betrayed partner as "the partner."

I also would like to clarify that we know addicts come in all sizes, shapes, socio-economic levels, and genders. I am using this book to speak to the largest population that I work with, which is male sex addicts and female partners. I recognize this requires that couples who do not fall into that category, like gay couples or couples where the wife is the sex addict and the husband is the betrayed partner, to adapt some of my writings to make it relevant to them. I regret that you who are a part of these underserved populations *cannot* read this book as if I wrote it specifically for you. I certainly work with couples of all types and recognize that you have unique circumstances that make the betrayal and the recovery more difficult. I am sorry that it is not simpler for you because it does add to your trauma to have to adapt to what is already a difficult situation. Contact me at carol@carolthecoach.com if you would like to partner with me to customize these books for your specific situation.

Introduction

A Beacon of Hope

This is a guidebook to help you both navigate the ordeal of sexual betrayal. Other than a child's death, it is likely the worst thing you will ever have to go through as a couple. Despite this pain and trauma, there is very little offered to get you through this crisis.

For the Addict: You have had to endure an addictive process that has stolen your identity and robbed you of your values. As a result, you have lied to the one whom you loved the most. Now since discovery, you are watching her get sucked into the darkest despair a spouse can ever encounter! You are waking up from the world of addiction and witnessing the consequences of your behaviors, and you are truly sickened by the devastation you have caused. You are trying to do damage control knowing you are the perpetrator of the damage, all while questioning every fiber of your existence.

As the spouse, your whole life as you knew it has changed dramatically. Maybe you sensed something was off, but like most people in a marriage, you attributed it to the rigors of life, the stress a couple can endure, and a development of the life stage you were in. You could not have, nor would you ever have been able to, imagine what was occurring without your knowledge. It has changed your entire sense of knowing, your sense of safety and your uncertainty about the future. How could the man you loved do this to you? Who is this man that you thought you knew so well? How could this have happened to you, and why would God have allowed this into your lives? Now you question everything, and you wonder if you will ever recover from such a breach of trust.

Yet you have purchased this book, and you are secretly hoping the relationship can be repaired. As the partner, you are afraid to admit you are hoping for a reconciliation because what person in their right mind would want to seek, repair, and accept what happened to her? But you understand he has a serious compulsion that he could not stop on his own.

This is not a man who purposely wanted to betray you. He is a man who got involved in unhealthy, unexplainable behavior and tried to stop repeatedly, but he could not manage the compulsion. As he continued to act, the compulsion got stronger, and his focus was on never letting you know that his behavior was uncontrollable and unforgivable, that his brain had been hijacked, and that it was getting worse and worse. There is a part of him that is relieved he has finally been discovered, but he is watching the devastation he has caused and questions if he can live with himself from having caused you so much pain.

As you read this book together, know that my style is to write as if you are in my office, and I am talking to both of you. If I want to write directly to either one of you, I will delineate this by stating "For the Addict" or "For the Partner."

Also, please read this knowing I am going back and forth in helping both of you through the next steps. I trust you will begin to understand my style and how I merge the work you are both doing to move you through this trauma dance you have been doing.

It is imperative you read all the material so that you know what I have said to both of you. You have survived the discovery, and now I will be sharing with both of you what you need to do to stay safe and decide on your future as a couple. It is likely you are both questioning your judgment, and your greatest fear is that this relationship is unsalvageable and you are both wasting your time. But you have hung in there and searched for the right tool, program, or professional that can help you both put this all back together so you can find happiness again.

Well, I want to be the beacon of hope for both of you individually and as a couple. It requires a lot of hard work on both of your parts, but if the willingness is there and he is in good recovery, you can restore the relationship. I hesitate to say that so early in this book, but you can recover together and deepen your relationship. This is because your husband will have learned very important relationship skills as he reads this book that actually will help you both rebuild trust. Couples who get to post-traumatic growth can find ways to give back and enhance the lives of others once they have healed. So there is hope for you as a couple, but it will take time and following the steps in this book for restoration.

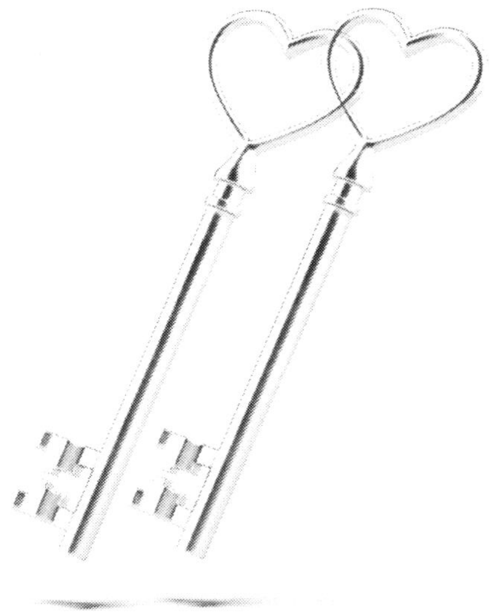

Chapter 1

Willingness is the Key to Restoring Your Relationship

ARE YOU BOTH WILLING TO DO WHAT IT WILL TAKE TO WORK THROUGH SEXUAL BETRAYAL?

You understandably are wanting to know what you can do to get through this ordeal. You both have many questions about whether that is possible and whether you can ever restore the relationship and live a loving, meaningful life. I have worked with many couples who have been able to get through this, but it requires you both to be willing to do the hard work to get through it together.

For the Addict: This means stepping up and doing 80% of the work to help her heal. It requires that you learn how to contain her pain and help her through it, and you must do this over and over again, even when it seems like it is not working. Even when it is met with pushback. And it will be met with pushback because she is unsure of every part of you. She is going to be testing you with every fiber in her body and soul because she cannot believe that your efforts are genuine...After all, look at what you have done to her for all of these years.

Men with sexual addiction or, as the World Health Organization (WHO) refers to it, Compulsive Sexual Behavior Disorder, historically have lacked empathy. The addiction caused you to be self-absorbed and self-interested in hiding your addiction from her so you could continue to feed it.

Look at the WHO's criteria for Compulsive Sexual Behavior Disorder and together identify how many indicators you matched for CSBD.

Compulsive sexual behaviour disorder is characterized by a persistent pattern of failure to control intense, repetitive sexual impulses or urges resulting in repetitive sexual behaviour.

Symptoms may include repetitive sexual activities becoming a central focus of the person's life to the point of neglecting health and personal care or other interests, activities and responsibilities; numerous unsuccessful efforts to significantly reduce repetitive sexual behaviour; and continued repetitive sexual behaviour despite adverse consequences or deriving little or no satisfaction from it.

The pattern of failure to control intense, sexual impulses or urges and resulting repetitive sexual behaviour is manifested over an extended period of time (e.g., 6 months or more), and causes marked distress or significant impairment in personal, family, social, educational, occupational, or other important areas of functioning. Distress that is entirely related to moral judgments and disapproval about sexual impulses, urges, or behaviors is not sufficient to meet this requirement.

As you both read this definition, does this sound like the addict?

To the Addict: Now that you are in recovery, you are going to show, learn, and practice empathy, even when it results in additional conflict. I know that can be very tough for you especially since you want to do the right thing, have reorganized your life, and are in the process of developing a good recovery program. You wonder why she can't feel more secure in all the work you're doing. But the truth of the matter is it takes a traumatized brain anywhere from one to three years to feel safe and stable. If you are in month three, month nine, or perhaps even sixteen months in and she still seems activated and triggered, that needs to be a sign that you need to be even stronger to contain her pain and do the right thing.

We will be talking about empathy in future chapters, but what I want you to realize and understand is that her "brain damage," if you will, is a trauma state caused by the betrayal. It matters not how long it takes to help rebuild this relationship; it is something you should want to do regardless of the outcome or amount of time it takes. I know it can feel very discouraging when it seems like she is not getting better, but I want you to continue to work on the all-important skills necessary to help her heal. Communication is your greatest skill.

In the next few chapters, you will both learn about reflective listening, which is an opportunity for the addict to allow her to vent about the emotional state she is in and concerns she has for the relationship.

As the Partner: You will be giving voice to how the betrayal has shattered the world as you knew it and how your entire world has been violated by his sexual transgressions. Your entire reality is riddled with doubt, and you don't know what is real anymore and are questioning your sanity at every juncture. You wonder how this could have happened to you. Did you miss the signs? Was there something wrong with you that contributed to his addiction? And now, is there something wrong with you for staying and seeing if there is a healing process? Can he really change? Will he return to the addiction? Should you cut your losses? Then you spiral into the anger that you are even having to ask yourself these things. You are a nice person. You would never have done this to him! You ask yourself, "Why am I staying? What is wrong with me? What will people think of me if they find out? Who already knows about this, and do they question my sanity?"

The self-doubt is overwhelming, and the rumination and racing thoughts have taken control. You fear that you are going crazy, and you are scared...You are really scared!

As a couple, you will need to decide if you want to invest in the time it will take to move through the recovery from sexual infidelity. It will be a long journey. Many couples do make the choice to work through it together.

This book is going to show you how to do it, and then you can decide if your relationship is worth the work it is going to take to heal. I always tell partners that now they are in the driver's seat because they get to choose whether to try the recovery road. Many choose it because they do not want to break up their families, finances, and their life more than it is already broken.

If you are both reading this book, you are both motivated to see what is out there to help heal the relationship. It can be done, and, believe it or not, it can be strengthened to a whole new level.

To the Partner: I know you may not feel up to the challenge, so move slowly and take lots of breaks for self-care. He is going to help you by getting better and proving himself to you. If he does not, you can decide how to proceed, but for now keep reading together and look at the steps to heal. You may be ambivalent about how to proceed, and you are reading this book to see if you both possess the stamina it may take to help each other heal.

Just as my first book *Help. Her. Heal.* suggests, if he can help you heal, it will help him grow exponentially. And when you, the partner, allow him to love you, it will restore the love that you thought you had but feared did not exist. This book is going to ask you to take risks, so there will be times when I recommend you try some exercises and activities you may not be ready to explore. Take your time and go slow, but know that therapeutically, it is necessary to try each exercise on to see if it fits both your desire and hope for the future.

When it seems impossible, I would ask you both to use the "Fake It Till You Make It" approach. Although it may sound like a disingenuous request, addicts and partners have found that if they fake it till they make it, they follow the principle of "Act As If." "Act As If" suggests that you decide what you would like for your life and act as if you had the power to make it happen. You cannot control the behaviors of others, but you can, however, control how you let their behaviors affect you both now and in the future.

When people want a particular relationship, specific job, or desired outcome, they should absolutely act as if they are experiencing the outcome of their desires. So if you want this relationship to not only survive but thrive, you should look for ways to heal so you can create a connection that is honest, open, and filled with integrity. If you can clearly name and claim what you want, you can look for opportunities to respond accordingly. In Chapter 18, we will go into more detail about this very important concept, but right now we want to focus on what can make you feel safe.

I would like for you both to practice some vulnerability as you start this book by agreeing to declare an intention for the relationship. If there were no obstacles and you could trust him to maintain a strong recovery program, what kind of relationship would you like to be in, and how could you contribute to it to make it loving and fulfilling?

To the Partner: I would suspect you are too hurt to trust him to give that relationship to you. And that is totally understandable. He has destroyed your sense of reality, and you are questioning everything about your life right now. You may be asking me how I could expect you to make a declaration for the marriage when you are not even sure you can continue it.

However, you are reading this book together and are wondering if you have a chance to rebuild your life together. So for the possibility of the relationship, just put it out there and ask for what you would like. When you write it down, you are more likely to make it happen.

Intention starts with hope. So let's start small and write out a statement that expresses what you would like to get out of reading this book. We will use this as a foundation for your intention statement.

WHAT I HOPE TO GAIN FROM THIS BOOK

Exercise: Both of you need to write out a statement (even though it may change) that "owns" why you want to get through this book and grow stronger. Now I realize you both may have doubts, but part of the intention of this book is to help you navigate through this betrayal and grow stronger so that you can lead the life you deserve!

To the Addict: Our marriage has been through so much, but what I hope to accomplish as a couple as I finish this book is to:

To the Partner: Our marriage has been through so much, but what I hope to accomplish as a couple as I finish this book is to:

Now that you have decided what you want to achieve by reading this book, it is time for you to create an Intention Statement for your marriage.

Despite the fact that there is much uncertainty, spend some quiet time and complete the following statement:

To the Partner: As we work through recovery together, what I want most for my marriage is:

To the Addict: As I work on gaining more and more sobriety and as I continue to improve my relational skills, what I want most for my marriage is:

____

____

____

____

____

Now I would like you both to find a space where you can move to chairs face-to-face and look at each other as you slowly read the Intention Statement. I know it will be difficult to share this level of vulnerability with each other, but it is necessary because it simultaneously plants a seed of hope for the relational recovery that is possible.

This is the first time since the betrayal that either one of you had the courage to dare to hope for more. I applaud you for writing the Intention Statement down and sharing it with your spouse. Hopefully, you both took it well and now feel more grounded to proceed both with caution and the expectation that if you do the work, it works. You will not only repair the relationship, but you will both get stronger!

Note: This small exercise will evoke lots of feelings, so make sure to find some time tonight to journal your feelings about it.

- What feelings came up for you?
- What level of vulnerability occurred?
- Did you believe your spouse?
- Did you recognize a seed of hope as you shared your intention?

As a coach and therapist with over 40 years of experience, I know that setting an intention and making a declaration for what you want in a relationship is very important. If your discovery has occurred in the past 18 to 24 months, it can feel daunting for you, the partner, to "put it out there" that you even want to invest in the marriage. But, if you are reading this book, there is at least a small part of you willing to consider the possibility.

If you are the addict, you probably feel unsure whether you have the right to set an intention or make a declaration, but I promise it will help you stay strong.

Now that you have created an intention for what you hope to get out of this book and what you hope for your marriage as you do the hard work of rebuilding it, I would like for you to take a deep look into what you personally are both willing to do individually to work together on the restoration of your marriage.

This assignment is a bit harder, so I am going to share some intentions and declarations from the couples I have worked with. That way, you will have some idea of what they look like. Later in the book as your relationship gets stronger, I will show you how to further use them to embed the changes you are seeing.

INTENTIONS FOR THE PARTNER:

- I am willing to watch him work diligently on his personal recovery and learn the skills to repair our relationship.
- I want us to build a strong, faith-filled, honest marriage, so I will be open to the changes he is making.
- I will watch my husband's progress, and I will assess whether I can be safe in this marriage.

INTENTIONS FOR THE ADDICT:

- I will do whatever it takes to help her heal and validate her anger as she works through this process.
- I will learn the skills to rebuild the relationship I destroyed and be patient when she pushes back and does not believe in my changes.
- I will develop my empathy skills so I can begin to be worthy of her trust.

Now it is your turn.

I would like both of you to write out your own declaration of what you are willing to do based on the recovery work you have started since discovery day. This declaration will acknowledge the effort and intention you have for this relationship by acknowledging your own work that you may have done or will need to do.

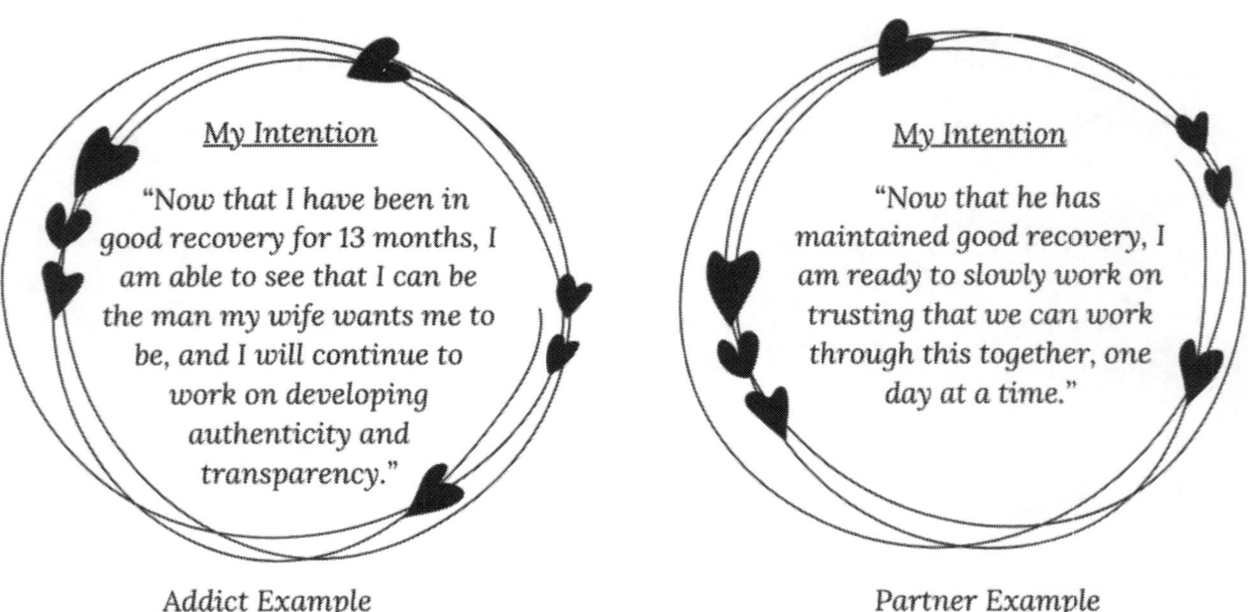

Addict Example

Partner Example

INTENTION STATEMENT FOR OUR MARRIAGE

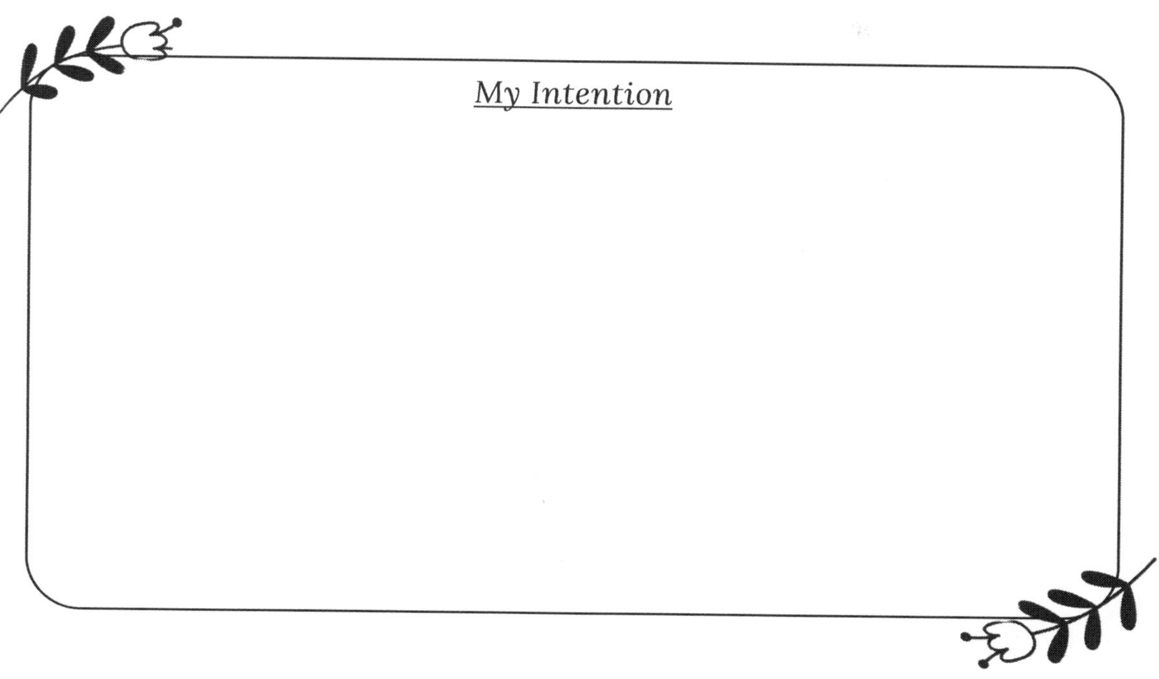

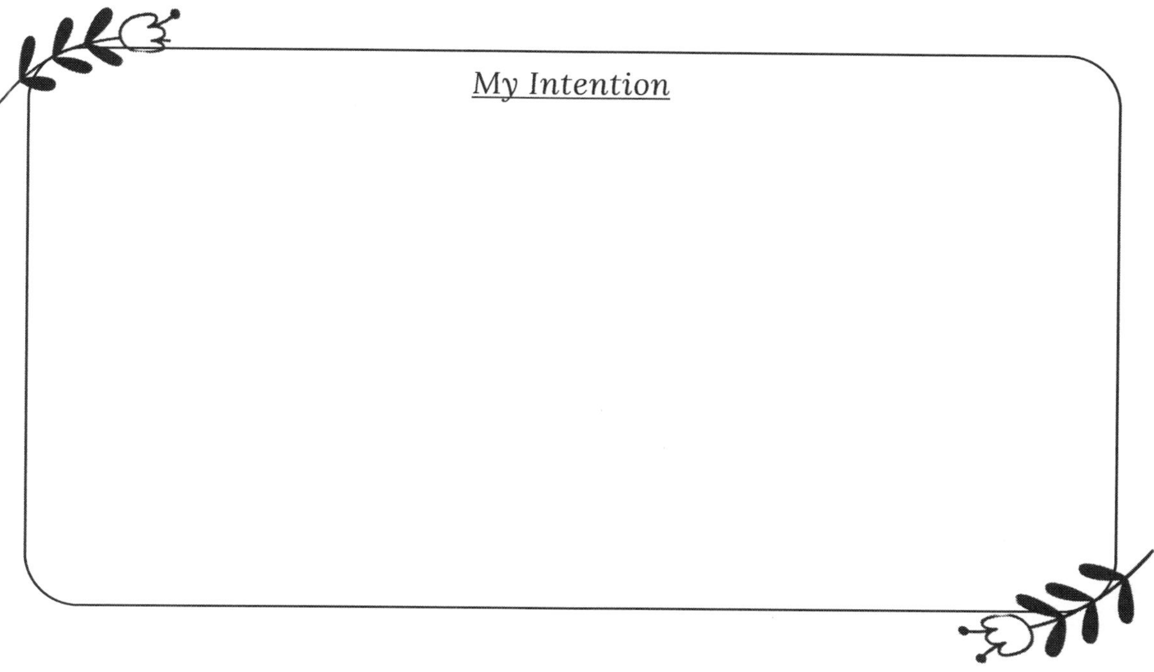

I want to commend you both for your vulnerability and hope. In the book Daring Greatly, Brené Brown, who is the leading expert on vulnerability, says that the definition of vulnerability is uncertainty, risk, and emotional exposure.

She describes it as "that unstable feeling we get when we step out of our comfort zone or do something that forces us to loosen control." Further, she says, "Vulnerability is not weakness, it's our most accurate measure of courage."

This journey to explore the creation of a new marriage is the epitome of acknowledging your own vulnerability. It is risky to take this book's steps for you both to heal. Just by your decision to read this book together, she has accepted that she is willing to slowly move towards repairing this relationship.

And for you the addict, you acknowledge that you are willing to do everything possible to create safety for her! I know there is fear and trepidation that you will not always do everything perfectly; however, if you follow the steps in this book, you will have a guide to helping her heal from the devastation of sexual betrayal.

You both can do this, but do it slowly and methodically—it is not an easy process.

> **"JUST REMEMBER THAT VULNERABILITY IS UNCERTAINTY, RISK, AND EMOTIONAL EXPOSURE." ~ BRENÉ BROWN**

Chapter 2

From the Beginning

YOU MUST COME INTO THE FIRST SESSION TOGETHER—NO MORE SECRETS!

To the Partner: I know you have spent a lot of time researching who can help you both work through this process, and more than likely your focus has been finding someone who can help your husband. Within my experience it is typically the wife that does the work. Why? Because she feels that she must ensure he gets the help he needs, even while she is wondering who she married and how this could have happened to her.

To the Addict: Your wife is in a state of shock, but she still goes into command mode, figuring out the best option for the two of you. She has done the research and has looked for a sex addiction specialist, a CSAT (Certified Sexual Addiction Therapist) who has training about your condition. She has put her own needs on the back burner because she knows that this deception is out of character for you, and she needs to find someone who can help you be the person she thought you were. She is in a traumatized state but is still worried about you.

To the Partner: It would have made sense if I had wanted to see him by himself, but that could not be further from the truth. I want to see you both, because I want to explain how I work and the model I am going to be using. This is a couple's issue that has impacted the both of you, and I believe that each of you need to understand how he lost control of his impulses, therefore changing his identity and keeping so many secrets.

You both need to know about his addiction, her trauma, and the tools and resources available to help you both.

I have developed the Early Recovery Couples Empathy Model (ERCEM), which helps couples simultaneously heal from the addiction. I believe you both have been so affected that it would be an injustice to work with you from the old model. In the old model he works on his issues while she works on hers, and in a couple of years you both can begin to do work to restore the marriage.

ERCEM is extremely partner sensitive, and that is why it is imperative that the partner agrees to work together to find healing. If she is not interested, the decision has been made, and ERCEM is not the appropriate intervention for you as a couple. However, if she is willing, then I would like you to come in as a couple. That way, I can share with both of you the protocol that is going to help you work through this crisis.

So if the partner is willing, I see you both for the intake. Remember, it is her decision when and how she decides to work on this relationship, so I always leave the option open. If a partner chooses not to come, that is her decision. Why? Because she did not ask for this, she did not sign up for this, and therefore, she gets to decide when and how she will participate in ERCEM.

The truth of the matter is most of my couples do come in together for the first time. It is important for her own sense of security that she gets to meet me and hear what I am going to recommend from the very start. That is how ERCEM Specialists work. They are partner-sensitive and want to help the couple work through the crisis of betrayal. Their desire is to disseminate information as quickly as possible to create a treatment plan that promotes safety and recovery from the time of intake.

To the Addict: You are both in shock! The discovery of your addiction has put you in a traumatized state. You never thought you would get caught, and now you are in an extreme state of shock. You have watched your wife experience the worst grief of her life, and you cannot believe that you did that to her. She is so traumatized by the discovery that it is quite possible she has not eaten or slept for days.

It is crucial to have both of you in the office at the first session to get valuable information from each of you and share resources so you both get some direction from the start.

Historically, the partner had been left out of the recovery relationship because professionals had not been trained to treat both simultaneously. There was no model like ERCEM to help you navigate this crisis together. The partner was told to take a back seat, and she had to sacrifice her needs so that her spouse could get immediate help.

To the Partner: Although this is a noble gesture, I cannot emphasize enough that you should not sacrifice yourself so that he can get help. You are bleeding out with angst and pain, and you need immediate help too! THIS IS A RELATIONAL TRAUMA, AND YOU BOTH NEED ASSISTANCE IMMEDIATELY.

This book is going to customize a treatment plan for you both that will undoubtedly increase the success of his individual treatment, in part because it is not solely focused on him.

For the Addict: I recommend ten recovery tools to help you get the needed support so you can build a strong recovery plan to decrease urges and cravings. While you are following those tools, I suggest that you the Partner become educated on what is happening to your mind and your body as a result of the trauma/stress you are feeling due to the sexual acting out.

Not every woman feels trauma, but research shows that the discovery of his acting out generally produces a trauma response. This can leave you feeling dazed and confused about what is happening to you, and your outcome is better if you seek immediate counsel with a partner sensitive treatment specialist. This is because you have someone normalizing all the reactions you are having.

By being together in the first session, you are both learning about the brain science of partner betrayal, and he is beginning to get the education he will need to help you heal. She will need safety, and since you betrayed her, that means you will need the immediate tools to get yourself healthy while simultaneously supporting her through this pain.

You both may be asking, what are the tools/treatment that promote good recovery? We will go into greater explanation in chapters 3 and 4, but typically the formula is that after ninety days of recovery and sobriety from all acting out behaviors, you both begin the therapeutic formal disclosure so that the partner will have access to the truth. She cannot make a good, informed decision about how she feels and what she needs until she goes through the process of hearing all the information about your acting out. I mandate that the addict take a polygraph afterwards to make sure he told the truth.

FORMULA FOR INCREASED SUCCESS OF RECOVERY

1. Come in together so that you can be informed by your ERCEM therapist about these 10 requirements for a successful first phase of recovery. (Your ERCEM therapist will help you decide when it would be helpful to meet individually during your early recovery couples work.)

2. Discuss the psychodynamics of sex addiction to insure that you both understand this brain disorder.

3. Educate both parties about the brain science of partner betrayal.

4. Create a strong recovery program that supports the start of betrayer's recovery for a minimum of 90 days.

5. Practice the 10 recovery tools for sex addiction.

6. Advocate for a full therapeutic disclosure (if desired by the partner) followed by a polygraph examination.

7. The partner participates in an emotional impact letter to release her feelings while simultaneously helping him develop empathy.

8. The addict will write a restitution letter that shows the partner he heard her and recognizes the damage he has caused.

9. The couple will start early recovery couples work if partner decides to continue with the marriage and addict maintains good recovery.

10. If either party chooses not to commit to the principles cited above, they may decide to separate in integrity. They understand the limitations that can occur in a coupleship if either person is not invested in working together to heal. When trauma or addiction goes untreated, it will impede the couple's ability to heal and keep the couple vacillating in phase 1 or 2 of partner betrayal.

Please reread the principles above and then answer the questions to the best of your ability.

Can each one of you agree as a couple to commit to supporting each other with the ten principles above? *Circle one*: Yes / No

Do you have reservations about any of them? *Circle one*: Yes / No

If yes, please answer the following:

The principle I worry about the most is:

____

____

because ____

____

____

Each of you needs to be honest so you can work together or leave in integrity. Share with your spouse what your fears are in proceeding further.

My greatest fear is that:

____

____

____

____

____

____

Share with your ERCEM therapist your fears and trepidation so he/she can work with you to make it less frightening and more realistic.

Chapter 3

Safety and Stabilization Requires "Extreme Partner Sensitivity"

ABOLISH THE CONCEPT OF CODEPENDENCY AND USE CO-CREATION INSTEAD

Couples have many questions about how to navigate the treatment they both may require to get through her partner betrayal and manage his sexual addiction recovery. The old school of thought told men and women they each needed to individually work on their own programs and remain separate from each other as they did their treatment. These 12-step groups (and other types of support) thought it was necessary for the sex addict to focus on his personal recovery solely to maximize his success. This kept things very private from her, kept her feeling isolated, and exacerbated her fears. The partner was asked to seek support from her own 12-step meetings and to work on her codependency. She was sent the message that in some ways, she had contributed to his sex addiction and now needed to figure out how to stay separate from it so he could heal. As helpful as the 12-Step Program can be in certain cases, this theory does not apply to sex addiction.

The 12-Step Model used for Sex Addiction was modeled after the 12-Step Model from Alcoholics Anonymous. When a wife has a husband who is alcoholic, she might throw away his bottle or call in his absence from work because he is too drunk. Her mission in life is to take care of her husband in hopes that he will get healthy. That is where the concept of co-dependency was born. She knew that when her husband was intoxicated, he could not deceive her because he himself was the evidence that he had drank again.

This is not the case for sex addiction. The partner had no idea her husband was cheating or meeting with prostitutes or escorts until he was discovered. There was no calling the boss and covering for him.

So, this current 12-Step Model does not apply to sex addiction or partner betrayal. This is a relational problem and needs to be addressed relationally. The partner should not be kept in the dark, and she should always know what her husband is doing to get healthy. Otherwise she is not helped into safety and stabilization, which prolongs the couple's recovery. This was considered the primary way that couples who faced sexual addiction could heal, but nothing could be further from the truth. Couples need to work together and co-create what is in their best interest.

Let me say it again to both of you so you can convey it to whoever you are working with: Sex addiction is a relational problem. It affects both of you and it needs to be addressed together unless the partner does not want to be involved in his treatment!

Partners get to choose what they need. Some partners do not want any information about sex addiction, and they would prefer that the sex addict work out his treatment program with his sponsor, fellowship, and therapist. However, most partners want very much to be kept abreast of the steps the addict is taking to find recovery.

The partner-sensitive approach to couple's work is that she should also have a say in what would make her feel safe within the coupleship and within his recovery.

There may be times she can make suggestions that she feels he would benefit from, and he should work on meeting those needs. ERCEM endorses co-creation, which is a new concept for sex addiction treatment, and it really does allow the partner to feel that she has an active role in his recovery.

There is no doubt that sex addicts want very much to help their partners heal, yet from time to time it can be frustrating when their wives are much more ambitious in their recovery program than they would be themselves. However, working together keeps the addict forward thinking to keep his brain recalibrated, and it allows his partner to heal from the betrayal at a more consistent rate.

As the Addict, what do you believe your wife needs for increased safety? This is your top priority. To develop your empathy muscle, I would like for you to list ten things you could do for your recovery that would help fortify her belief in your recovery.

10 THINGS THAT I COULD DO TO INCREASE/STRENGTHEN/FORTIFY HER SAFETY

1. I could increase ____________________
2. I could add ____________________
3. I could learn ____________________
4. I could participate in ____________________
5. I could start ____________________
6. I could stop ____________________
7. ____________________
8. ____________________
9. ____________________
10. ____________________

To the Partner: When you think about your husband's sex addiction recovery, what could he add, alter, or change to make you feel more safe, secure, and confident that he is taking his recovery seriously?

What do you wish he would do to upgrade his program? Although we know that his work is his to do, we also know that you can be incredibly helpful in helping him determine what you need to heal. Part of your healing is dependent on the energy he puts into addiction management, but the other part comes from your willingness to see his progress and acknowledge the work he is doing. Let's look at what you need to feel more secure as you watch him work his program and and witness the progress he is making.

Ask yourself, what might you need to feel better about his individual recovery?

I WOULD FEEL MORE CONFIDENT ABOUT MY HUSBAND'S ADDICTION RECOVERY IF HE:

1. ______________________________
2. ______________________________
3. ______________________________
4. ______________________________
5. ______________________________
6. ______________________________
7. ______________________________
8. ______________________________
9. ______________________________
10. ______________________________

These fears or issues are great check-in material that helps him to identify what you need to feel safe. In Chapter 10, you will find out more about check-ins and how they improve both your communication and awareness of how recovery is going for both of you. It also provides an opportunity to assess what would help you move forward in your healing. When you both decide to move forward, it is important to validate the progress you each are making. With ERCEM, the Connection-Shares focus on struggles and appreciation for the work.

AS THE ADDICT CONTINUES TO STRENGTHEN HIS OWN RECOVERY

To the Addict: You have experienced in your coupleship where the partner is doing some ferocious reading, listening to podcasts, and searching online for the best treatment therapists and coaches in the country. It is not uncommon for the addict to allow her to take on that role as he continues to do his new recovery steps. After nine months, twelve months, or even a year and a half of good recovery, it can feel laborious for the addict to have to follow the requests of his wife. This may have happened to you, where you come into therapy and say, "I'm working a good recovery program—why is she expecting me to continue to work so hard when my recovery is solid?"

A partner-sensitive therapist will help you as a couple decide what is realistic in terms of treatment. Because the partner has so much at stake in the relationship, she is wanting you to participate with 150% of your energy. Recognizing that this can feel as if she does not think you are doing enough requires you to be open and honest with her and work on the skills of acknowledging her feelings while being open and transparent about your own vulnerability. For the addict who is working good recovery, it is common and normal for you to feel like you are getting messages from her that you are just not working hard enough or doing it well enough.

If your intentions are pure and you are 100% stable in your own recovery, you will need to figure out a way to pay attention to her needs for ongoing enlightenment. You may be asking yourself, "When will I get to share my needs and wants?"

For the first twelve to eighteen months your focal point will solely be on your wife. You will be learning relational skills that include focused listening, direct communication, reflective listening and empathy strategies to make her feel heard and understood. This has to be your primary focus so that you can build the safety and security she will need to trust you again. Initially it can feel overwhelming and one-sided to put her first and keep her at the center of your attention, but it is a necessary step to rebuilding the trust that your infidelity has destroyed. Practicing the all important empathy skills immediately will show her that you recognize the damage your addiction has caused and that you are willing to do anything to earn her confidence in you again.

It will take many months before she lets her guard down and joins you in a more mutual relationship because she is reeling from what has happened to her. As she begins to trust you and lets her guard down, you will have opportunities to share more of your needs and wants. However, for the first year, it will be your responsibility to put her first.

This addiction is considered a process addiction, which is different from other addictions because it is characterized by strong impulses and cravings that result in harmful behaviors. These behaviors result in emotional, physical and interpersonal maladaptive behaviors and harm both you and your significant relationships. Because you have done significant damage, your focus needs to be on your recovery and her healing first and foremost. When you put her first to help her heal, you will be working towards a living amends to increase trust.

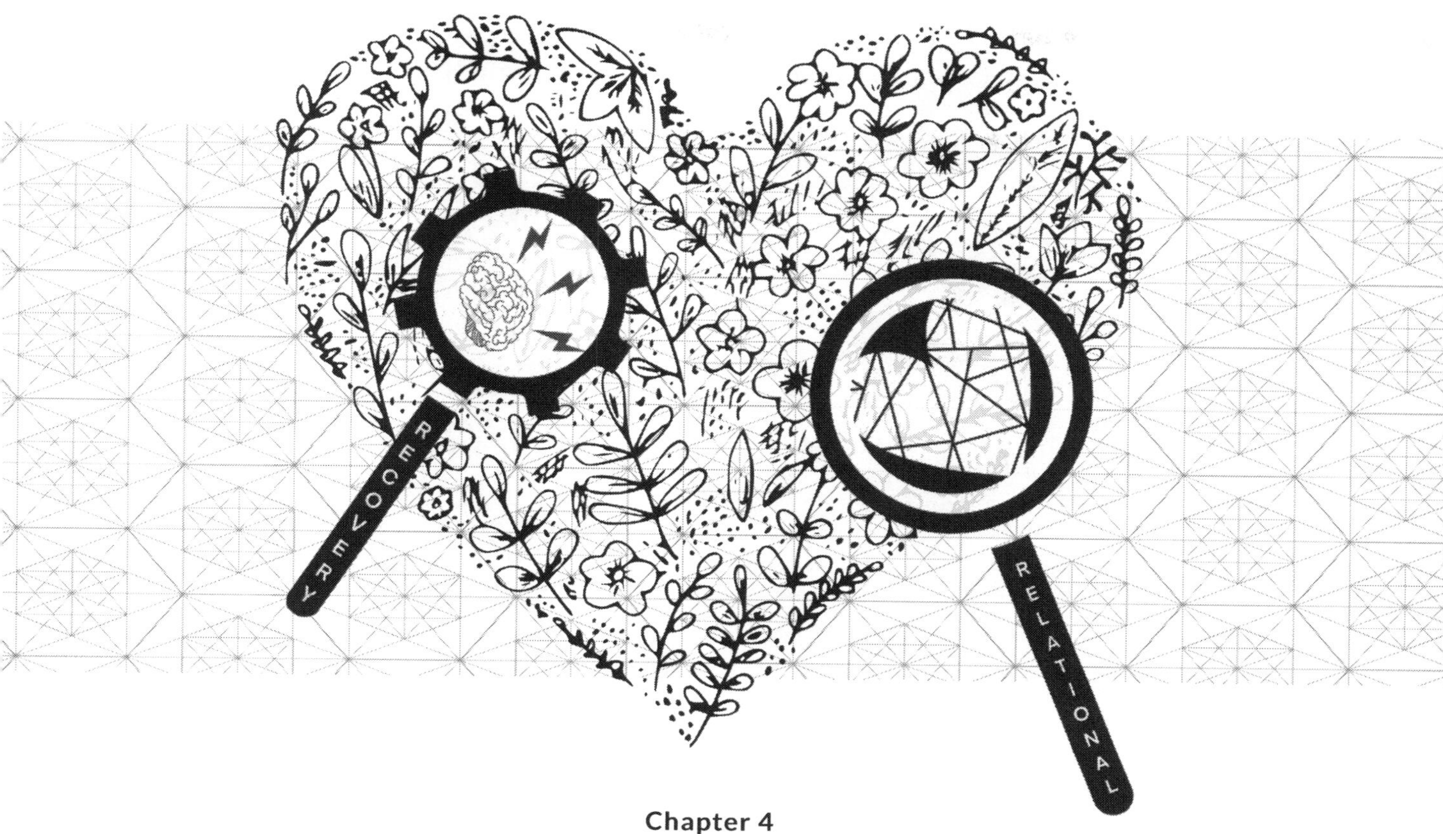

Chapter 4

Sex Addiction Requires Two Perspectives

IT IS A RECOVERY ISSUE, AND IT IS A RELATIONAL PROBLEM

For the Addict: If you are like most men that I work with, you are now dealing with the aftermath of your addiction and are watching your wife in a very traumatized state. Most men who walk into my office have been referred by their wives. It makes sense that a wife would want you to reach out to an expert in the field. For that, I am grateful she has found a partner sensitive therapist because we work differently than many therapists.

When I was contacted, I made sure to let you both know I wanted to see you together for the first session. What I know for sure is that I can help you with your addiction if you are motivated to change. Your treatment plan must deal with your own personal recovery from sexual addiction. But it will require more than addiction recovery; it will require relational recovery because you have fractured the most precious partnership that was ever bestowed upon a couple. Your addiction robbed you of your sanity, and, as a result, you participated in horrendous behaviors that have left your wife shell shocked and bleeding out.

Certified Sexual Addiction Therapists (CSAT) understand that the addiction kept you chasing different forms of sexual acting out, like compulsive pornography and masturbation, perusing the internet for provocative images, web chatting, video sharing, sexting, prostitution, massage parlors, strip clubs, and/or affairs. You may have participated in one or two forms of sexual acting out for sexual pleasure, or you may have engaged in them all. Problematic sexual behavior always escalates in intensity and frequency, so had you not confessed or been discovered you would never have stopped. The addiction would have gotten worse and worse and worse.

It is difficult for your wife, whose brain has been severely compromised due to the discovery of what you have been doing, to understand how you could have continued in this immorality and madness, but CSATs know you could not stop. You thought about stopping hundreds of times, but the compulsivity took over and was more powerful than your ability to discontinue the behavior.

Over the course of our work together, I want you to read books on your addiction, so you can understand that addiction is a brain disorder and that once an addiction develops, it is invariably uncontrollable until the wakeup call of discovery.

I have never met an addict who did not try to stop their behavior.

I know you probably told yourself you were going to stop acting out, whether that was pornography, prostitutes, web chats, massage parlors, strip clubs, or any other gratuitous form of sex. In most cases, your sex addiction really had very little to do with sex. It more than likely included the pursuit, the seduction, or the fantasy that lit up your brain and produced an abundance of dopamine.

As with all addictions, you had to increase the dopamine hit to experience the same high that you initially got when you first started to act out sexually. What seemed so pleasurable initially did not have the spike it once had, and therefore, you looked for something new and different to produce real results. The cycle continued, and sex addiction became less erotic and less stimulating. It was time to up the ante again. Like all addictions, you could never really reinvent that first high, but the search was on until you got discovered or arrested.

Now if you were addicted to pornography, you are likely to say "Carol, that did not apply to me. I never physically cheated on my wife, nor did I ever do anything illegal." But, pornography addiction also intensifies in frequency and intensity. I know that as you were sitting with the wife and kids, you were wondering what pornography was out there that you had not seen. Your addiction stole your focus and your being present with the people you loved. It may not have been a crime, but it was living a lie, and it was a horrendous relational betrayal.

Now the work you need to do entails shutting down that reward center and allowing new neural pathways to develop.

So next I am going to ask you to do some things that yesterday would have seemed inconceivable.

As the Partner: It is unimaginable that he could not stop. Most women go back and forth and internally debate whether it was an addiction or if their husband was just a "plain old cheater." I would like you to go over the criteria for Compulsive Sexual Behavior Disorder on page 16 and count the number of criteria that fit your husband's behavior.

He could not stop! After talking to thousands of men about the self-loathing they felt about their sexual acting out, I know they go through the process of hating themselves for what they were doing to themselves and the relationship. They would promise that they would stop and 20 minutes, two days, or two weeks later they were back acting out.

Patrick Carnes calls it the Sexual Addiction Cycle* and uses this depiction to illuminate the auto exacerbating cycle a sex addict is in before recovery.

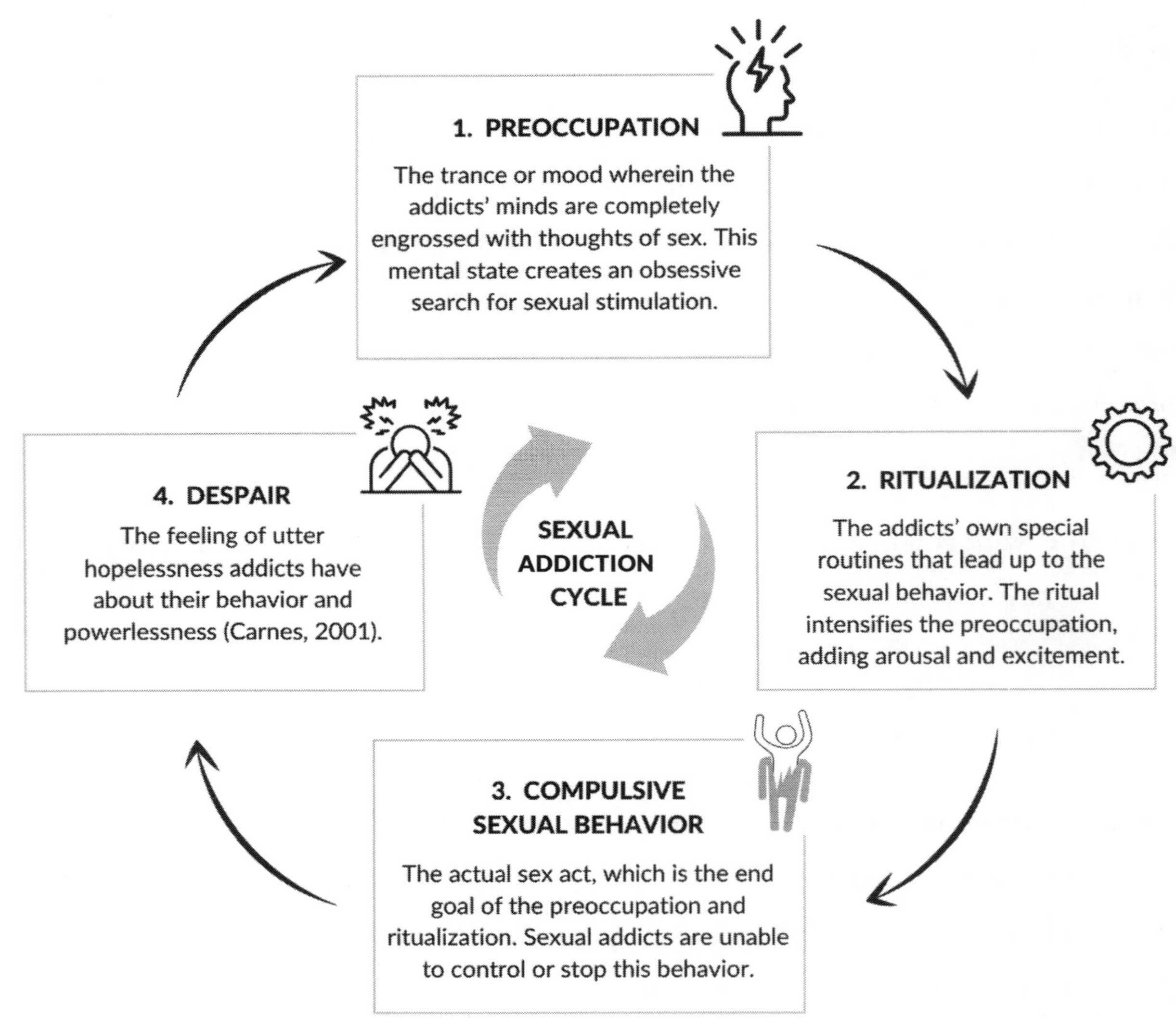

*The Sexual Addiction Cycle © Gentle Path Press. Adapted for use with permission.

Most of the men I work with are relieved once they are discovered. They wanted something to stop the addictive cycle, but they weren't strong enough to stop it themselves. What we know about sexual addiction, or CSBD, is that it is the strongest of all addictions and cannot be stopped without following an entire arsenal of tools that promote recovery.

The addict wants to restore the relationship and "stop the bleeding" as they watch their wives go into a trauma state like no other.

For the Addict: You feel horrible that you have put her in this place, and you wonder how the addiction could have robbed you from your conscience, mental well-being, and sanity. Somehow, someway, because of the nature of this addiction, you were able to do the unthinkable and believe that she would never find out. That is why it is so important to do whatever you can to make her feel safe.

This is not a "you" problem; this has become a couple's problem. However, you are the crucial element in helping her heal. If you can put her first, contain her pain, and work a good recovery program, you are much more likely to find success and bring the relationship into a new state of being.

I am not sure if your wife is in the fetal position on the floor or if she is raging at you nonstop for betraying her. Perhaps she is in bed 24 hours a day, unable to find the strength to get up, go to the bathroom, eat, or shower. Shock, rage, and depression are three trauma responses women frequently have when they have been betrayed.

ERCEM: THE NEW RECOVERY MODEL

IN SUMMARY

Together, all three of us are going to work on strengthening your recovery tools. As a Couple, you will no longer be ascribing to the old school of addiction recovery where you do your own personal work while she does hers separately without input from each other. This relational problem will require her letting you know what will make her feel safe and you finding ways to increase your recovery to show her you have addressed her issues. You will keep her informed of your recovery program, and she will be able to ask you to modify it.

As the Partner, you have every right to know what he is doing and what his treatment plan consists of, and you will get to weigh in as to what you believe would strengthen your relationship. You are an active part in the process of recovery and will want to check in with him to determine the efficacy of his program.

I recently had a partner request that her husband find a partner-sensitive CSAT to maximize his success. The addict was comfortable with his therapist and did not want to change, but he agreed to interview other therapists who had specialty in sex addiction and partner sensitivity. After he met with several professionals, he was able to see her point and added the ERCEM Specialist to their team. ERCEM is the "Gold Seal" in helping them heal because it incorporates empathy into the therapy from day one and works with the addict to continuously look at the addiction and damage through her eyes.

If you do not have an ERCEM Specialist in your area, check the directory at www.sexhelpwithcarolthecoach.com for a list. There are ERCEM coaches that can work with you virtually anywhere in the world. Your next choice would be to go to either a Certified Clinical Partner Specialist at APSATS who has training in addiction and partner trauma (Check out the list on apsats.org) or seek a specialist that is both a CSAT and CPTT—Certified Partner and Trauma Therapist (Go to www.sexhelpwithcarolthecoach.com).

If you can put her first, contain her pain, and work a good recovery program, you are much more likely to find success and to bring the relationship into a new state of being.

As a couple you will need to engage in reconnecting together but first, you need to develop the empathy, compassion, and resiliency to stand alongside her in her pain. You will be learning a process to help her heal, and the coupleship will go through the stages of recovery together. This will require that you learn about trauma and how it has affected your wife, and you both will work on developing the skills and techniques necessary to work through the three stages of partner betrayal. This is done while the addict continues to strengthen his own addiction recovery. It is an arduous undertaking for both of you, but you can get through this and grow stronger!

That is why I need you both here for the first meeting. You both need to know about the treatment recommendations I will be making for both of you and the resources that are available to supplement your work. Unlike the old school of recovery, you will be working together to create more healing. The partner is an active part of his treatment, and you need to know what to expect and see his work so you will feel safe.

A trained specialist is always the best choice to help you on this journey. However, if you don't have the finances to seek a specialist, you can use this book as a guide to do the work. It is a roadmap to help you both work through the 3 phases of partner betrayal.

THE 3 STAGES OF PARTNER BETRAYAL—SEEING PARTNER BETRAYAL THROUGH THE EYES OF TRAUMA

As you navigate through working together as a couple, it will be important to find a specialist who has been trained in partner sensitivity. I ascribe to the APSATS model that seems to be the most partner-sensitive, and it was derived from trauma pioneer—Judith Hermann. Hermann's trauma work was groundbreaking—she conceptually identified three phases of trauma treatment that a survivor would need to work through the trauma.

You are a trauma victim. Although his sex addiction was never meant to hurt you and certainly not meant to cause extreme trauma, that kind of relational betrayal undoubtedly causes trauma, which is why you need a partner specialist!

Dr. Barbara Steffens and her colleagues adapted and developed a trauma model for partners of sex addicts in 2011. What followed was the creation of a premier training organization—The Association of Partners of Sex Addicts Trauma Specialists. APSATS was the original partner-sensitive training organization created by Dr. Barbara Steffens, PhD to ensure that partners were treated from a trauma perspective. She and its founding members developed the Multidimensional Partner Trauma Model which advocated utilizing a trauma perspective in treating the traumatic impact of sex addiction upon the partner or spouse. These founding members created the curriculum and were visionaries in the field of partner sensitive treatment for betrayal.

This resulted in the clinical world viewing partners as being trauma survivors. This has caused a shift in perspective and techniques that have changed how professionals navigate their clients through their pain and trauma of sexual betrayal. This model seeks to provide a sound foundation for assisting partners in their healing process. I know because I have been teaching this model alongside Dr. Steffens, and, out of the APSATS MPTM training and the *Help. Her. Heal.* book, I developed ERCEM.

APSATS and the MPTM model have helped thousands of partners view themselves differently and understand their reactions from the lens of trauma. It has taught professionals all over the world about partner sensitivity and the brain science of partner betrayal.

To the Partner: You have been overwhelmed by what has happened to you and did not know that you likely qualified as a trauma survivor. When he acted out, he had no idea he would cause you such pain. He more than likely used all sorts of denial and defense mechanisms that kept him from thinking about the potential consequences of his actions, and that kept you from having any idea of what he was doing. His addictive thinking caused him to believe that "what you didn't know wouldn't hurt you," "he was going to stop after this last time," or "men have done this for centuries and this acting out has nothing to do with the fact he really does love you."

Having an addiction required that he make it his full-time job to lie to you and keep you as far away from his addiction as he could. When you later discovered all the deception and excuses he told so he could continue his behavior, you began to feel that your betrayal was layers deep. Not only did he live a double life and keep his secrets airtight, but he also spent hours producing plausible stories as to why he missed your daughter's birthday event and used the birth of your child to pick up prostitutes, meet with affair partners, or go on a 17-hour porn binge.

This has thrown you into the first phase of partner betrayal, and what you need now are tools to increase your sense of safety and stabilization. You no longer feel safe, nor do you feel stable, and you fear for your sanity.

As we work together as a couple to navigate this tsunami of pain, we discuss how both of you can work together and separately to ensure that you find, as Dr. Barbara Steffens says, "safety in an unsafe situation."

This requires you to ask yourself, "Can I make these three commitments?"

THE THREE REQUIREMENTS FOR ADDICTS AFTER DISCOVERY

To the Addict: Now that she has discovered what you were really doing, you will need to do whatever it takes to redefine yourself in recovery.

The three requirements to restoring the relationship after discovery are:

1. A period where you have proven good recovery so she has more assurance that you want to get healthy and are willing to do what it takes to get healthy. Your wife needs to know that you have the right support in place to be healthy.

Patrick Carnes the "Father of Sex Addiction" and co-creator of Sex Addicts Anonymous says that your recovery is dependent on a strong support system which he calls "the committee." You will need to build a strong "committee" to assist you through the transformation it takes to maintain good sobriety. He believes that no one is strong enough to do it by himself, and he feels that there are lots of ways to build in support. He supports the 12-Step process which contains an abundance of longevity, hope, strength, and recovery to get you through the tough times.

There are many support groups that can provide assistance as you gain recovery. Sex Addicts Anonymous, Sexaholic's Anonymous, Every Man's Battle, Recovery Nation, Pure Desire, and L.I.F.E. Recovery International are just a few of the groups that are available to support you in this process. You cannot do this alone, and your wife will be watching to see how you navigate recovery. You must treat this process as if your life depended on it because having a process addiction is by far the toughest addiction to navigate. You cannot get lazy or complacent because you will not only relapse, but you will return to your addiction worse than before.

2. A formal therapeutic disclosure so she has the full truth and can determine how she wants to proceed.

3. The ability to develop empathy so you can contain the pain you have caused and help her heal.

The three requirements are crucial in providing you both with the needed elements to make her feel safe and begin to start the process of reconciliation. Next I will provide more detailed information to start the process of helping her heal and helping you begin to live a life free of addiction so you can learn how to be your best self.

To watch a short video on partner betrayal, go to: www.sexhelpwithcarolthecoach.com/about. Scroll down to the 2nd video, *The Brain Science of Partner Betrayal.*

Chapter 5

The 10 Recovery Tools to Increase Your Success with Recovery

To the Partner: Understandably, you wonder what recovery tools could work for a man who has chosen to be deceitful and lie to you every step of your marriage. I do not blame you for being skeptical and would expect nothing less. I have recommended these ten recovery tools because they are an incredible resource to assist the addict in good solid recovery. These tools also act as ways you can observe his due diligence with his recovery.

So many partners ask, "How will I know that he is really in recovery? He has lied our entire marriage, and I am so afraid that he will deceive me again." These tools provide a measurement of his continued commitment to the recovery process and will help you gauge his efforts.

For the Addict: Utilizing these ten tools is a tangible way for you to practice the skills you will need to learn to cope with urges and cravings, and it will keep you strong while you recircuit your brain and develop new neuropathways to replace the old neuropathways of addiction. The tools are diverse and help a man integrate and transform addiction from many different levels. It is a step-by-step formula for promoting habits that reinforce the man you want to be. It will be a measurable tool to help your wife know that you are being diligent in your recovery. I tell wives, "You will know your spouse is genuinely serious about his program if he has excitement for his meetings and protects the schedule he has set up to do his ten tools. If he begins to get lax, he is telling you indirectly that he does not think he needs the assistance, which could not be further from the truth." When he becomes complacent, he moves closer to relapse.

Meetings are crucial to help you find a safe place to be with other men who are learning how to manage their addiction. The first five recovery tools have to do with attending meetings. I highly recommend meetings that are either faith-based or 12-step-based because I have seen them be the most effective. Sex Addicts Anonymous (SAA) and Sexaholics Anonymous (SA) are two valuable 12-step groups that provide an opportunity to live an authentic, transparent life.

In a 12-step program, you are expected to recognize that your life has become unmanageable and that a power greater than yourself can restore you to sanity. For many men, a Higher Power is God. For other men, it's the program, their fellowship, and/or a good Certified Sexual Addictions Therapist. Regardless of what it is, it can help you be the person that you have always wanted to be, and the 12-step program reinforces the need for connection. It has you do the hard work of looking at all your past feelings, failings, and wounds so you can acknowledge and process them and stop medicating yourself with addiction. Once you have gone through the steps, then it is up to you to make amends to the people that you have hurt, recognize when you are falling back into old behaviors, and give back to your community because you are a changed man. As Patrick Carnes says, "It is out of great suffering, one experiences the process of transformation and once transformation occurs, you will want to give back to other men that are fighting this addiction."

Unfortunately, I work with so many addicts who go to meetings, but never work the steps! When you do the 12-Steps, you actively work on transforming your life! Don't shortchange the work that needs to be done.

The difference between Sex Addicts Anonymous and Sexaholics Anonymous is in part, the philosophy of objectification versus lust. In SA, the program stresses the fact that you must stop lust in every way imaginable so that you can decrease the dopamine hits to the brain.

Faith-based organizations like The Living Truth or Pure Desire, work from a very similar process, in that they want you to look at your life, see where the wounding and holes are, and determine what needs to occur spiritually to feel whole again. There is much connection with other men, and oftentimes they offer opportunities for you to hear from men that are in excellent recovery or women who have been devastated by the sexual integrity issues. It becomes an arena for you to understand your problem and get the fellowship you need through God and the connection with other group members.

The first five recovery tools include:

1. Going to meetings. As a newly recovered addict, I ask you to go to at least three meetings a week while you are achieving that first 90 days of sobriety.

2. Find a sponsor/mentor/guide who can hold you accountable but also help work you through the steps of your recovery program so you are not doing it alone.

3. Read the book that is predominant in the organization you are a part of to better understand the philosophy behind the work

4. Do the hard work that is required. If you are in a 12-step program, that means you must work through all twelve steps.

5. Have a list of the men in the fellowship: people you can call at any time of the day or night when you have urges or cravings, when you are doing well and want to celebrate, or when you are having a rough time with your spouse or family.

The next five steps have to do with ongoing work that will keep you present, focused, and moving forward in your recovery:

6. Seek a professional who has been trained in sexual addiction. I always encourage you to see a Certified Sexual Addictions Therapist, but remember that the professional you see should also be partner-sensitive. Again, we recommend an ERCEM Specialist who has been trained in early recovery couples work from an empathy model. To find ERCEM Specialists, go to the appendix in the back of this book.

7. Go to a therapy group for sex addicts so that you can crosstalk and really explore where you are at with your addiction, relationships, and yourself.

8. Pray, meditate, or journal because you need to become self-reflective. You do not have to do all three; you need to at least do one out of the three. But of course if you do two or three, you are increasing your results.

9. Read information so that you understand how your addiction has affected the brain. This will require that you understand how the addiction has created neuropathways that need to be replaced with new neuropathways that are healthier and relational. You want to develop these new neuropathways so that you can be the man you really want to be.

10. Accountability tools. Maybe you will seek a polygraph test twice a year to help keep you accountable, or perhaps you will put Covenant Eyes on your phone, laptop, and PC. It is a tool that can send a report to your wife when you have made a bad choice, looked at provocative images, or have gone back to porn. Having accountability tools is important. It allows your wife to feel safe and allows you to think about the outcome of your behavior before you give in to your urges and cravings. Even though it can feel like a restraint, it provides much liberation.

These tools are a guide for you and for your spouse. As an addict, you need to be aware of the tools you need to be safe. And as the spouse of an addict, you need to be able to assess if he is doing the hard work it takes to maintain recovery.

To the Partner: Unfortunately, I have never met a man who could do recovery by himself. If your husband is not following these steps with rigorous focus and attention, he will likely fall back on old behaviors which will reactivate his sex addiction. Knowing these steps keeps you safe because it keeps you informed about what he should be doing. Some men resent the extra set of eyes and will complain that this keeps you “in his business,” but for the first three to five years your responsibility as the spouse of a sex addict is to keep yourself safe. That means he needs to do the hard work to beat his addiction, and these tools will keep him on the right path.

A man in good recovery is pleased to work with these tools because it helps reassure his spouse that he IS doing the hard work for himself, for her, and for the relationship.

To get a copy of these tools, go to sexhelpwithcarolthecoach.com/resources

Chapter 6

As a Recovering Addict, Your Job Is to Provide Safety

THE FULL THERAPEUTIC DISCLOSURE

For the Addict: Once you have established some good solid recovery, you will need to participate in a formal disclosure by a partner-sensitive trained therapist who will be able to provide your partner appropriate safety and stabilization while she hears the entire truth for the first time. I also recommend that you have a therapist who has been trained in doing formal therapeutic disclosures.

My colleagues, Janice Caudill and Dan Drake, have written a series of books helping both of you to understand why this is so important to the relationship and how it can provide safety and stabilization once she learns the truth. Not only does it help you both work through the process of finding out the truth, but it also helps her brain stop ruminating about what else she does not know. In my endorsement, I called their series of books "the Bible for helping couples utilize the disclosure in the safest way for the sake of the partner." The book series, *Full Disclosure*, is the gold standard for helping clinicians and coaches know how to properly set-up this important process.

We know how tough this is for you, the Partner, to try to put the pieces together and continue to wonder what really happened and, more importantly, how this could have happened to you.

There is no way to right the wrong that has occurred when sexual addiction robs you both of the integrity and trust needed in a healthy relationship. You have both been deeply affected. If trust is ever to be restored, it will require that you learn the truth so that you can make an informed decision about what you want or need to proceed.

Partner-sensitive professionals recommend that you participate in a formal disclosure **only if you feel the need to go through that process.** Most women feel it is necessary to know the truth to determine what has preempted their marriage and more importantly, what has been going on with their husband that they would have never in a million years imagined. Some women explain that they already have enough information to know how damaged he is, and they do not want to put anymore thoughts or images into their brains. There are no wrong or right answers here...it is whatever you need!

In a formal disclosure, a therapist works closely with the addict to create a timeline of all his indiscretions from the time of meeting his spouse until present.

The spouse may want to understand the history of how the addiction began, so ask the partner where she wants the disclosure to start. Although this process is gut wrenching and raw, it helps the addict reveal all his secrets, and it allows the partner to hear the truth.

This process of the addict writing out his timeline usually takes three to six weeks.

- His spouse is asked to list all her questions that have to do with the "facts" of his acting out. Sometimes a partner will have 20 questions that she wants the addict to answer in his disclosure and timeline (I recently had a spouse who had 139 questions that she needed answered. It took us quite a bit of time to pair those down to the basic information she was needing. But ultimately she determines the number of her questions).

- He is to answer all questions that are fact based in the disclosure in conjunction with his acting out.

- After the disclosure, he is asked to bring his wife to the polygraph appointment to assure that he did reveal EVERYTHING about his acting out. She is not allowed to sit in on the examination but is available to review the results with the polygrapher. An examiner needs to be willing to include the spouse as he reports his/her findings. Sometimes, couples must travel hundreds of miles to seek out a good polygrapher who understands sex addiction and is sensitive to partner betrayal.

The disclosure can affect partners in many ways, but in general, most partners reported that they felt the disclosure was helpful in "stopping the bleeding." They were tired of the staggered disclosures and wanted a safe way to hear it all. They were now able to see the addiction for what it was and have felt some compassion for their husband. The disclosure showed her the compulsivity that predominated the behavior. Although most women feel devastated by the facts, they also express relief at finally knowing the truth.

There is a lot of controversy about the reliability of a polygraph. I know there are a lot of people that believe you can fool the polygraph examination. Also, there are some personality types that might be proficient at deception. If we are dealing with a man that has no conscience and is sociopathic or severely narcissistic, chances are that he may be able to skate through a polygraph. This is because he has no feelings; his feelings only revolve around him. He is so well-defended and guarded that he can hide from his own feelings. Therefore, when he is asked the three to eight questions an examiner would ask, he can lie without any perceptual change in his heart rate or breathing and pass without suspicion. More than likely, your spouse does not have a serious personality disorder, does have a conscience, and would not be able to fool the examination. Very few of my clients fall under the criteria of sociopath or narcissist.

A polygraph ensures honesty. Most men may still want to minimize and lie to avoid causing you more pain and themselves more anguish, but taking the polygraph adds an extra dimension of pressure to be authentic, honest, and transparent. Some people question the authenticity of a polygraph, but if you have a good polygrapher and a good measurement tool, it is unlikely that your spouse will be able to deceive a polygraph.

There are many different types of polygraphs, so you will need to educate yourself on what you feel is the most effective. It is important to seek an examiner trained in sex addiction because you will need to work with him for the next three to five years if you fear your spouse has relapsed. The process of polygraph testing keeps you both safe. It helps him to be accountable for his actions, and it helps the partner to feel protected and become more stabilized. Addicts in good recovery tell me that regular polygraphs in the first two to three years helped them to "do the next right thing" as their brain calmed down and developed new neuropathways that reinforced healthy behaviors.

THE EMOTIONAL IMPACT LETTER (TO BE DONE BY THE PARTNER)

An extremely helpful tool in developing empathy is for the partner to write her emotional impact letter. This process originated out of the work of Schneider, Corley, and Irons, 1998. This tool is an important adjunct to the formal disclosure because it helps you give voice to the atrocity you have undergone and for your spouse to know how profoundly you have been affected. It is an opportunity in a safe place to make sure you are heard. You are able to share your thoughts, feelings, and pain while the addict quietly listens. It is a chance for the addict to hold her pain in an empathetic way when he quietly listens, and the emotional impact letter gives him an opportunity to accurately hear the pain.

This can be done after you have processed the formal disclosure. I have found that most partners feel compelled to share their feelings two to four weeks after the disclosure has occurred. You may need to take more time before you feel ready to write out your thoughts and feelings. The important thing is that you feel ready to write out your thoughts and give them a voice. It is also good to externalize your feelings so that these thoughts do not remain silent.

THE PROCESS

Once you have participated in the disclosure and heard the truth, you are to write about how your spouse's actions have affected you. This typically results in you highlighting times when your spouse had deceived, manipulated, and gaslighted you. In the EI letter you may want to describe the anguish of being abandoned during the birth of your second child, being left at home during an appendicitis attack to fend for yourself, or not being able to locate him when your teenage daughter was in a near-fatal car accident. The impact may have included the pain of feeling increasing separation, never having sex anymore, and the many nights you would wake up to him "surfing the internet" downstairs when he was really engulfed in web chats and pornography.

This letter is a way to convey the pain and is a direct result of what you heard in the disclosure. It is a formalized way to give your pain "voice," and it can be very cathartic. The addict's responsibility is to stay quiet and listen to your pain. He will then use the information to write a restitution letter.

Most partners report feeling like they have found a safe way to purge the pain in a contained place. It almost always provides a sense of relief, and it provides a profound opportunity for the addict to show empathy when he completes his restitution letter.

THE RESTITUTION LETTER (TO BE DONE BY THE ADDICT)

The restitution letter is not an amends but an opportunity to share with your partner that you heard the pain and sadness your addiction has caused her. You are acknowledging what you did, yet you are not asking for forgiveness.

You start by receiving a copy of her emotional impact letter and use that to write your restitution letter. In this letter, you show her that you heard her pain, and you acknowledge the trauma she described. You are not explaining, defending, or apologizing for your behavior. You are repeating back verbatim what she described in the emotional impact letter. When you do this, you are validating her feelings, thoughts, and beliefs that she described. You are practicing empathy by gaining perspective on how she feels.

You are expected to have your letter ready for her within two weeks of her emotional impact letter. It creates an opportunity for her to feel validated and reaffirmed. For many couples, it is a chance for you and your partner to get closure on the secrets and begin to rebuild your relationship.

Many partners say that after their husband does the Restitution Letter and shows her that he heard her feelings, thoughts, and truth, it shifts her thinking and is a game changer in their relationship!

Note: Not all partners want a formal disclosure, and it is her prerogative as to whether she wants or needs one. This applies to the emotional impact and restitution letters as well.

Remember, that it is imperative to use a partner sensitive therapist or coach to guide you in all 3 of these processes to ensure that there is a "safe place" for both of you.

I have used Early Couple's Recovery Work to do the emotional impact letter and restitution letter without the disclosure. It is an equally powerful empathy exercise! If you decide against the disclosure, we can still do these processes referencing the addiction and the destruction it has caused you.

Regardless, when a partner has a safe space to share her anger and pain, she can get clear about her feelings and then decide what she is going to do about them. When the addict allows her uninterrupted time to share feelings and can address each point, she again feels heard and validated. She then feels a bit safer to communicate about other things.

ADDITIONAL ACTIVITIES TO HELP HER KNOW THE TRUTH AND UNDERSTAND YOUR ADDICTION

THE ENLIGHTENMENT EXERCISE: WHY DID HE DO THIS TO ME?

My colleague Dorit Reichental recommends the following exercise as extremely helpful in breaking the addict's denial about how his actions have impacted his wife and his life. She believes it can be done after disclosure and can add to what Reichental refers to as "the missing link" to the "Why did he do this to me?" that typically occurs for the first 12 to 18 months after discovery. She clarifies that this process is what Patrick Carnes refers to in *The Recovery Tasks* as "Breaking Denial."

Reichental explains that resentments are at the heart of sex addiction and the natural by-product is denial.

Resentments may look like many things. Sometimes they are things that you are angry about from your childhood or early adulthood. Perhaps, you were abused as a child. You may have experienced a parent who walked out on your family and you were forced to stuff your feelings resulting in unexpressed anger that protected you from trusting others. This anger resulted in feeling resentful that others seemed to have parents who were loving and connected. Oftentimes resentments have developed because of unmet needs that were never fulfilled.

Brené Brown's research in *Atlas of the Heart* has described resentments as belonging to the "Envy family" and is often a by-product of envy. In other words, oftentimes we will form resentments because we really wished we had experienced a nurturing mother or father. Or we were envious of the kid who did not have to return to a home with a raging, alcoholic parent.

Patrick Carnes shared in our Sex Addiction Certification that neglect can cause more wounding than abuse.

Regardless of your trauma, addicts are encouraged to look at their resentments in the Fourth Step of their 12-Step Process to promote accountability for their choices. When a sex addict choses addictive behaviors, he typically resorts to the natural state of medicating the pain and the wounding by using defense mechanisms like rationalization and justification to account for his sexual and relational acting out.

You, as the partner, have no idea what the addict's distortions or resentments were or how they were rationalized and justified. Many partners experience all the traumatic, abusive, betraying, and violating behaviors that underlie the resentments but continue to wonder what was happening and why was their spouse so angry, distant, or cold.

Some partners say they felt the resentments, but because the addict denied it for so many years, she was blinded by the gaslighting and denial that occurred in the relationship.

To the Addict: Relationally, Reichental has found it helpful for both of you to augment the Fourth Step with an additional process that helps to enlighten the addict by showing how your resentments created the link to further acting out.

Denial of these resentments kept you, the addict, locked in a cycle that legitimized your addiction and further entrenched the disconnection with your spouse. Now that you are in good recovery and wanting to help her heal, you must excavate the many defense mechanisms that you used to feed the addiction.

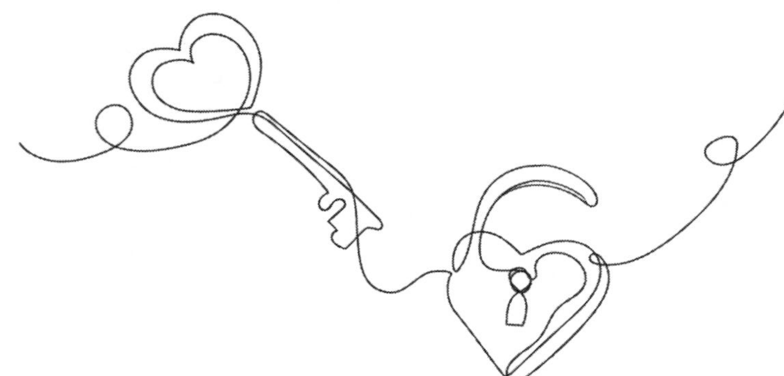

Currently in your 12-Step Work you do a very emotional deep dive into the many feelings that contributed to your addiction. You write them down and then read them to your sponsor to cleanse your psyche.

Again, because sex addiction is a relational addiction, we ask you to go one step further for both of you.

Withholding the vital information the Fourth Step contains is the ultimate secret that endangers the couple's recovery, if in fact we believe the recovery principle "we are as sick as our secrets." We would also encourage you to add to the process by incorporating the following steps.

Once you are both stabilized, the addict can:

1. Share his revised Fourth Step in session with his partner and the couple's therapist who is helping them with Early Recovery Couple's Work.
2. The addict adds two columns to his Fourth Step: "The Impact" column" and the "And Now" column.
3. Under the "Impact" column he shares the impact that his distorted thoughts, beliefs, actions, and resentments had on his partner.
4. Under the "And Now" column he includes, but is not limited to, his reframed resentments.

This has incredible healing power for the partner. It is another way we are building on a process that is incredibly helpful on its own and making it more partner-friendly. Currently, the addict reads his Fourth Step to his sponsor, not his wife. But it is his wife that deserves to understand how he could have allowed himself to do the things he did in his addiction.

We want the *full disclosure* to provide safety, but as Dorit Reichental has surveyed with her clients, she feels that partners are missing the most valuable information that she needs to make sense of the crazy-making of addiction and to keep herself safe in the future.

We both believe that you are entitled to all his thoughts, feelings, beliefs, frustrations, resentments, and justifications for acting out in the first place.

This modified Fourth Step is an opportunity to go back and disclose this crucial information that you need to protect yourself if he relapses. If you do not understand the underlying resentments, you may not see the relapse coming.

Many men get into a 12-Step Program but do not start actively working the 12 Steps. More reason for you to ask your spouse to do his 12-Step Work in a workshop or with his sponsor. Then you can go to your ERCEM Specialist and ask him or her to help you write the two columns to help complete the full-circle experience of why he acted out.

The disclosure is typically about the "How Did You Sexually Act Out?" process and this Fourth Step relational addition helps you understand the "Why Was He Able to Do This to Me?"

Although there is no specific time frame for each addict to complete the disclosure or his Fourth Step, Dorit believes the 4th step comes right about a year after disclosure and becomes the foundational work for moving forward.

We believe that the "Enlightenment Exercise" should occur as soon as he does his Fourth Step and should be done both for his recovery and the relational recovery simultaneously.

Again, I want to reiterate that the Enlightenment Exercise should be done with an ERCEM Specialist because it is filled with lots of emotionality, anger and pain. The addict needs support to navigate through this process, and the partner needs the structure and stability to be a witness to the origins of his acting out. ERCEM Specialists are the only professionals who has the training to take you through this exercise. Go to www.sexhelpwithcarolthecoach.com and find an ERCEM Specialist who can support you in this process.

I WOUNDED MY WIFE EXERCISE

In this book, we will expect the SA to work on doing whatever he can to help you stabilize, but that is no easy feat.

To the Addict: In the book *Help. Her. Heal*, I ask you to identify the wounding you have caused because you will be using it to show her that you see her pain and know you caused it. You immediately hold yourself accountable by taking ownership for the pain. When you can correlate your actions with the impact it has had on her, you are more likely to understand how she feels, and it is the beginning of building that empathy muscle. I know that as you examine the damage that your addiction caused, it can leave you feeling shame and guilt. But I promise that as you begin to see the damage and hold yourself accountable, you can feel the growth of the man you want to become. As she sees that you understand her pain, she will begin to believe there may be a chance to rebuild the relationship and create a new marriage that is built on the foundation of trust.

In this book I would like you to take it a step further. I want you to think of all the ways that you have hurt her:

- Emotionally
- Physically
- Socially
- Intellectually
- Spiritually

Please write out ten ways you have wounded her in all these areas. First start with how you have wounded her emotionally.

1. I know I have wounded you emotionally by causing you to question my love I have for you.

2. I wounded you emotionally by causing you to doubt your sanity.

3. I wounded you emotionally by flooding your brain with feelings that are overwhelming.

4. I wounded you emotionally ______________________________

____

____

5. I wounded you emotionally ______________________________

____

____

6. I wounded you emotionally ______________________________

____

____

7. I wounded you emotionally ______________________________

____

____

8. I wounded you emotionally ______________________________

____

____

9. I wounded you emotionally ______________________________

10. I wounded you emotionally ______________________________

Now do the same for how you have wounded her physically.

1. I wounded you physically when I endangered your health by exposing you to sexually transmitted diseases.

2. I wounded you physically by risking you and our unborn child to disease.

3. I wounded you physically by causing your brain trauma.

4. I wounded you physically ______________________________

5. I wounded you physically ______________________________

6. I wounded you physically ______________________________

7. I wounded you physically ____

8. I wounded you physically ____

9. I wounded you physically ____

10. I wounded you physically ____

Now look at how you wounded her socially.

1. I wounded you socially when I made you doubt who in our community may have known about my deception.

2. I socially wounded you when I made you wonder if the women you saw in the grocery store may have been old acting out partners.

3. I wounded you socially because the friends we know may think less of you for staying with me.

4. I wounded you socially

5. I wounded you socially

6. I wounded you socially

7. I wounded you socially

8. I wounded you socially

9. I wounded you socially

10. I wounded you socially

Now it may be difficult for you to imagine how your sexual behavior wounded her intellectually. Sexual addiction impacts the partners brain, and it affects her ability to reason, make decisions, speak, or problem solve. She is in a state of shock, and her brain is flooded with chemicals that are preventing her from thinking rationally. This ordeal has caused temporary brain dysfunction.

As you think about the impact of your choices, complete the following:

1. I intellectually wounded my wife by causing days of sleeplessness.
2. I intellectually wounded my wife because she is not able to think at work.
3. I intellectually wounded my wife because she has taken off several days from work.
4. I intellectually wounded my wife ______________________________
____
____
5. I intellectually wounded my wife ______________________________
____
____
6. I intellectually wounded my wife ______________________________
____
____

7. I intellectually wounded my wife ________________________________

8. I intellectually wounded my wife ________________________________

9. I intellectually wounded my wife ________________________________

10. I intellectually wounded my wife ________________________________

Most women report their spiritual life has been compromised because of the betrayal. They now question their relationship with God and themselves. Put yourself in your wife's shoes and imagine how this might be true.

1. My wife was spiritually wounded because she questions where God was when I was cheating on her.

2. My wife was wounded spiritually, because she wonders why God did not get me to repent when she has been a faith-filled believer.

3. My wife is spiritually wounded and wonders if she can trust anything in her life.

4. My wife's spirituality has been compromised because ______________________

____

____

5. My wife has been spiritually wounded ______________________

____

____

6. My wife questions her spirituality ______________________

____

____

7. I wounded my wife spiritually ______________________

____

____

8. I wounded my wife spiritually ______________________

____

____

9. I wounded my wife spiritually ______________________

____

____

10. I have wounded my wife's sense of spirituality because ______________________

____

____

It can be helpful for you to read this list to her and if she is willing, ask her to add additional ways that your compulsive behaviors affected her.

You will need to work on yourself to increase your recovery while beginning to communicate and connect with what she needs. Because she is in a traumatized state, you will have to be very consistent and show her that she is your top priority. Understandably she will not trust you, but she will desire seeing your efforts as they leave her a feeling of hope.

Note: The two of you can do this work in the privacy of your own home, but it can be helpful to have a professional to support you as you work through this process. You may decide that this would be a good exercise to present to your therapist so that you can do the work together in a safe environment like a therapy or coach's office.

Chapter 7

You Both Need to Understand Your Feelings

As you start this journey, we will be talking about feelings and emotions. We have found it helpful when identifying emotions to reduce them to five basic feelings:

- Anger
- Sadness
- Happiness
- Fear
- Loneliness

As a partner, you are flooded with feelings, and as the addict, you may be afraid to express your feelings—you believe you are not entitled to having them after the betrayal. Nothing could be further from the truth, and you both must express them to feel a sense of authenticity. To keep it simple, I ask you both to identify the primary feeling you are experiencing. All emotions can be condensed down to any of these five feelings.

The difficult task is to determine which feeling is predominant at the time. You may be aware that you feel several feelings at one time. Oftentimes, the feeling most uncomfortable for you is the one you avoid. Women typically feel and express sadness when the main feeling that they are experiencing (and avoiding) is anger. This frequently changes when partners are in the betrayal trauma state because their amygdala is activated, and as a result they go into the fight part of "flight, fight or freeze" stage and feel uncontrollable anger and rage. When this occurs, it can further compromise their sense of safety because they wonder what is happening to them. They have never felt so out of control with anger before, and they wonder if they are going crazy.

Using feeling self-regulation will allow you to recognize the feeling, describe it, identify where you feel it in your body, and then determine what helpful message it might be trying to send you so that you can take better care of you. Partners who use the "Feeling Check-in Method" no longer feel controlled by their feelings. Instead, they use their feelings to guide them to better self-care.

THE DAILY FEELINGS INVENTORY FORMAT

The following format allows you to take some quiet time and assess what you want for the day. This simple tool empowers you to put yourself on the front burner—you get to decide how you want to live your day and what direction you want to take. It is a simple exercise of self-empowerment. The belief is that when you tune in to what you need, you are more likely to have enough energy for yourself and others.

You can create any structure you need to set aside time for a feelings check-in. Most people find it helpful to find a quiet time and place to write a paragraph or two on what was their primary feeling throughout the day and where they felt it in the body. Each person is different and will store their feelings in their body differently, so this process is teaching you to take an inventory of how your mind and body processes feelings. Journaling your feelings helps you honor them and decide how they can motivate you to make necessary changes for yourself.

As illustrated in *Unleashing Your Power: Moving through the Trauma of Partner Betrayal*, The daily "Feelings Inventory" has many benefits, allowing you to:

- Be in the moment
- Pay attention to what is going on inside of you
- Nurture yourself
- Let go of all things of which you have no control

For the Partner: Although you are trying to ascertain what you might have control over in order to keep yourself safe, it can be freeing to let go of the need to manage all his whereabouts and activities. Now that you know what he did, he will never be able to fully deceive you again! The "Feelings Inventory" is the vehicle that allows you the opportunity to let go of the need to control and stay focused on yourself.

This book is about you both working together to increase your safety, with him doing much of the work to repair the damage resulting from the addiction. That being said, I would like you to stay present with your feelings in order to work through them. This will require that you encourage yourself to be accountable for your own life.

To the Addict: In *Help. Her. Heal*, you learned that you needed to be present with your feelings so that you develop empathy. Both you and your spouse should make a regular practice of spending five to ten minutes linking up your thoughts and feelings with the day's activities and your interactions with others. Let it be the compass for what you are needing for yourself and from each other.

As you identify your primary feeling, you may find that it correlates strongly with guilt and shame. When you do the hard relational work and watch your spouse agonize about what has happened to her, it is easy to go into a shame cycle. When this occurs go back to Chapter 7 of *Help. Her. Heal* to find an affirmation that you can tell yourself to put things back into perspective. Many of my clients report that they use Principle #6, which reminds you to practice saying, "This is not who I am today, this is the consequences of my past actions. I need to realize that I can only stay healthy and support my wife properly if I stay focused on who I am today."

It can feel like a juggling act to practice good recovery, help her heal, and stay out of the shame cycle, so I would encourage you to re-read the "7 Principles of Conflict After Betrayal" (found in Chapter 7 of *Help. Her. Heal*) and customize them based on what you need to stay strong as you continue to do this important relational work with your wife.

Couples oftentimes report an impasse when they are working together on finding connection. Where do you both feel personally stuck? Take a few moments and think of which part of the betrayal seems the most problematic.

For the Partner: Most women report that they feel most stuck because their safety has been compromised. Does it affect your sense of safety? If so, how does that make you feel?

For the Addict: How do you feel about having robbed her of her sense of safety? Do you go into sadness or fear? Or does it catapult you into guilt or shame? What do you

do when you feel guilt or shame? Do you feel discouraged? Do you feel like you will never be proactive enough to stay ahead of potential triggers that take her down the spiral of fear? Does it make you feel unworthy? What is the primary feeling that links up to "unworthiness?"

To the Partner: Has the betrayal shattered your sense of the world? What feeling does that evoke in you? Have you generalized it to not trusting anyone or anything? Has it morphed into not trusting your family, your community, your work environment, your religious community, or God?

Which feeling is the most overwhelming as you both think of the betrayal? The two feelings that frequently come up in our sessions and typically stop women from moving through their issues are fear and sadness. For men, it is sadness and loneliness. It is imperative that you identify what feeling is immobilizing you. Spend some time sharing your feelings with your spouse.

You may be flooded by your feelings, which makes it feel impossible to sort through them. Your brain is trying to process normally but is in shock, and you are feeling a whole host of feelings that can seem overwhelming. This is a normal reaction to partner betrayal, and what you need to do is self-regulate and co-regulate.

There are many ways to self-regulate when you feel flooded by your feelings. Part of doing your own work is to learn how to ground yourself and find resources that will diminish the terror that can naturally occur when you are flooded (otherwise known as resourcing).

Partners report that there are many things they can do to honor their feelings and process them to move forward on their journey. Some examples are:

Prayer	Meditation	Journaling
Therapy	Support Groups	Coaching
Mindfulness	Intentional Self-Care	Retreats

In the recovery world there is a slogan that encourages a person to "face your fears head on." This encourages you to accept them for what they are but not be controlled by them. It is important for you to sit with your feelings to ascertain what they might be telling you. When you are in trauma, you are flooded with feelings, but now that you are resourcing, I want to reinforce how you can use your feelings to motivate you to make some needed changes in your life. I would like you to explore some situations that have felt problematic and observe what they might be telling you.

IDENTIFYING THE POWER OF FEELINGS

1. What situation have you encountered and felt personally overwhelmed by?

2. What was the primary feeling, and how did it affect your choices?

3. How could you use this feeling to motivate you to make some needed changes?

Let's try another one.

4. What is another situation that you have encountered and felt personally overwhelmed by?

____

____

____

5. What was the primary feeling, and how did it affect your choices?

____

____

____

6. How could you use this feeling to motivate you to make some needed changes?

____

____

____

I will share some examples of how other partners identified how sitting with their feelings contributed to some forward movement.

1. One partner used her anger to create boundaries that would empower her. She might not have been able to control his frequent slips, but she certainly could make her bedroom a safe haven by explaining that she had no desire to be around him when he didn't prioritize better recovery. As a result, she took over the bedroom and excluded him from the opportunity to be close to her. She explained that she needed ongoing distance to process her anger.

2. Another partner recognized that her loneliness was a sign that she needed more connection, so she purchased not one, but two French bull terriers to love on. The puppies were no substitute for a healthy husband, but they distracted her from focusing on him. A secondary

gain was that she and her husband would walk the dogs together, which inadvertently brought them closer.

3. One woman was flooded with feelings. But as she sorted through them, she identified that her primary feeling was fear. As she sat with her fear, she recognized that she needed to calm down her emotions. She felt disoriented because of the dysregulation. She committed to spending more time looking at her fear as a gift instead of "the enemy." This resulted in her asking herself, "What is fear trying to show me?" As she power walked each day, she would ask God to reveal to her what she needed to know most about the fear. One day, she clearly heard God telling her that her fear had more to do with not trusting herself. She started to weep and recognized that she had lost her connection to herself. She committed to focus on intentional self-care to get to know herself again and separate from the betrayal. She spent extra hours in yoga classes learning how to slow down her mind. She felt more control in her body and began to get her intuition back.

   She also decided to resume playing the piano, which she had abandoned in adolescence. She committed to taking lessons so that she could practice thinking about something else instead of the betrayal. She found it liberated her from the old fear and reminded her that her feelings could be used to guide her towards something that empowered her instead.

To the Addict: Feelings have always been hard for you too. Your addiction has interfered with "feeling development." There is much research that suggests addiction helped to medicate your feelings. This meant you never fully were able to understand them, nor could you feel them because your goal was to suppress them with your addiction. In *Help. Her. Heal* we went over these same five feelings so you could become more comfortable identifying them for your benefit and recognizing them in your wife. You must recognize feelings to have empathy for yourself and for others.

I want you to list the earliest time you felt each one of the five feelings. After you have completed this exhausting list, I would like you to share it with your wife so that she can understand the evolution of your feelings. This may bring up vulnerable emotions for you, which may act as a detour to expressing them, but push through them anyway. As you do this work, you will want to find opportunities to express your vulnerability. The act of vulnerability is a "trust builder."

- The first time I felt anger was

- I dealt with the anger by

- The messages I received from my parents/caretakers about anger was

- The first time I felt sadness was

- I dealt with the sadness by

- The messages I received from my parents/caretakers about sadness was

- The first time I felt anxious was

- I dealt with the anxiety by

- The messages I received from my parents/caretakers about anxiety was

- The first time I felt lonely was

- I dealt with the loneliness by

- The messages I received from my parents/caretakers about loneliness was

- The first time I felt happy was

- I dealt with the happiness by

- The messages I received from my parents/caretakers about happiness was

- Were there any common themes in how you experienced your feelings?

- What were the messages that your parents/caretakers gave you about feelings and particularly your feelings?

- How did each parent express feelings?

- Which feelings are you the most comfortable expressing?

- Are you afraid to express feelings? And if so, do you know why?

Now let's look at present-day circumstances that involve your ability to identify, process, and express feelings, and let's take a hard look at how you express them when you are around your wife. I realize this might involve some real excavation of what causes your feelings and how you express them. You may also notice a relational pattern of not expressing your feelings to your wife. To create connection, you must learn to share vulnerable feelings with her.

Once you are done with them, you will want to share them with your wife.

- The last time I felt anger was

- I dealt with the anger by

- The messages I received from my wife about how I dealt with my anger was

- The most recent time I felt sadness while I was with my wife was

- I dealt with the sadness by

- The messages I received from my wife about how I dealt with my sadness was

- The most recent time I felt anxious with my wife was

- I dealt with the anxiety by

- The messages I received from my wife about how I dealt with my anxiety was

- The last time I felt lonely and was with my wife was

- I dealt with the loneliness by

- The messages I received from my wife when I expressed loneliness was

- The last time I experienced happiness was

- I dealt with the happiness by

- The messages I received from my wife when I showed my happiness was

To the Addict: As you get more and more comfortable sharing your feelings, you will be better able to contain her pain as she describes her feelings. This process is called co-regulation. For it to be effective, it has to build on the foundation of you being able to process and express your own feelings.

Co-regulation is when the addict helps his wife to regulate her emotions. This can be done with the two of you following the formula in this book, but you may want to use a specialist who can co-facilitate and create a structure that will help both of you to feel safe as the partner begins to share feelings. Because she is in a traumatized state, it may require small doses of communication (it may even require small doses of time together initially).

To the Partner: When you express your fears, anger, sadness, and grief to your husband and he can hold them for you, you are much more likely to manage them because you are not suppressing or repressing them.

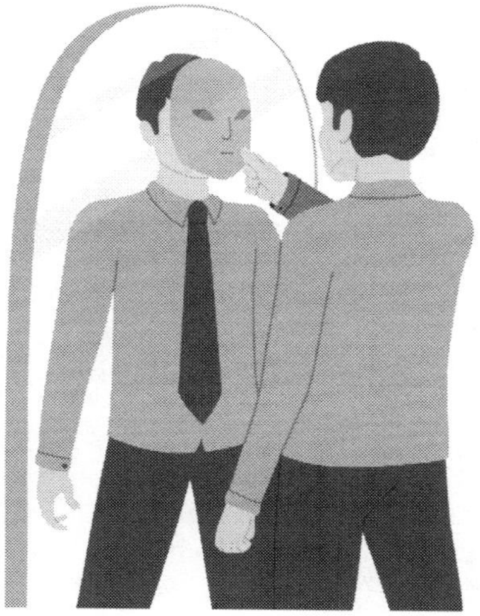

What is suppression and repression? Suppression is when you stuff your feelings away and try to ignore them because it does not feel safe to express them. You may have learned this early in your childhood, and now that this betrayal has occurred, you have gone back to using suppression as a natural defense mechanism to keep yourself safe. It is not good to suppress or stuff your feelings because the body keeps score, and these feelings will cause you great distress later.

Repression is when you bury your feelings and thoughts so deep that you no longer consciously know they are there. This is an extreme form of denial. Even though it may feel like it is serving you to have amnesia shielding you from the effects of the feelings and the events from your past, it will play out in how you function, your mental health, or even your physical health. "What you resist, persists" in one form or another, and that is why you are so brave for facing your fears head on and working to assess both your current situation and the state of your relationship.

Both addicts and partners have been known to repress feelings. If you are a partner who has repressed your feelings, you will likely be unable to find connection no matter what he says or does. Although your defense mechanisms are there to protect you, they can be problematic. When defense mechanisms are used too frequently or with too much intensity, they can end up blocking you from restoring your relationship. You may even find that they rob you from enriching relationships in business, at church, with other family members, or in life.

Men suppress and repress feelings too. If you are an addict who feels numb and does not believe you have any of the five feelings, you will want to work on this with your therapist with great determination. The truth of the matter is that if you cannot identify and express your feelings, you will be a shell of a man to her. She needs to know how you are feeling. She needs to know when you are afraid—when you are afraid she might leave you, when you are afraid you are not good enough, when you are afraid the relationship may not heal. When you express those feelings to her, this will more than likely start a dialogue where you may find her reassuring you that she wants to know your feelings.

CONNECTION-SHARES ENHANCE SAFETY AND CONNECTION

To the Partner: You may ask, "What if I don't feel safe sharing my thoughts and feelings with him?" Maybe he does not seem to be working hard enough, so you don't want to be that vulnerable. When couples go through that impasse, I encourage them to make sure to talk about their feelings in a check-in, since that is a structured process that allows you to identify the number one feeling you are having. You will learn more about check-ins in Chapter 12.

The important thing is that both of you own your feelings. It is a natural defense mechanism to put them on the back burner and hope that a time will come when you feel comfortable enough to share them, but if you do not start sharing them now, that time may never come.

One thing we know about partners who have been through discovery is that they oftentimes are unable to express themselves in this crisis state. Partners report that since discovery, their mind is no longer clear, and they have trouble communicating clearly. They cannot find the right words, and sometimes they cannot speak at all. This is because trauma affects the part of the brain that receives and expresses communication. Your frontal lobe has functions linked to speech production, and Broca's area of the brain serves a vital role in the generation of a speech network. It is no wonder why you are having trouble producing words to describe how you feel or what you think!

As you work through your trauma and he helps you to co-regulate, you will be able to gather your thoughts together and work towards expressing yourself slowly. As your brain heals, the words will come back as well. But after recognizing how the trauma has impacted your frontal lobes, you have all the more reason to move slowly into safety and trust your intuition to know how much of your feelings to share.

If you are having trouble expressing yourself and cannot find the words to convey what you are feeling, I would encourage you to go slower and find somebody very, very safe to share your feelings.

If your fears are preventing you from grounding and resourcing, then it may be time to do some processing on an unconscious level. Brain spotting, EMDR, and Somatic Experiencing are all extra resources to use when processing your wounds and the wounds of your childhood, and doing so may free you up from your tendency to always appear in control.

When you process beliefs and reactions that may be tied to childhood issues, it frees you up to live in the present. Doing this will motivate you to take care of yourself differently.

LEANING INTO TRUST

As you work as a couple to heal, I am going to ask both of you to lean into trust. I know that feels impossible, but you must let a sliver of hope and light in to continue to strengthen yourself and the coupleship. This process of trust begins with trusting yourselves on an individual basis.

To the Partner: You must begin to believe that this relationship is worth fighting for and that you are the reason he is fighting so hard. I know it feels scary and even humiliating to begin to trust him again. You wonder if other people are doubting your judgment and are secretly thinking that you are crazy. You have some naysayers telling you that you are too good to put up with "his garbage," and they do not want you to be a "sucker."

Do not let their criticism confuse you and make you doubt your feelings. Identify them and then use them to propel you toward your desired transformation. Making the decision to stay together and to work on rebuilding the relationship is your choice. Although other people can be concerned and protective, they do not understand the science behind sex addiction, nor do they understand the many multitudes of times that he tried to stop and could not. They cannot put themselves in your shoes and reckon with the thought of divorce, the importance of your vows, or splitting time with the kids or grandkids.

No one can know the sacrifice you have been through or the love you have in your heart for the man you hope he can be.

Let me remind you that when a man is in good recovery and is practicing the principles, he is healthier than 85% of married men out there! Understandably, there must be a part of you that wants to take advantage of a renewed commitment with integrity. It can really help to have a partner-sensitive specialist who can also support you as you work through your fears and help you find yourself again. The more support you have, the more you will be able to use those feelings as a compass to point you in the direction that is best for you. You will become confident in your own intuition and will make decisions that work best for you.

I have had so many couples hold back from sharing their feelings because they are afraid they will be rejected or their feelings will be used against them. It is understandable that during the crisis of sex addiction sharing feelings comes at a high cost.

If you, as the addict, want to share your true feelings with your wife, you fear she will resist them. Many addicts have even said to me, “I have no right to share my feelings with her because of the atrocities I have caused.” This is a negative mind story that you tell yourself. Depending on her wounding, she may not acknowledge, validate, or trust your feelings, but deep down inside there is a place within her that does want to know how you are feeling. She yearns to know the real you, but she fears that you are not capable of being honest since you have lied to her for many years.

Reconnecting can feel terrifying for both of you. If you need more support, have your therapist use this book as a guide to support you in your desire to heal together. Having a neutral person to provide structure can be a key ingredient to your healing.

Chapter 8

The Ultimate Goal of the Early Recovery Couples Empathy Model (ERCEM): Restore Safety, Trust, and Intimacy through Empathy

ERCEM was designed to set up a structure for you to begin to feel safe and work through the anger and grief of learning that your husband had an addiction. In working with couples, I could see that he wanted to help you but he did not know what to do because he was the perpetrator of your pain.

You, as the partner, may not want to be vulnerable because he is not worthy nor has he earned your trust. You are devastated by the betrayal and fear that your relationship will never be restored. You have not felt safe enough to even begin to share your true feelings because you do not know who your spouse really is. In the last chapter, you learned to look at your feelings a bit differently and hopefully you have been encouraged to identify and express them to begin the process of allowing him to create a safe haven for trust. Remember that this process can not be accomplished quickly, but every day that you work on letting him help you heal is another day that renews trust.

If you look at this diagram that my colleagues Janice Caudill and Dan Drake use in their book, *Full Disclosure Volume* 1, you can see that you must know the truth to determine if you can increase your sense of safety. You are suffering from a relational trauma and there are no guarantees that the relationship can rebound from it.

We do not expect you to put yourself into a vulnerable position as safety is your number one concern. It is, however, important for you to notice his ability to be vulnerable because that is part of his treatment requirements. It is not imperative that you acknowledge it, but it is helpful.

If you have been working on the relationship either through a couple's recovery group or with a therapist, it would benefit him and the relationship if you could acknowledge the changes he is making with others and his attempts at sharing his feelings and being vulnerable.

If you can work on those first steps, you will be more likely to work towards trust, vulnerability, and increased intimacy. Intimacy can be increased in many ways, and you will learn in Chapters 10 and 14 how to increase behaviors that work towards more closeness and connection.

My colleagues, Janice Caudill and Dan Drake who wrote a series of books on full disclosure for the addict and the partner explain in their books, *Full Disclosure: How to Share the Truth After Sexual Betrayal* and *Full Disclosure: Seeking the Truth After Sexual Betrayal*, that "intimacy is the highest point on this pyramid.* It is built on a foundation of vulnerability, trust, safety, and ultimately, honesty. With these components, relationships flourish in love and health. They are satisfying and connected." (Dan Drake, Joanna Raabsmith, and Matthew Raabsmith have updated this pyramid, placing honesty at the base to reflect intentional action steps taken to provide truth).

Unfortunately, when couples are devastated by sexual betrayal, it is not just their intimacy that suffers, it is the whole pyramid that crumbles, starting with the foundation of truth. The relationship the betrayed partner thought they were building for weeks, months, years, or even decades shatters when lies and sexual secrets are discovered.

You, as a couple, need to agree to authenticity, honesty, and transparency for how you feel, what you need, and what you believe for the coupleship. And that includes when there is conflict. You must be able to know that you can get through the

*The Trust/Intimacy Pyramid © Kintsugi Recovery Partners LLC. Adapted for use with permission.

conflict and get closer as a result, because conflict breeds intimacy if you are working on creating a healthy relationship.

I always tell my partners to utilize other safe people to share their stories. Many partners recognize how helpful groups can be because they offer safety and support. When you access group support, you will have a safe place to share your feelings and thoughts with other women who have similar shared experiences. The group is anonymous, so you need not worry about confidentiality or any of your family and friends finding out your private information. A group allows you to express yourself freely without judgment. What we know about group work is the more you practice using your communication skills, the more you will regain your ability to use your expressive skills. And then you can practice those skills at home with your spouse. Your spouse can speed up this process if he can be patient with you and encourage you to share anything that is locked deep inside of you.

To the Addict: You should be experiencing the same phenomena when you attend your groups. As you share your story with the men in your support group, you should feel great relief that these are people who understand. You should feel a closeness (intimacy) that you receive and benefit from. This process will occur with your wife but since it is a slow process, you must be patient. Keep practicing that vulnerability in your group so you can use it at home and create a sense of closeness with her. I recognize how difficult this can be because in normal relationships when you work on trust and vulnerability, it usually is reciprocated. Because of the betrayal, you have to initially practice the concepts without reciprocation. She is going to need to see you walk your talk over and over again before she will be able to believe it.

YOU WILL BE INCREASING THE HEALING PROCESS BY LETTING HER KNOW THAT YOU KNOW YOU CAUSED THIS PAIN AND WILL DO EVERYTHING POSSIBLE TO HELP HER HEAL FROM THE TRAUMA OF SEXUAL BETRAYAL.

It is important that both of you know what can happen to a partner once she has experienced the trauma of discovery. Although not every partner experiences a trauma response most partners experience at least ten out of the 20 symptoms below.

Janina Fisher is an expert on trauma and she has created a graphic that really depicts the many symptoms of trauma. How many trauma responses are you dealing with as a result of the betrayal?

For the Couple: It is important for you, the partner, to share with your husband the many trauma responses that you may be experiencing intermittently.

*Trauma chart adapted from Janina Fisher with permission.

To the Addict: We will be talking about what you can do to help her stabilize. But first, you need to know how she feels to know how you can support her to experience increased safety and stabilization. Many partners express that they want to see the addict go above and beyond to see him put her first! This is why the willingness list is so important. It is a vehicle to show her what you are willing to do to be open and transparent with her to begin to restore the trust.

To the Partner: Is your husband willing to do WHATEVER it takes to make you feel safe? In Chapter 1 of *Help. Her. Heal.*, I asked the addict to write down 25 things he could do to make you feel safe.

He can get out that list and share it with you in a check-in.

He may say:

- "I am willing to give you all my passcodes."
- "I am willing to quit my job so you no longer have to worry about the affair partner whom I see daily at the office."
- "I am willing to talk to your family so they can support you through the stress."

If you have not read the book or done the exercise, I am going to ask you to do it now. We are going to be elaborating on this list now that we have your wife involved in this process.

THE WILLINGNESS EXERCISE

List 20 things you are willing to do to make her feel safe. Write them out here.

1. I am willing ______________________________
2. I am willing ______________________________

3. I am willing ________________
4. I am willing to ________________
5. I am willing to ________________
6. I am willing to ________________
7. I am willing to ________________
8. I am willing to ________________
9. I am willing to ________________
10. I am willing to ________________
11. I am willing to ________________
12. I am willing to ________________
13. I am willing to ________________
14. I am willing to ________________
15. I am willing to ________________
16. I am willing to ________________
17. I am willing to ________________
18. I am willing to ________________
19. I am willing to ________________
20. I am willing to ________________

Now I would like you to read this list to her but to do that you must be in the proper position.

You must sit facing each other with your knees touching each other.

Look into her left eye and share your willingness list slowly so she can hear and process it. Read one statement at a time and watch for her reactions. Give her time to respond, if she so desires.

Be open to her critiquing your list. You may have said that you are willing to take polygraphs once a year and she responds that she will need two tests a year for her own sense of safety. After she has critiqued your list, she is given the assignment to create her own list of additional things she will need.

To the Partner: You have three options. You can request the list, take some time to contemplate how you might add to it, and bring it back to share with him once you have finished it. Or, you can begin to dialogue with him and discuss what you would like him to add in the here and now.

Your third option is to share the assignment with your therapist and do it in the office so that the therapist can be a third set of eyes and ears and help guide you through this process.

Sometimes there are things he is already doing that are no longer needed in your life?

An addict may say he is willing to do a polygraph and his partner says she no longer needs it because she wants to start building trust without the safety prompts.

I had another couple do the list and he had added that he was willing to tell her family about his addiction. The partner thought long and hard about it and responded by saying that she needed her family to stay non-judgmental, so she would not want him to divulge his indiscretions.

Not only does this exercise show his willingness to do the right things, but it also opens the dialogue for what she needs out of the relationship for her healing.

Note: I forewarn you....if you commit to doing something on this list and you do not follow through it will feel like another betrayal to her. Spend time talking about an action plan if the list involves complicated situations like telling the kids, or changing jobs, or moving to new cites.

And if your list includes doing regular check-ins and you begin to get lax on follow through, it will further deepen her wounds. Good relational recovery involves following through with your word. Your integrity is at stake here and so is her safety! Don't make promises you can't keep.

To the Partner: Sometimes your willingness requests will change. One of my clients told her husband, "You no longer need to do polygraph examinations because you have been in really good recovery, and I want to start trusting you without the accountability tools." Then a year and a half later she confided, "I need him to take a test because as I was working with my support group, one woman felt it was good assurance for her husband to be obligated to take the test, and I keep ruminating on that point. I want him to know I will intermittently need this from him just to give him extra incentive to do the right thing." I assured her that it was always ok to change her mind and that from time to time her safety needs will change.

What things might you like him to add? Is it time to talk to your pastor together? Is it time to tell the kids?

This exercise helps you both clarify with him what you need for safety. You are allowing him to show empathy and do whatever it takes to increase your safety. You are also expressing your vulnerability. You both are being very courageous.

Side note: Brené Brown also says he must earn it. The Willingness Exercise is a way he can show you that he wants to earn your trust.

Couples need to make each other feel safe. You as the partner may want to create your own willingness list to show him what you are willing to do to provide more safety for him! Trauma brain can result in erratic and volatile behavior.

Showing him that you are willing to work with him can increase connection and safety. The following script that Dorit Reichental created will also show both of you how to increase safety. Both of you should practice using it with each other.

SAFETY AND RELATIONSHIP AWARENESS

In order to keep our relationship safe, when you say/do ______________________,

it makes me feel ______________________.

The impact it has on me is ______________________,

and I will ______________________

until you can say/do ______________________

and I can see that you understand the impact it has on me.

That will help me to feel ______________________.

(loved, valued, respected, cared for)

As a result of feeling truly seen and heard, you have given me the gift of restored trust and safety.

Chapter 9

The Brain Science of Triggers

As a Partner you are struggling with much right now. Not only are you reeling from the realization that your husband was not who you thought he was, but you are now struggling with the fallout from sexual betrayal. He never meant to traumatize you but did, and now your mind and body are on full alert. You are waiting for signs that you are not safe when you are also looking for signs that you are.

This book is going to help you both find ways of coping with this tragedy and grow stronger from it. You are going to learn to lean into the trauma when your triggers are activated.

Triggers are the by-product of trauma. They can feel frightening and uncontrollable, but they are there to help you stay safe. It used to be that when a woman was triggered, she was left to fend for herself or deal with it on her own. ERCEM suggests when you are triggered, you should work on defusing the trigger together. This means that he needs to be astute at noticing when you are triggered, and you need to be able to tell him when you are in that triggered state.

Many women will complain that they do not understand their triggers. They realize that some of the triggers are linked to specific dates like their marital anniversary, the date of discovery, a love song that was "their song" but no longer has the same meaning, a hotel where the betrayal happened, or the make and model of the car the affair partner owned. These triggers can be identified and understood. They have been consciously linked, and she can make sense of them. Yet, some triggers are locked in the unconscious part of the brain. They are stored there for safe keeping. There is no recollection of what they are or why they are stored in the brain. These triggers haunt the partner because she never knows when one will occur or why she is having one. She feels hijacked by them.

In *Help. Her. Heal.*, I wrote about a woman who could no longer tolerate going to her favorite restaurant, and she did not know why. She would go with friends, feel claustrophobic, and would need to leave. She felt like she was going crazy. One morning as she was slowly waking up, her memory moved from unconscious to conscious, and she realized that she had learned of her husband's acting out with prostitutes in their yellow kitchen. That yellow was triggering to her, and her favorite restaurant had colorful, bright yellow walls. As she was waking, she made the needed association to why she felt so uncomfortable there. She had no previous understanding of the association, but her body had kept score and was telling her to beware of this yellow building because it could hurt her like the other yellow room had.

Sounds crazy? Well, that is trauma.

To the Partner: As frightening as it can feel, I want you to know that triggers are your mind and body trying to keep you safe. When you experience an unknown trigger, you can take pause, look for an identifier, and if nothing comes up, you can silently remind yourself that nothing bad is happening in the here and now. Some women even thank their triggers for being so protective.

To the Couple: Here is how you can work on trigger-busting together.

When the partner is triggered, she becomes activated. Often the addict can see that something is going on with her, but he may not know why.

The left part of the brain goes offline, while the right brain takes over. She is flooded with emotions and feels a sense of being out of control. The spouse must guide her back into the "Window of Tolerance" to decrease the helplessness and confusion she feels.

To the Addict: You can assist her in feeling safe as she experiences the trigger, but you must be patient and present for her as she works through the triggers. When you acknowledge that she looks like she is triggered, you are showing her you recognize the pain of the trigger.

To the Addict: In this chapter, you will learn how to help her deal with her triggers. When you notice she is unexpectantly different, you will want to ask her if she is triggered. This seems like an obvious assumption, but many men have avoided questioning their wives because they fear it will make things worse. They sense that something is wrong, their wife has gotten markedly angrier or has withdrawn for no apparent reason, and it is a typical reaction for men to leave the room to give her space, not realizing how alone and frightened she feels. They do not know they can help her through the trigger by staying with her and helping her co-regulate until the trigger has subsided.

Trigger-busting is a process you will both need to learn to work through together.

To the Partner: I am sure you have noticed that he is working hard to help you heal. It can take a lot of emotional maturity to sit with you when he can visibly see that you are in pain, and he knows that he caused it. When you notice him staying present and watching your pain, you might remind yourself that he is really wanting to help you heal. When you appreciate his effort, you defuse the trigger that has occurred involuntarily.

You may feel indignant that I would even suggest that you appreciate him for helping you through the very event he is responsible for having created from his past actions. Yet your trigger is holding you hostage to the past, and if you want to break the effects of your triggers, you must stop hating him for being the cause of these triggers. This will release you from the current day trauma and cause you to feel more at peace with what is occurring for you in the moment.

To the Addict: Having worked with thousands of partners, it has become apparent that all a spouse wants to do is feel safe again. Whether she felt like she had a good marriage or knew that the relationship had problems, she had no idea you were living a dual life that entailed lies, deception, and secrecy. As a result, this trauma has deeply affected her brain and her brain has gone into overdrive.

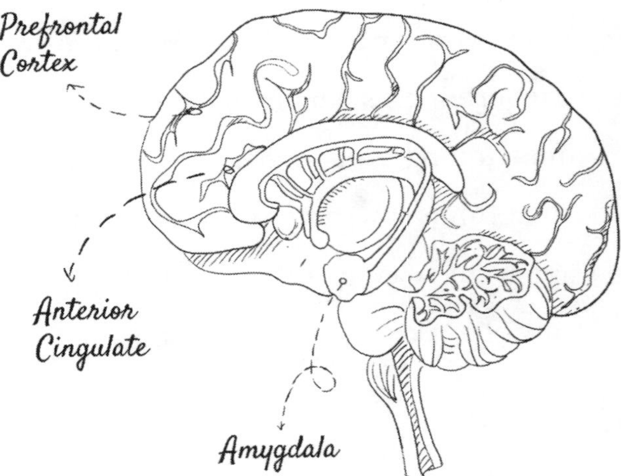

This information has impacted the amygdala, which exists at the bottom of the brain above the brainstem. This part of the brain stores and processes information, and its main function is to keep your spouse safe. Therefore, it guides your wife to react to her pain, anxiety, and anger by going into fight, flight, or freeze mode. If the protective mechanism moves her towards fight, she will go into "attack mode" and say mean and hurtful things. She may become physically aggressive—pushing, shoving, and hitting you as her emotions feel more and more intense. Many wives tell me they are reacting to their emotions in ways they could never have conceived. They wonder if they are going crazy because they have never resorted to name calling or aggressive behavior in the past.

To the Partner: Have you felt like you were going crazy? Has your normal functioning been compromised? Are you having trouble remembering words, dates, and simple tasks that have real impact on your daily functioning? Are you experiencing emotional highs and lows that seem insurmountable? Are you having trouble with impulse control and wanting to yell or cry all the time because of something he has done or not done?

Your brain is being hijacked by trauma. Unfortunately, you are experiencing a trauma reaction that can feel uncontrollable. It will be necessary for you to calm down your brain and work on lots of grounding and resourcing to bring some safety and sanity back into your life. So just like in *Help. Her. Heal.*, I will be showing you how to manage the triggers you are facing because of partner betrayal.

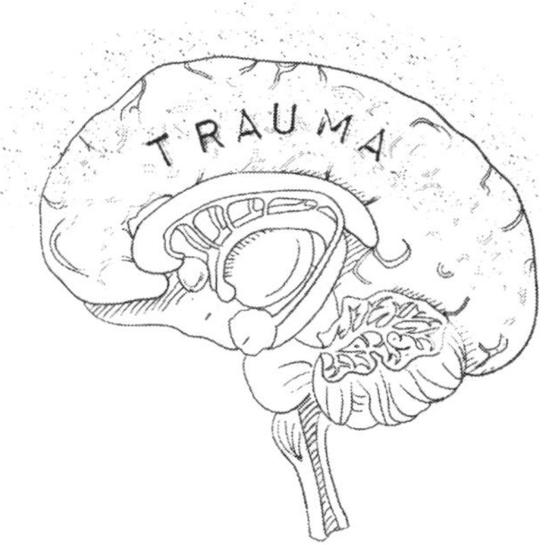

Here is my message to the Addict:

It can feel scary when you notice your wife is triggered. One minute she may be fine, and then BAM, she appears to be struggling with thoughts and feelings that have overcome her. Neither of you necessarily know why they've shown up.

It is important that you understand what happens when your wife is triggered so that you can empathize and spend time using empathy exercises or trigger-busters to help ground her. You will be learning about empathy in the next chapter, so for right now let's focus on how to deal with the triggers.

TYPES OF TRIGGERS

Triggers may have origins you both can trace.

You came home and told her you were overcome by shame as you saw another adult bookstore going into the strip mall. You questioned how this would impact her since you both travel this busy highway every week.

You may have taken your daughter to an ice cream social at school together, only to run into an affair partner from the past.

You both drove by a hotel or massage parlor where you acted out. You try to distract her, but she is obviously triggered and affected emotionally.

She can experience triggers everywhere, and her brain goes into immediate overdrive. She might be aware of the anniversary date of her first discovery. In other words, there may be an actual connection to a person, place, or thing that triggers your spouse.

There may be sensory triggers. For example, she sees a billboard on the highway that advertises a hotel where you have acted out and her brain takes her into the past. It may be auditory, and she becomes triggered by the ding of a text on your iPad because it was a text from a prostitute that was the origin of discovery for her. It might be olfactory, and she's triggered as she smells the Italian meal she was preparing for you when she got the phone call from the affair partner.

Those types of triggers, once identified, can help you both decide how you are going to manage them.

As the addict, it is your responsibility to let her know if a trigger is coming up—that way, you can pre-plan how you can deal with the potential trigger together.

However, sometimes the triggers are not associated with anything conscious.

Triggers may occur without any direct link to a situation that is associated with your acting out.

What we know about trauma is that there can be associations that are unconscious. Many times, as I mentioned, triggers are associated with the five senses, but unfortunately, they can be stored unconsciously too. Just like the woman who was triggered by the color yellow, the partner may be triggered for no known reason and all the more reason for the addict to realize a shift in her behavior and ask her, "Has something triggered you or it seems like you are triggered."

Your partner does not necessarily know why she is being triggered. The best way you can be helpful is to decipher when you believe she is being triggered and ask her if she is being triggered.

She may not tell you when she experiences triggers, but you can tell that something is off with her. She seems angry, cold, or distant, and you do not know why.

Can you imagine how scary that would be to not know why your brain has gone offline? One minute she is going through her normal day and then instantly, and for no apparent reason, she is thrown back into post-traumatic stress. She must navigate through the fear, panic, and fright that accompanies the association.

As you experience the trauma, it may feel unsafe to share what is going on with your mind and body, but I plead with you to be more vulnerable and help him know what is going on inside of you. I want him to learn how to help you, and it works better if you share your thoughts in present time. I know that he has hurt you beyond belief, but you two are working on rebuilding your relationship. He needs your guidance to get better at empathizing with your trauma responses and pain.

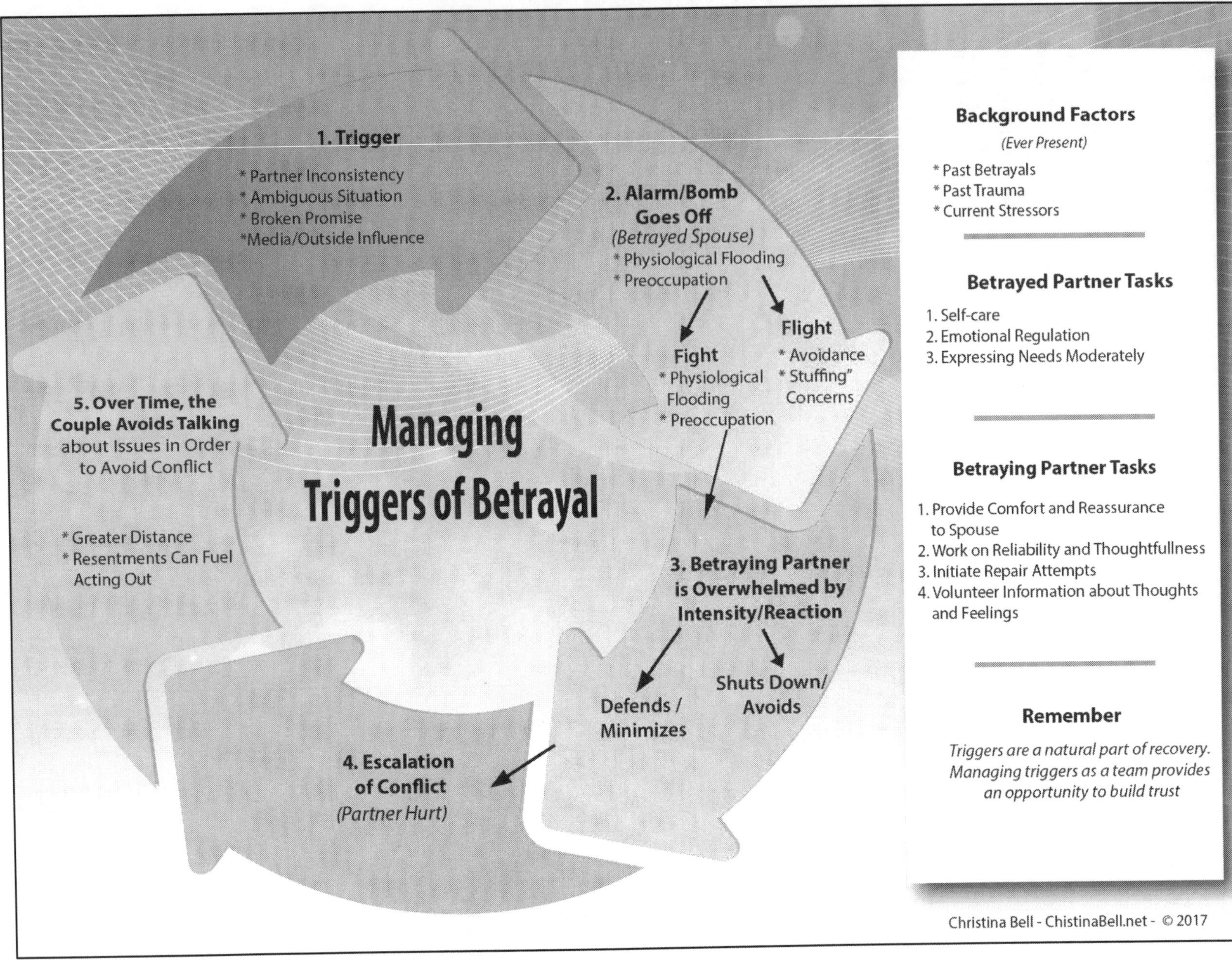

 Reprinted with permission from Christina Bell.

Christina Bell has a wonderful chart that helps you both understand what happens as you are being triggered. Please go to sexhelpwithcarolthecoach.com/resources and print this out so you can add to it and begin the discussion of what happens when you are triggered. I would also recommend that you visit her site at ChristinaBell.net to access her tools for working through triggers. She has a lot of great free tools to help you heal!

So as your wife heals, she will need you to be patient as she experiences the frustration, sadness, and anxiety that accompanies the triggers. She will remind you that she is going through this "hell" because of your acting out.

An addict who is not in good recovery will either lash out or go into isolation to avoid feeling the shame that normally accompanies her anger/fears. As Christina Bell exemplifies on the diagram, it is important to deal with the triggers as a team, and when you assist your wife in working through the triggers, you are building trust. You will need to provide comfort and reassurance to your spouse. Of course, the first step is to have good recovery so she can begin to trust that you have changed. Then you need reliability—reliability in all you do!

- Therefore, you must be predictable and put her first.
- You must be reliable by letting her know when you are leaving and coming home. You will need to follow through with promises and commitments.
- You can help her by taking over the household duties and kids. You will need to step up and provide a true team approach to your family.

When she experiences a trigger, you will need to acknowledge exactly what you are noticing in the here and now. Christina believes it is helpful to provide repair attempts, which John Gottman defined as partner requests. In his book *The Seven Principles for Making Marriage Work*, Gottman defines a repair attempt as any statement or action—verbal, physical or otherwise—meant to diffuse negativity and keep a conflict from escalating out of control. Dr. Gottman calls repair attempts the secret weapon of emotionally intelligent couples.

When an infraction has occurred, it is helpful to ask your spouse, "What can I do for you right now?" or "What do you need?" Maybe she needs more space, or perhaps she needs you to hold her. Maybe she needs you to sit with her in silence as she goes through the trigger.

Unfortunately, many therapists do not know how to advise you to help your wife. They do not know how to help you both to work through the triggers that leave you both feeling inadequate, insecure, and increasingly more fearful. Now she not only fears the triggers but also wonders when the next one will come, and the cycle becomes auto-exacerbating.

You are likely to go into shame and want to do nothing, but this is the time to move into the process of trigger-busting so that you can assist her in getting through it. I am going to share with you a trigger-busters activity sheet that will help you with this process. It takes lots of practice and patience for both you and your partner. Remember to stay patient and gentle; when she experiences triggers she is in full blown trauma and needs to feel reassured that you can work through them together.

IF YOU ARE ACTING OUT OR ARE IN MIDDLE-CIRCLE BEHAVIOR, YOU SHOULD NOT PRACTICE TRIGGER BUSTING. TRIGGER BUSTING, AS A TEAM, "REQUIRES" THAT YOUR RECOVERY IS STRONG AND THAT YOU ARE NOT HIDING ANYTHING FROM HER.

My colleagues Dorit Reichental and Janice Caudill have produced a Trigger-Busters Protocol which can help you and your partner work through the triggers together. They have broken it down into four stages:

1. First calm yourself so that your voice, tone, and demeanor are comforting and soothing. Then identify what you believe you are noticing with your partner in the here and now. You next ask, "Are you triggered?" and validate what you are seeing, which in most cases is the trigger. You can say, "It makes sense to me that you would be triggered," or if you are confused about the trigger, simply "I can see that you are triggered."

2. Help her to stay grounded in the here and now by orienting her to the present. Remind her that she is safe and nothing bad is happening now.

3. De-escalate the experience by saying something nurturing and safe. "I am not doing anything now that would put you in harm's way. This is a bad trigger, and I imagine it is reminding you of my past acting out. I am not acting out now, you are safe, and I am right here with you." If your spouse is open to comforting touch, place your hand on her back.

4. Once the trigger is defused, your partner will be able to anchor onto your regulated nervous system and come fully into the present moment to re-engage and reconnect with you. We call this co-regulation. You have gone through the trigger-busters cycle together!

On the following page is Reichental and Caudill's "cheat sheet" for what they call "Relational CPR for Sexual Addiction and Triggers."

TRIGGER-BUSTERS: RELATIONAL CPR

FOUR STEPS TO SAFETY & CO-REGULATION

Trigger Activation:

Partner: Left brain goes offline; right brain takes over as she becomes triggered Addict must actively help the partner calm her nervous system.

STEP 1: IDENTITY THE TRIGGER

- Clarification: Clarify if spouse is triggered.
    - "I can see X, Y, Z. Are you triggered?"
- Accountability: DO NOT defend, blame, shame, minimize, invalidate, judge, criticize, debate, stonewall, correct with irrelevant detail, withdraw, escape, or project anger.
- Validation: As soon as addict realizes partner is triggered, s/he validates partner.
    - "I can see how scared and unsafe you are, it must remind you of... It makes sense to me that you feel triggered, scared, angry, unsafe, etc."

STEP 2: ORIENT TO HERE AND NOW

- Addict gently reminds the partner that s/he is safe and nothing bad is happening right now (triggered partner cannot differentiate between past and present).
    - "I am not doing anything now to put you at risk or in danger; it's a bad trigger as a result of something that happened when I was acting out."
    - "I am not acting out now, you are safe, and I am right here with you."

STEP 3: DE-ESCALATION, SAFETY, & STABILIZATION USING TRIGGER BUSTERS

- What does the nurturing/protective addict need to continue saying and doing to help the partner down-regulate? The Addict may need to reassure and repeat the message multiple times.
    - As the hijacked brain comes back online, the addict empathically attunes to the partner and states:
        - "I can see this was a really bad trigger. You are safe right now. I am right here with you."

STEP 4: SOCIAL ENGAGEMENT

- Notice the somatic signs that the trigger is being defused. For example, partner's eyes, voice, and face softens as the body begins to relax and breathing regulates. Now the two of you can have a real conversation. In fact, the partner may even want to connect with you.

To the Couple: You can both defuse the intensity and frequency of triggers if you work together to identify them, decide what safety precautions need to occur, and work together as a team to manage them.

To the Addict: It is so important for you to be proactive and inquire about what you are noticing and validate what you are seeing. Sitting with her and going through the trigger with her is an act of empathy. When you put your guilt and shame away and show up for her while she is triggered, you are reminding her that you know that you are responsible for her pain and that you are willing to do what it takes to help her heal!

Chapter 10

Couples Need a New Model to Help Them Heal from Sexual Betrayal: Empathy to the Rescue

In working with men who suffered from compulsive sexual behavioral disorder, I noticed that they knew that they had no skills to make things better. More importantly, they too were traumatized by the trauma they caused their spouse, which further complicated their inability to know what to do to help her. They reacted in ineffective ways to their wife's devastated state. They were floundering in a relational pool of trauma.

I wrote Help. Her. Heal as an elementary guide to help him learn relational skills like reflective listening and feeling identification. However, what he needed most was a crash course on trigger busting and empathy.

In the beginning, I discovered that he really needed a professional to coach him through the relational tsunami occurring at home. Men reported that the skills were helping, but they wished I could be a guide on their shoulder assisting them with the next relational piece. That is when I started bringing in partners to talk about what he was learning and practicing. We were turning his individual sessions into couple's work and practicing the work in the office. Partners were showing me what they needed and wanted for safety, and I was customizing the assignments for them. The addict was experiencing much more success, and the partner was feeling much more safety. I knew that this field needed a new movement that would help couples rebound from this terrible ordeal.

That is when ERCEM was born, and I developed the Early Recovery Couples EMPATHY Model to help professionals work differently with couples who were experiencing sex addiction and partner betrayal. The major component was finding empathy tools to incorporate into the work and to help both of them heal simultaneously.

WHAT IS EMPATHY?

In Brené Brown's video on empathy, she sites Theresa Wiseman, a nursing scholar, who found that empathy consists of four qualities. These qualities are perspective taking, staying out of judgment, recognizing emotions in other people, and communicating that recognition. Basically, empathy is feeling with people. This video is three minutes long and does a great job of describing empathy, so I recommend watching it. It can be found by googling “Brené Brown video on empathy.”

In partner betrayal, empathy is that ability to show you that he can see and feel the pain he has caused you.

To the Couple: Know that his heart is aching because the addiction caused him to do despicable things. He questions whether he will ever be forgiven, and he fully understands if he is not. He ruminates about what he has done to you, and he questions his own sense of sanity. He never meant for it to get this bad, and he hates himself for the pain it has caused you and the family.

He wants to show you empathy, but he is afraid to be close because he believes that he does not deserve your forgiveness. This makes the process of empathy more difficult because empathy naturally opens the door to connection and closeness. He is fearful of the reaction he will get from you. In Help. Her. Heal, I mention that a common response I hear from sex addicts is, "I have tried to use empathy, but she doesn't trust it. Why should she after all I have done to her? She will likely never trust me."

To the Partner: After discovery, you are more than likely coexisting to buy some time in deciding what you are both going to do. It will be necessary for the addict to work diligently on his empathy skills so he can assure you he not only wants connection but knows he must act to restore your sense of safety.

To the Addict: Learning the new skill of empathy would be easier to practice if your partner believed you and accepted it easily, but the truth of the matter is that you need to learn the skill of building connection so she can begin to trust you again. It is a natural process that she will reject initially because she cannot believe that you are seeing things from her perspective.

I understand that learning this new skill would be reinforced if your partner believed and encouraged you, but you must gain the skills to show her you are no longer that dual personality that fed your own needs by sacrificing hers. You will run into the roadblock of defensiveness on her part because she is afraid to let her guard down and let you back into her life. Her trauma response is initially involuntary and requires you to continue to address her pain by seeing it through her eyes.

Empathy is a skill you need regardless of whether this relationship survives the infidelity. Part of your job is now to make a living amends to her to show you are going to be a man of integrity and the man she deserves and desires. "Living amends" is a term that originated out of the recovery world. It is the commitment to keep working on those qualities that make you a better person. The addict is always looking for ways to heal the relationship and prove his commitment to be trustworthy. A living amends cannot occur unless empathy is at the heart of it. Developing empathy shows her you are in sync with how she feels, what she believes, and what she needs. This is counter to your old addictive cycle, and she will reject it because she fears it is not real. She must protect herself until you practice empathy long enough that she gets comfortable with it and the new man you have become. When that occurs, the empathy cycle will come full circle because then you will feel good about yourself, which will restore your integrity.

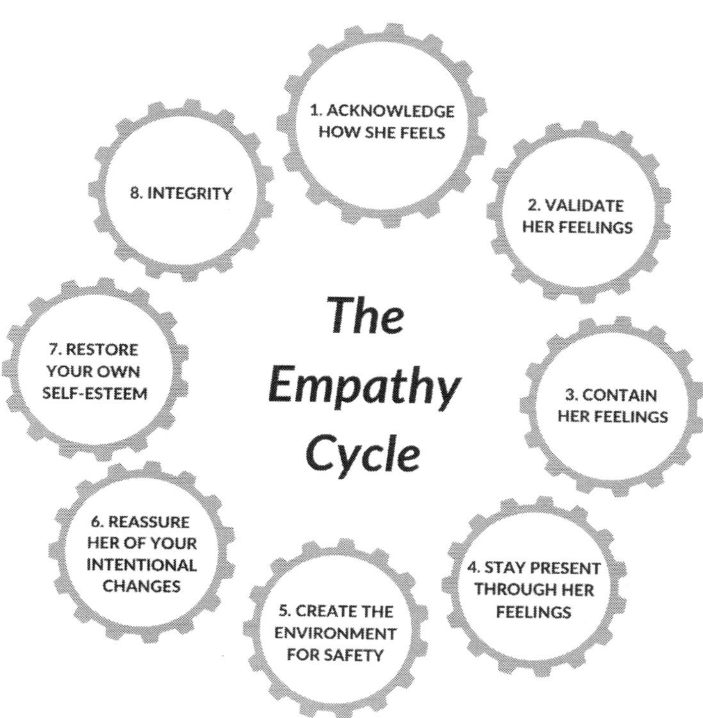

THE OLD ADDICTIVE CYCLE:

Some sex addicts will report that they had marital problems before they started acting out and will say "We didn't communicate prior to the discovery, and we really aren't communicating now that she knows about the betrayal." Empathy can be used in those situations too. Empathy is a form of communication and shows your partner that you heard what she is saying and are noticing the collateral damage. You want to support her by being accountable for the pain you caused.

Your sexual addiction has created a lot of guilt and shame. When you feel your partner start to reject, criticize, or mistrust you, you may want to revert to the old style of communication whereby you get defensive, want to check out, give up, or fight back. When you make the conscious choice to use empathy it can defuse her angry feelings and your protective stance.

Therapists know that problems in a marriage are never the result of "just one person," and yet it is extremely important you remember that ANY problems that you had in your relationship are now secondary to the damage that was caused because of you sexually acting out. You must take full responsibility for the betrayal and consistently show empathy before you can attend to the other normal marital issues that were there prior to the discovery.

Remember, you never want to send her the message that your previous problems prior to discovery caused your acting out. Previous problems were the justifications and rationalizations that you used for your acting out.

In other words, you will not be able to get to the inherent problems in your marriage until you "right the wrongs" regarding your acting out.

This process requires that you show up and develop the skills to right those wrongs, rebuild the trust, reassure her that you are new and improved, and consequently take your marriage to the next level.

Can you imagine how incredible the marriage would have been if you had learned empathy, healthier communication, and true connection? Can you imagine what it will be like to build a sacred space to give and receive the love you always wanted? I have seen couples achieve this and have the relationship they have always wanted, but they must learn the skills for connection and trust. It is up to you to practice healthy relational skills that will begin the process of a living amends. Empathy is the muscle in that living amends.

Empathy will look like two different things depending on whether you are the addict or the betrayed. It will be difficult for you both to be empathetic for a variety of reasons. As the addict, it will mean that you must make a specialized effort to see the world through the eyes of your partner. This requires asking yourself at all times, "How does my partner feel?" I teasingly tell my clients that it is symbolic of the old rubber bracelets that Christians wore which said, "What would Jesus do?" This bracelet was a reminder to always act like Jesus. Well, it would not hurt to wear something on your wrist to reinforce the need for constant empathy. I have had couples go out and buy a bracelet to remind him to consistently work on imagining *how is my partner feeling, and what does she need?*

Empathy might look like, "I have noticed a trigger and need to ask her if she is triggered so I can use trigger busters with her," or "I know that the anniversary of D-day (Discovery) is Friday, and I need to let her know I recognize that day is coming up. I know it is going to be a hard day for both of us, and I am wondering if there is anything I can do to make it easier for her." Or, out of the blue you say, "I just want you to know that it must be hard for you to drive past 'her' (affair partner's) house, and I am absolutely willing to move if that is what you think we need to do to make you feel safe."

When you create this type of mind state, you are working the relational side of the brain that brings forth understanding, compassion, and responsiveness. It feels good to put her needs first and grow your heart relationally. The secondary gain to this is that it makes you feel better about the person you are becoming, and that increases your self-esteem. You feel good about yourself, perhaps for the first time in your life.

I want to give you hope that this is the person you can be! I want to give her that same hope, but that requires you to work empathy with vengeance. Your vengeance is against the addiction that robbed you of so many things. We know you had no idea about how medicating yourself sexually would become so compulsive and result in losing everything that ever had meaning to you—your wife, your family, your self-esteem.

Do you believe that you ever had empathy? After working with addicts for many years, I have often wondered if the addiction robbed you of your ability to empathize. Or, did you lack empathy from the beginning but somehow still functioned and provided for your family? Did this lack of empathy feed into your need to self-medicate with sexual acting out?

DID THE ADDICTION ROB YOU OF YOUR EMPATHY?

For the Addict: To be an addict in active addiction, you must ignore what the addiction is doing to you and her so you can maintain it. You learned to compartmentalize so you could act out your sexual fantasies in total deception and then close that box or compartment to come home to her at night and maintain your old routine filled with love, family commitment, and routines. It also kept you from truly loving yourself because you were holding such a shameful secret. Secrecy feeds the shame that chips away at your self-esteem. When your self-esteem is compromised, so are your relationships. You cannot give what you do not have!

We know that addiction interferes in empathy because you could never have participated in incomprehensible behaviors if you had it. Your inner demon stole your ability to put yourself in her shoes because then you would have had to confess and gotten the help you needed. You were not stronger than the addiction. Your focus was to maintain your secret and the addiction. Then discovery occurred, and all hell broke loose!

Now that the secret is out, it gives you the freedom to commit to empathy. It is imperative to see it from her perspective. You want to put yourself in her shoes to the best of your ability and keep reminding her that your addictive behaviors are at the root of her pain.

In a normal empathetic exchange, a person describes what he or she believes the other person must be feeling. However, your situation is different because in many cases, your actions caused betrayal injury and you can only "imagine" how that could feel. You see it, you are witnessing her struggle, and it is causing you great pain to watch it. You are very much aware of the pain, but you cannot know the devastation she feels from it. That is hers alone.

This book is going to teach you the concept and skills of empathy. This will require that you try to understand her feelings and validate them to show her you know you caused her this pain.

This model will teach you to meet her where she is. If she is unbelievably angry, you will need to let her know you see her anger and you know you caused her that pain. It will show her that you can hold her pain. Sex addicts in recovery can be containers for the pain to keep from immersing themselves in the shame. This lets the spouse know that her choice to share feelings is welcomed in the relationship. This is a huge undertaking and typically requires the assistance of an ERCEM Specialist who can help you navigate through your partner's feelings. You have traumatized her, and now you must prove that you can meet her emotional needs, perhaps even for the first time in your partnership.

These points are so important that I would like to highlight them again.

1. This book is going to teach you the concept and skills of empathy.
2. This will require that you work on understanding her feelings and validate them.
3. You will need to show her you know you caused her this pain.
4. When you use this model, it will teach you to meet her where she is and accept all her feelings.
5. It will demonstrate to her that you can hold her pain.
6. This lets your spouse know that her feelings are welcomed in the relationship and that she is safe.
7. This is a huge undertaking and typically requires the assistance of an ERCEM therapist who can help you navigate through your partner's feelings yourself and as a couple.
8. You have traumatized her, and now you must prove that you can meet her emotional needs and help her heal.

So many women confide in me that yes, they despised the acting out, but even more than that, what they could not live with was the manipulation and "gaslighting" that occurred while their husbands were acting out. They report that their husbands made them feel crazy when they asked too many questions or shared their fears that something was not right.

Even though she may ask the same question one hundred times, her questions are always welcome because you traumatized her brain, and she will ruminate with questions until her brain heals. And the healing is dependent on your recovery and your patience. This work requires you to be very gentle and patient with her. Now that you are in recovery, you will need to learn how to be direct and ask inquiring questions to clarify how she feels and send her the all-important message that her feelings and needs really matter.

You see, "in healthy relationships, conflict breeds intimacy," so the hope is that you can restore your relationship and bring it into a state of health and well-being. Then when conflict occurs, you will have the strength to know that even though it feels scary, once it is externalized and you work on your empathy, your spouse will feel safe and your relationship will move towards more closeness.

This is the goal of empathy and intimacy: to restore the relationship and bring it back into a state of health and well-being. When conflict occurs because of the betrayal trauma, you will have the strength to know that it needs to be externalized through empathy, leaving your wife feeling safe and your relationship feeling more intimate.

THE AVR FORMULA©

As I worked with couples after discovery and disclosure, I noticed how difficult it was for addicts to directly share empathy. When he was face to face with his wife, he lacked the verbiage and the skills to convey how he wanted to help her heal. It was then I decided that I needed to break empathy down in a way which he could use it consistently with his wife.

I experimented with different formulas to convey what he was seeing, what he believed she was feeling, and what he wanted to do to help her heal. Out of these sessions AVR was born.

For the Addict: AVR helps you acknowledge all the damage you had caused. It may feel counterintuitive because you are afraid that if you identify with the fact you are responsible for the pain, she will go on a tirade and be filled with more contempt for your actions. But actually, nothing could be further from the truth. When you see her pain and acknowledge it, it has just the opposite effect. It brings her defenses down because you have made her aware of your accountability, and it reinforces that you not only recognize her pain and struggle but also know you are the source of her pain.

It was then that I realized how your acknowledgement was a game changer for helping her heal. So let's go over this three part formula that will be the foundation for using empathy with your wife.

The "A" stands for "Acknowledge." When you acknowledge the pain that your addiction has caused, or her current struggle or challenge, you are connecting with her on an emotional level. It is so important to remind her at every juncture that you see and hear her pain and that you know you have caused it.

The "V" stands for "Validate." When you use this formula, it will help you to identify how she must be feeling—which is no easy task due to the trauma she has endured. I encourage you to keep it simple and only include the five primary feelings which consist of anger, sadness, happiness, loneliness, and fear. As you determine how the issue or pain is making her feel, you can begin to understand which feeling is the most predominant, which leads to understanding her better emotionally. You will be checking in with her and assessing how she must be feeling. When you validate her primary feeling, you are reinforcing that you are connecting with her on an emotional level. Brené Brown says that empathy is "perspective taking," so it will be your job to "take her temperature" so to speak—identifying which feeling appears to be primary and validating it to build that emotional connection.

The "R" stands for "Reassurance." In this last part of the formula, you are sharing the changes you have made and will continue to make to be in good recovery both relationally and in sobriety. Secretly, she wants to be reassured that you are in good recovery and are making strides relationally to put her first and help her heal. I say secretly because she has been so betrayed and traumatized that she is scared to believe you and believe in you. Her heart cannot take more disappointment, so she stands before you in a guarded position, not sure if she can trust this new reality. Your job is to be consistent, work on the relationship skills in this book to build trust and show her that you will "contain her pain," and sit with her as you both work together to heal from this addiction and from the damage you have caused.

As you practice looking for opportunities to use AVR or, as I prefer to call it, to AVR her, you may question whether it is helping. She may continue to send discouraging messages that she does not believe you, but keep doing the next right thing because she really does want to see you work on relational repair.

Partners consistently tell me that they want the addict to understand the depths and devastation of their pain. Although the addict is living with the pain they have caused daily, part of the partner's healing process is to be reminded that her husband "sees the pain" and can link it back to the "knowing" that he is the reason for the pain. This process must happen consistently for her to feel safe enough to trust his recovery. She wants to believe that you, her husband, will never do this again, but she has no guarantee. Her heart wants to trust you, but her head and experience is telling her it is not safe to be this vulnerable. So, she keeps her guard up and looks for reasons to reject your attempts at honesty and authenticity. This is going to require you to consistently practice empathy in all sorts of ways.

I'm going to repeat that again because I want you to believe the following with all your heart:

1. She wants to believe that you, her husband, will never do this again, but she has no guarantee.

2. Her heart wants to trust you, but her head and experience is telling her it is not safe to be this vulnerable. So, she keeps her guard up and looks for reasons to reject your attempts at honesty and authenticity. She is protecting herself.

3. This is going to require you to consistently practice empathy in all sorts of ways.

WHY DOES AVR WORK?

Using AVR assures her that you are linking up your previous actions to her feelings. It also reminds her of what you are doing to rebuild her foundation of safety.

Often in Early Couples Recovery Work, the addict needs a formula to help him respond to his spouse in a way that shows her he realizes the damage he has caused and how his sexual addiction has affected her.

We have been trained to know that the quickest way an addict can redeem himself, and also prove to his spouse that he will do whatever it takes to build the trust back, is to recognize the pain and remind her he knows he caused it. It is then important for him to validate her feelings, make sure he can assess them appropriately, and then reassure her that he will do whatever it takes to rebuild the confidence she once had in him. Again, let's break down the formula and look for situations to use it.

THE AVR FORMULA

ACKNOWLEDGING THE ISSUE AND THE PAIN YOUR ADDICTION CAUSED

- Practicing the A in AVR requires that you acknowledge the situation and accompanying pain. At first it can seem counterintuitive to bring up the damage your addiction has caused her. She wants to know that you remember her pain is a result of your actions. It assures her that you have not forgotten, nor are you in denial.

- "It makes sense to me that looking at our Memorial Day picnic pictures causes you great pain..."

VALIDATION OF HER FEELINGS USING THE FIVE PRIMARY FEELINGS

- It can be difficult to ascertain how she is feeling, so it is helpful to focus on her primary feeling (and see if you got it right). If you were indeed able to figure out the primary feeling, you will be able to validate it later in your day if it comes up. Remember to identify one of these five feelings: anger, sadness, loneliness, happiness or fear.

- "I can see as you look at the pictures from the Memorial Day family picnic that you feel sadness because now you question the reality of what really happened on that day. It feels like I contaminated the joyful event."

REASSURANCE THAT YOU HAVE CHANGED, AND YOUR TOP PRIORITY IS TO HELP HER HEAL

- It will be necessary to share how you are changing and what you are working on to focus on your recovery and her healing (You do not want to be cocky or arrogant. Instead, you want to gently remind her that you will work diligently to build back her trust in you).

- "I hate that I have ruined some important holidays for you, but I want to reassure you that I am working a good recovery program and will work on creating new memories that you can trust."
- Empathy is putting yourself in her place. You cannot possibly know the intensity of her feelings, but when you are able to look at what she is struggling with through her eyes, you are better able to assess what she needs.

To the Partner: I recognize that the AVR formula will sound scripted and rote. I promise you he does not know how to empathize, so he must learn the skills before it becomes natural to him. I would like to tell you that this process could take three months, but unfortunately it will be 12 to 24 months before this becomes organic. So please be patient with him and try to refrain from rejecting him for his empathy statements. You can make this process smoother if you acknowledge his attempts—no matter how scripted or feeble. All humans need positive reinforcement, especially when they are working on relational repair.

Throughout this book, I am going to share situations which I am sure you will find some parallels or pieces to relate to as you examine your own relationship. You will also see how relational skills help repair the present-day problems that are buried in relational trauma.

STORIES: FROM PORN TO EXTORTION

Sam and Tami came to see me after Tami discovered Sam's visits with married women he had met on "hookup" sites. They had been married for 18 years. Sam had looked at porn from age 11 until discovery at age 43. He knew that something was not right about porn, but he ignored his discernment and rationalized that looking at it was "boys being boys." Over the years his behaviors escalated, and his visits to strip clubs advanced to private encounters in the back of the clubs. He knew that what he was doing was wrong, but his brain could not wait for the next encounter.

He met Tami at his work at the hospital. He fell in love with her immediately and spent all his energy winning her over. He loved her children like his own and after a year, Tami was sure she had met the man of her dreams. They married, bought a home together, and both climbed the corporate ladder at the hospital. They had so much in common and both felt a love they had never felt before. Sam stopped his acting out temporarily and convinced himself that he did not need to act out because he had found the love for which he was searching.

And then his compulsion returned. His visits to the clubs became more frequent, and he started to experiment with other forms of acting out. It was as if his addiction had become even stronger than before he had stopped. It escalated, and he got on websites that advertised "hook-ups with married women." He reassured himself that this would ensure that he did not become emotionally involved. Somehow, he rationalized that if he remained detached emotionally, his sexual acts were harmless. He continued to cheat on Tami until one day, an affair partner started demanding money from Sam. He had initially given her money after she had separated from her husband and could not pay her rent. Her requests became more frequent, so Sam decided to stop seeing her and blocked her calls.

Through social media, she contacted him and threatened to expose him to his wife and the hospital. Sam panicked and gave her $5,000 hush money, but her threats to expose him continued. He eventually went to his wife and shared his infidelity. Tami was in disbelief that he had put both himself and their family in jeopardy. Together they went to the police, but the police said they could do nothing.

They waited together wondering if she would threaten Sam again. The extortionist did contact Tami through social media and demanded more money. Tami told her to leave them alone or they would have her arrested. The extortionist said that Tami and Sam would be sorry, but then she disappeared from their lives. However, her ghost haunted them for years.

When they came to my office, they appeared to have lost all passion for life. They both wanted help, but they admitted that they were just going through the motions. Tami wanted me to help Sam and was not sure if she really wanted to follow my recommendation to come in for the first session. It was as if she had become a skeleton of a woman and wanted to detach from the horror of Sam's addiction.

I acknowledged the intense pain that she must be going through. Tami had thought she had met her Prince Charming who had presented himself as the perfect man. They shared so much together, and now their life seemed ruined. Neither of them had the strength nor the desire to end things. They both expressed a deep love for each other, and yet Tami questioned whether she could really be in love with him because she did not know him. She questioned her sanity because she was not ready to end the relationship. It was as if they were both in purgatory and were not sure what might happen in their future.

She wanted me to fix Sam, and as the session continued, she realized that she too wanted guidance as to how this could have happened and what she should do next.

I talked about the brain science of addiction. I explained that she would not be able to determine what she needed next until she knew what she was dealing with. I talked about the intense work Sam would need to do, and he admitted that he wanted to go somewhere to get that intensive help. Together we talked about treatment centers that could provide him the time and the treatment to reset his sense of self.

Tami admitted that this would also give her the needed space to evaluate what she might need in the future. We sent him to a treatment center specifically for sex addiction, and she worked with me and a psychiatrist who specifically worked with trauma to help regulate her emotions. Tami was very bright and had hundreds of questions, so I knew that together both the psychiatrist and I could help her understand the nature of her husband's addiction.

I encouraged her to write out all the questions she would need to have answered knowing that some of them would be impossible for Sam to answer. The treatment center wanted to do a disclosure. However, I intervened and told them that I would be preparing Tami for the disclosure, so they could help Sam prepare his timeline—which, of course, would start from the time Sam was 11 years of age and saw his first porn video.

I explained to Tami that it was important for her to have lots of preparation and support if she was going to do the disclosure, and I would rather that the couple work with me to ensure that each person was fully supported during it. She agreed to wait for the disclosure until after he returned from treatment.

Tami went out to the treatment center for the week and learned about Sam's compulsions and his sexual addiction. She found that she had learned how to detach from how he had hurt her personally, and she was able to understand how Sam was unable to stop.

She was still devastated, but the 60 days away had given her some perspective. When Sam returned, he remained motivated to stay in recovery and work his program.

Together we worked out the guidelines for the disclosure, and when the day came for Sam to bare all his secrets, he did so with the goal of giving Tami the information she needed to determine how she was going to proceed. He took the polygraph and passed it, and Tami told me at the next session that she felt ready to go on and assess whether they could repair the relationship.

We spent many sessions practicing ERCEM. The couple learned how to use reflective and focused listening. For the next four months Tami had ongoing questions about "how" he could have led such a double life. She understandably was frequently triggered and honestly disturbed by the reality of what she had gone through. Sam worked diligently on using AVR with her to show her the empathy she deserved as they battled this problem together.

As with all my couples, they would come in and talk with each other about the events of the past week and the feelings that accompanied them. They sat in their chairs knees-to-knees and intently focused on each other as they communicated their struggles and successes.

The session started with me asking the couple to discuss with each other how their week had been. Sam stated, "Things were better this week, less fighting, although we were really busy."

Tami said, "I tried to be easier on you because it was your birthday."

Sam replied, "Yes, I had a good birthday. I felt very grateful to be with you celebrating it."

Tami retorted, "Yep, it started out ok, but when you pouted at the end, I just wanted to throw my hands up and say I give up." She looked at me and said, "Sam didn't get everything he wanted for his birthday."

Sam started to explain himself, but he realized that he should AVR Tami because she was understandably upset with him. He said:

- A: "I realize it hurt you that I was selfish with my high expectations for the evening. "
- V: "It must have made you angry when I wanted you to lay close to me so we could hug and cuddle with each other."

- R: "But I want to reassure you that I am going to keep working on my neediness. The next morning after the party, I berated myself for not having gratitude that I had gotten the most important gift for my birthday, and that gift was you."

Tami looked at me and explained, "I baked Sam his favorite cake and we watched a movie, so he automatically assumed that we could be close because we were getting along. I knew what he was thinking, but I absolutely did not feel it was fair for him to think that just because it was his birthday that physical closeness which might have led to sex was automatically on the table. So when I told him after the movie that I hoped he had a good birthday and that I was going to bed, he got sullen, did not thank me for the night, stayed up, and didn't come to bed. I was glad that I stood up for myself, but I was mad that he thought we were normal."

Sam started to explain, but instead he said, "I wasn't able to process it right away, but the next day I was disgusted with myself that I automatically assumed that since our night seemed so normal that we would take it to the next level." He looked at Tami and said, "I promise I will get better at sharing my feelings with you when I begin to feel entitled or assume that you might be ready for that closeness."

- A: "It had to have put you back in that place of wondering how I could be so arrogant."
- V: "You had to have felt very lonely lying in bed that night."
- R: "I can only say that I will continue to work on putting that self-interested side of myself away, and I know that I can do that if I continue to put myself in your shoes."

THE AVR FORMULA EXERCISE

The formula is simple, but it takes lots of practice. So together I would like you both to help him to get comfortable using the formula. After several months of practice, you can change it up and not follow the script verbatim. But I find that following the script gives him a good chance to develop the language behind empathy. Be patient with him...This stuff is hard for men!

USE AVR WITH HER FEARS

To the Addict: So now it is your turn to think back to some frequent fears your wife has experienced.

Fear/Concern # 1

Acknowledge her Fear/Concern/Issue

Validate her feelings

Reassure her

Fear/Concern # 2

Acknowledge her Fear/Concern/Issue

Validate her feelings

Reassure her

Fear/Concern # 3

Acknowledge her Fear/Concern/Issue

Validate her feelings

Reassure her

AS A PARTNER, WHAT WOULD YOU LIKE TO SEE?

To the Partner: I would like you to channel your husband—think of three fears that you currently have and write out an AVR for each one of them. This is an opportunity to let him know what you wish the dialogue would sound like.

Fear/Concern # 1:

If you were channeling him, this is how would you like him to:

Acknowledge the Fear/Concern/Issue

What feeling would you like to have validated?

Validate the feeling

How would you like him to use **R**eassurance to remind you that he is making changes?

Fear/Concern # 2

Identify a Fear/Concern that You Have:

If you were channeling him, how would you like him to:

Acknowledge the Fear/Concern/Issue

What feeling would you like him to validate?

Validate the feeling

How would you like him to use **R**eassurance to remind you that he is making changes?

Fear # 3: Fear/Concern

If you were channeling him, how would you like him to:

Acknowledge the Fear/Concern/Issue

What feeling would you like him to have validate?

Validate the feeling

How would you like him to use **R**eassurance to remind you that he is making changes?

To the Addict: I know that writing these fears and concerns out can feel laborious, but this is a very important process and one that will really make the difference in your relationship. Therefore, you want to get it right and do it well.

Remember that you spent a lot of time lying to her, deceiving her, and denying there was a problem. Now it is your opportunity to be heartfelt, honest, and authentic.

My experience with working with the male population in general, is that men did not learn empathy skills in their childhoods. As a result, this may be the first time you have concentrated on learning it and using it, so it will take some work. There is a saying the 12-Step Community uses that "when you work it, it works!" That saying applies here, so do not shortchange the process!

To the Partner: This exercise may have come easy for you or you may have had some difficulty with it. It is not as easy as it looks. Yet, this is a great opportunity for him to see what you would like to see as he is "AVRing" you. The secondary gain is that you may begin to develop some empathy for what he is trying to do.

Some people have questioned if ERCEM is teaching an addict how to deceive his wife further by teaching him empathy. In my history of working with men, I have never known a man to deceive his wife by practicing this process. It is my experience that he wants to help you heal. He just did not have the tools by which to do it.

By going through this process together, you will be able to understand the effort behind the outcome, and it will hopefully help you both see the progress that you are making.

AS HE GETS HEALTHIER, YOU WILL NEED TO SHOW HIM EMPATHY TOO

To the Partner: After discovery, your whole world seems unreal. As a spouse, you are shell-shocked from what you have learned. You wonder who this man is that I thought I knew and how could he have done this to me? You cannot figure out who you are living with, and you question whether you are living with a sociopath, a narcissist, or both. You not only are reeling from the horrible shock while your brain is offline leaving you unable to think or speak, but you also worry about your future, your children, and your family as a unit. You have had the wind knocked out of you, and you say repeatedly, "Who is this monster and why is this happening to me?" You possessed a lot of empathy prior to discovery, but now you are in survival mode. It is understandably all about you. There is no way that it would be safe to empathize with him or his addiction because you cannot even comprehend what happened, let alone understand in the first few months how an addiction could cause such a thing.

Your hypervigilance, which is a survival skill and a trauma response, watches everything he does. You make a deliberate effort to watch him walk his talk, and when he does so it will be hard to comment. This is because he has hurt you so badly, and you are not going to reward him for "doing what he should have done all along."

At some point, as he continues to work good recovery and has proven that he wants to be the man in solid recovery, he will need your feedback and reinforcement that you can tell he is changing. You will resist this, and you will find a million reasons to push him away. You have been so badly hurt that you could not conceive of trusting him again ever. But as you learn the guideposts for good recovery and assess that he has used the right tools, you will begin to let your guard down. When this miracle starts to occur, you will begin to do what you have always done, and you will start to acknowledge the changes you are seeing. You will resist this at first because you will not believe that it is true, but then you will see it with more regularity. You will feel the relationship take a turn in the right direction. You will begin to use empathy and identify the good work that he is doing in recovery, and you will breathe a bit easier as he continues leaning into helping you heal!

(Actually, I see women who are able to practice empathy as soon as they see that their husbands are practicing the skills diligently. We know that empathy is innate in women, so oftentimes it is a natural by-product of his work.)

It doesn't matter where you are with your trust level to begin to practice empathy. It will be harder if your guard is up but you will still see opportunities to use it. Please practice it so that you will begin to let that huge wall down just enough to really assess the situation. Remember, now that you know what he did, you will be able to protect yourself and still be able to work on the skills you need to heal.

Chapter 11

Mindfulness Based Addiction and Trauma Work Can Change Your Perspective

We are all pioneers in the field of problematic sexual behavior and partner betrayal, so when I started in this field there were very few treatment modalities that felt effective. We already talked about the codependency model that was way off base. Then I continued to see couples who had just gone through discovery being thrown into couples therapy when they required crisis work and early recovery couples empathy work.

No one was doing formalized empathy work with them, so they floundered and were flooded with treatment modalities that they could not even begin to assimilate. This left them feeling scared, overwhelmed, and shamed.

I kept thinking we need to find a treatment modality that helps to quiet the minds of both people in the relationship.

It was no accident that I met Darrin Ford, who is the President of Sano Press, my book publisher. Darrin is a CSAT who also ran a publishing company and catered to professionals who worked with addiction. I must be transparent here; Darrin Ford is a CSAT who I sought out to be my publisher because of his knowledge about sexual addiction. I thought he would well-represent me and the books that I wanted to write because of his knowledge base and sensitivity.

As I got to know Darrin and his publishing company, I realized he had his own story about addiction and addiction recovery. Darrin Ford is also the Founder and Chief Executive Officer of The Mindfulness Academy for Addiction and Trauma Training, (TMAATT.com) and the Chief Executive Officer at Mindful Centers for Addiction and Trauma Therapy (MindfulCenters.com) with offices in Long Beach, West Los Angeles, and Newport Beach, California. Mindful Centers also sees clients from all over the state of California via telehealth services.

After years of reviewing the work of Daniel Segal, Richard Davidson, and John Kabat-Zinn, Darrin has come to the realization that the research supports mindfulness as a necessary step in working with compulsive sexual behaviors and partner betrayal. "Our mission is to provide comprehensive, inspiring, research-based mindfulness training to addiction and trauma therapists around the world. We are dedicated to helping mental health professionals learn how to incorporate mindfulness tools and techniques as they support their clients in long term recovery, growth, and healing."

What was especially appealing to me was that his strategies were simple, straightforward, and incredibly effective in reducing addiction and trauma symptoms while improving the overall health and wellbeing of my clients. His curriculum gave me practical tools to work with addicts, partners, and the coupleship.

Darrin Ford teaches in his Mindfulness Based Addiction and Trauma Work that he wants addicts to gain the ability to identify their mind states and mind stories. This allows them to recognize the ability they have to alter their relationship to these states and stories, providing a new perspective that will move them into healthy, non-reactive behaviors.

He describes the work with partners as the following: "Our goal as therapists is to allow partners to recognize that the trauma has their thoughts, feelings, beliefs, which are all constructs designed for survival." Their minds are seeking the certainty they believed they had in the past before they discovered the betrayal. The betrayal trauma reactions are now causing distress that intensifies uncertainty and discomfort. Their mind's resistance or "aversion" to this uncertainty creates greater suffering.

You as the addict are working hard to create safety, which is a new truth. The mind is conditioned to create certainty, which is a survival mechanism.

The traumatized partner's mind is on a perpetual search to find more certainty, which can lead to more suffering, and yet it is the survival skill attempting to keep the partner safe." A partner's attempts to find safety can exacerbate her fears because her primary need is to feel safe and survive. This can create more suffering because she is in that hypervigilant state to know the truth. It can be an auto-exacerbating cycle that results in more pain.

To the Partner: My goal is to teach you how to become aware of your emotionality and identify what emotion is driving your mind state. My job is to help you use compassion so that you can surrender to what has happened to you and through compassion find an identity that is separate from partner betrayal. When you do this you decrease reactivity and begin to trust yourself again so that you can appreciate who you are and your own intuition. You develop an improved sense of confidence that allows you to attune to the reality that the addict's behaviors affect you but are in no way, shape, or form because of you. The addict acted out because he is an addict. He did not act out because you were not good enough or not worthy of his love. You did not cause or contribute to his acting out.

A secondary gain of mindfulness is that over time, you can learn to be present with the uncertainty, which is a normal response that is manifested out of betrayal trauma. You will learn to react with less intensity. When you acquire this skill, you will not only survive, but thrive because of the self-growth that has occurred because of your trauma.

FORD ISOMORPHIC PATH TO INTIMACY WITH OTHERS

Ford explains in his "Isomorphic Path to Intimacy with Others" that in order to gain intimacy as a couple it needs to begin with self-intimacy, and furthermore, partners need to practice distress tolerance and be present with the uncomfortable emotionality that is an inevitable outcome of a partner's natural state manifesting from the betrayal. That is no easy feat!

He states that it is only by having a mind focused on the utilization of "constructively compassionate" interventions will the partner then be able to gain the ability to remain present with herself.

"Constructively compassionate" is defined as allowing oneself to be fully present with the experience of one's self, while fostering a mutual acceptance of suffering, in an effort to bring a kinder reaction to distressing emotionality. This is intimacy with the self.

That intimacy then ripples out into every other aspect of the partner's life. This allows the betrayal trauma response to calm as you gain the ability to be present with the natural normal distress resulting from the discovery that the addict has betrayed you. Your reactivity decreases and your distress acceptance takes the charge out of the fear equation.

The secondary gain is that you begin to apply this constructively compassionate mindset to others as well.

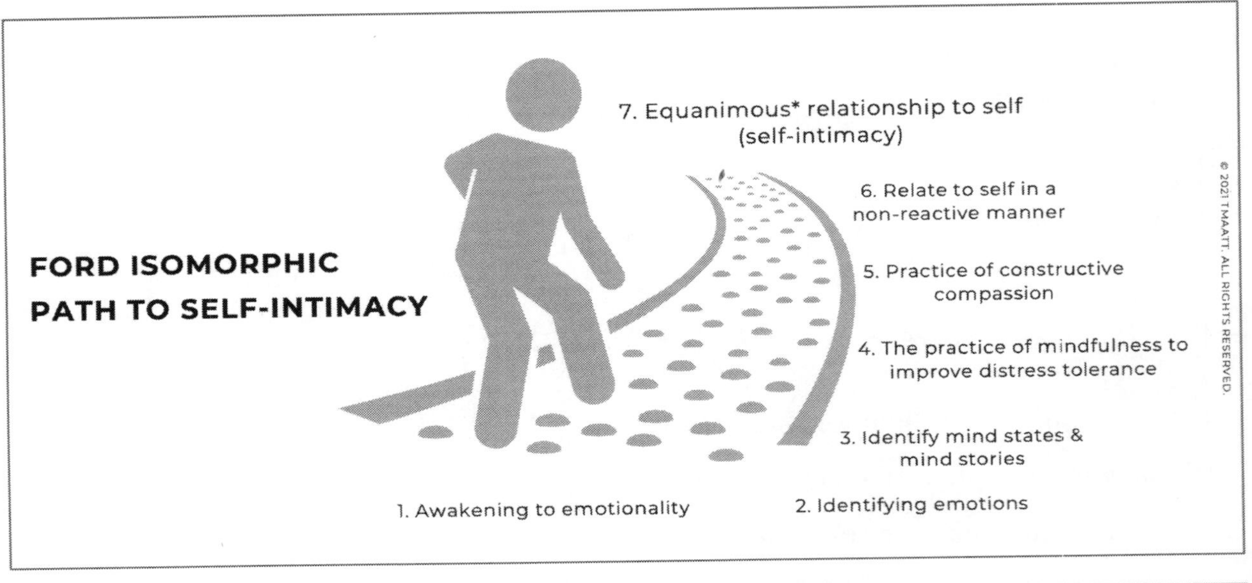

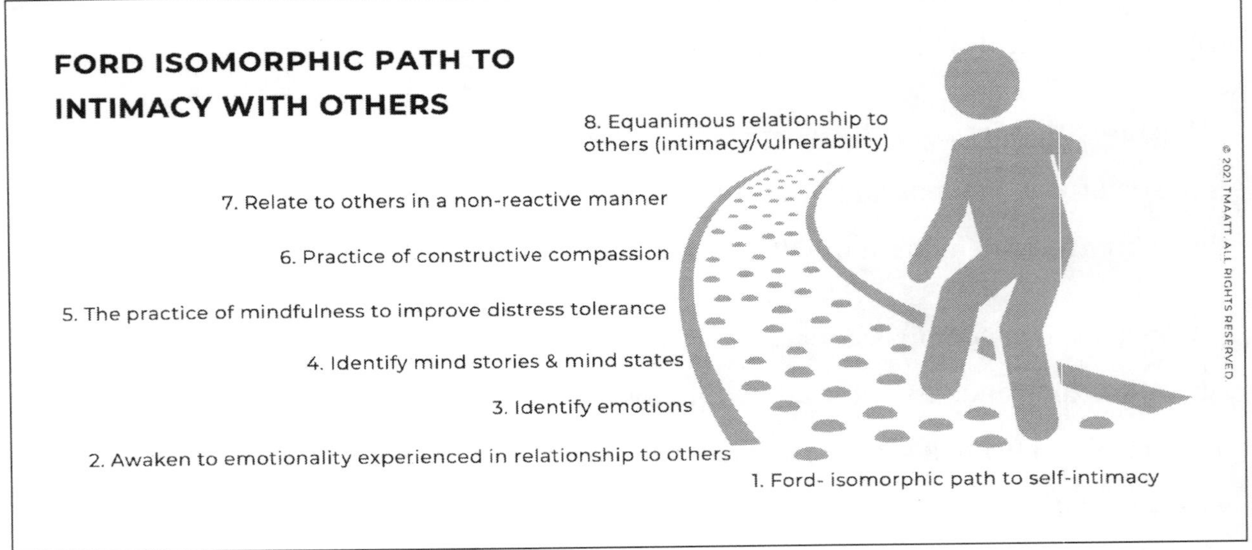

*The definition of "equanimous" means calm and composed.

The Early Recovery Couples Empathy Model incorporates these skills to help you to become less reactive to your environment and the reality of the betrayal. You replace the fear with a constructive compassion that is cultivated using the Ford Isomorphic Path to Self-Intimacy.

I know that you want to be less fearful of the unknown, and yet, you are afraid to stop looking for clues that he is acting out because you do not want to be betrayed again. It is an auto-exacerbating cycle.

THE AUTO-EXACERBATING CYCLE OF PARTNER BETRAYAL

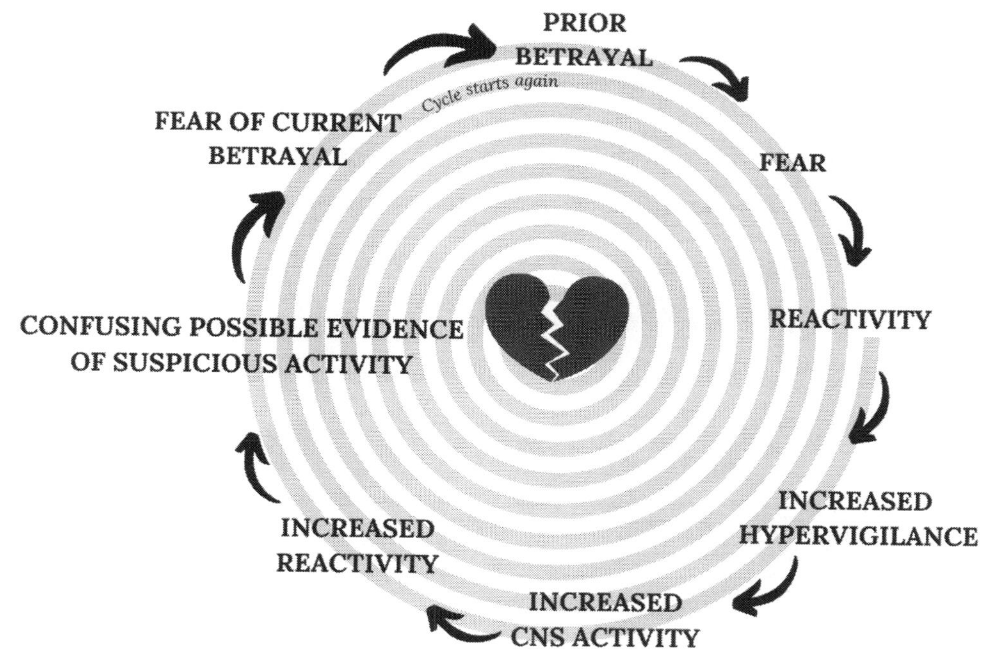

Unless others have lived with your uncertainty, they cannot know how exhausting this cycle is. You likely create a reactive mind state with mind stories that sound like "I will never be able to trust him. What he did was inexcusable, I do not know this man that I married, and I fear I will never be able to recover. How can I ever trust him again, and worse than that, how will I ever be able to trust myself?"

In trying to protect yourself you create "destructive compassion," which Ford explains is when you attempt to reduce the reactivity of the mind at the expense of your long-term healing. You do this by thinking that if you find the potential activity you may be able to detour it and keep yourself safe. Instead, it does exactly the opposite! It keeps you from being able to enjoy life and trusting that if a potential betrayal would occur again, your intuition would take over and you would have a plan that will keep yourself safe.

It is a normal protective reaction to want to search for evidence that you will not be deceived again, but that hypervigilant cycle that makes you look for things ten times a day can become addictive too. It robs you from having your own life. A more constructively compassionate response might be, "I am going to keep my searches to twice a day, and I am going to spend more focus on the in-between moments. I am going to concentrate on my breathing. I am going to read more spiritual material, so I can create more serenity in my life. I am going to call an old friend and attempt to find other things in my life to talk to her about to remind myself that I do have 'other things' to focus on."

The antidote is "constructive compassion" because working together in ERCEM allows you to repair the damage caused by the addiction. You get to focus on the new changes that are occurring in the relationship while you trust in yourself and practice a new form of self-compassion that frees you from that auto-exacerbating cycle.

Here is the path we want you to focus on:

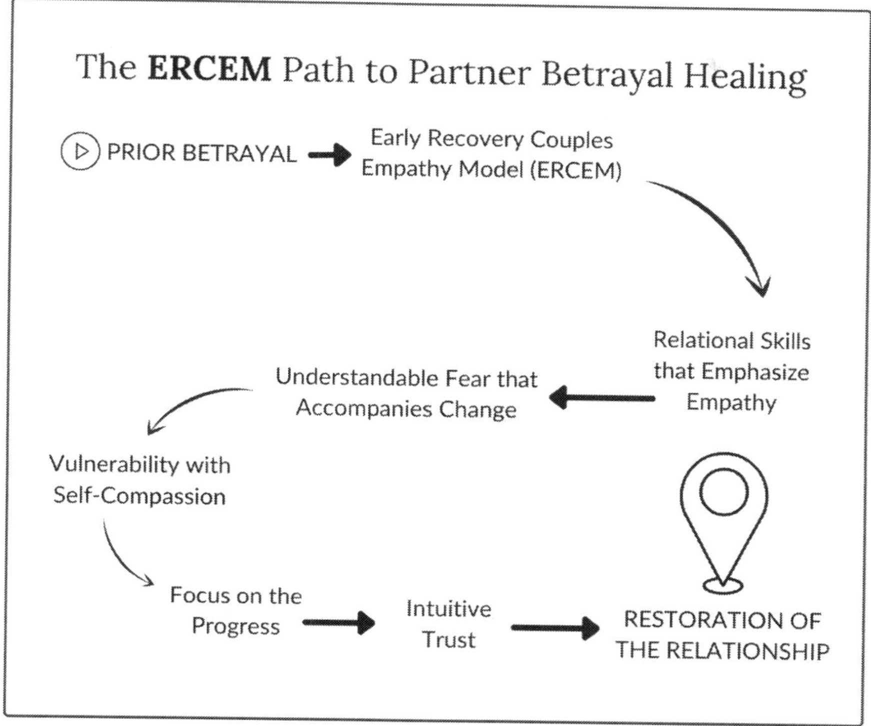

This process results in what Ford calls "equanimity," which refers to you being able to develop a state of psychological and physiological stability. Equanimity is considered neither a thought nor an emotion. It is a steady conscious realization of your new reality, congruent with a knowing of oneself, and the calm that accompanies the new sense of self. As a partner it is where you want to live so that you can enjoy life again.

Mindfulness is an excellent way to explore your feelings as an observer and gently remind you that "you are not your mind." All the thoughts, feelings, and beliefs that are swirling inside of you right now are the result of trauma brain, and you can begin to calm them and take back your life.

It starts by identifying your mind state. "A mind state is a foundational unit that the mind uses to develop a story," and it develops out of the experiences in the environment in conjunction with our biology.

According to the Mindfulness Academy for Addiction and Trauma Treatment, there are five mind states that contribute to both Addiction and Partner Betrayal Trauma. As you both read the five basic mind states decide which one or ones that are predominant in the process of sexual betrayal.

THE FIVE MIND STATES

AVERSIVE: *WHEN THE MIND SEES AND UNDERSTANDS REALITY BUT PUSHES AWAY FROM IT*

Some examples of this would be:

- When an addict is in active addiction, he may recognize these behaviors are harmful to himself and to his partner, like my client who frequented prostitutes. He left every encounter disgusted, promising himself that he would never participate in this type of behavior again. He hated himself and wondered what was wrong with him, but later in the day or that week, he would be compelled to call another prostitute and set up yet another meeting.
- When a partner sees that her husband is working on his sobriety and relational recovery but pushes away from it for fear that it is not real and she will get hurt again.

DENIAL: *CHARACTERIZED BY SOME AWARENESS OF REALITY BUT REFUSING TO ACCEPT IT*

Some examples of this would be:

- An addict in denial would be the man who understands the neuroscience of addiction. He knows that he can not look at pornography because it will light up his reward center and start the cycle of abuse. However, he clicks on a lingerie ad while he is at work and lies to himself by saying that the behavior is a poor choice but not activating like pornography. In reality, it activates the brain in the same way and can contribute to a slip or relapse. Denial is a chronic state for an addict both in and out of recovery. Patrick Carnes states in the 30 Recovery Tasks that addicts will naturally fall back into a state of denial. As trained Certified Sexual Addiction Therapists, we are always working with the addict to have him examine his own thinking and keep him out of denial.

- A partner goes into denial when she *knows* she should take better care of herself and is actively working towards that, but then she stops the behavior and forgets the importance of intentional self-care. She tells herself, that it is more important to monitor his behavior to keep herself safe.

JUDGMENTAL: *WHEN YOU HAVE CRITICAL THOUGHTS OF YOURSELF AND OTHERS THAT KEEP YOU FROM SELF-ACCEPTANCE*

Some examples of this would be:

- An addict goes into a lot of self-loathing when he thinks of his past or makes a poor relational or sobriety choice. He ends up hating himself and believes it won't get better.

- A partner will believe that his addiction means she is not "good enough." A partner in a judgmental mindstate frequently believes that her husband acted out because she wasn't pretty enough, their sex wasn't adventurous enough, or she wasn't a good enough wife.

CLINGY: *CHARACTERIZED BY THE DESIRE TO HOLD ONTO SOMEONE OR SOMETHING BECAUSE IT REPRESENTS SAFETY OR SECURITY (EVEN IF IT DOESN'T)*

Some examples of this would be:

- When an addict is in a clingy mind state, he might cling to the perceived relief his acting out brings to his trauma. He may see it as a medication when ultimately it complicates things and creates more chaos.

- A partner may watch her spouse struggle with being sober and cling to the belief that he will eventually gain good recovery. She clings to the hope that her husband will find sobriety. She is unwilling to set healthy boundaries despite the reality of his real life condition. By clinging to her fantasy, she avoids having to set healthy boundaries with consequences for his irresponsible recovery attempts.

DELUSIONAL: *CHARACTERIZED BY A DISCONNECT FROM REALITY*

Some examples of this would be:

- For the addict: This might have looked like believing that the addictive behaviors could continue with minimal or no consequences while you were in active addiction.
- For the Partner: She may take full responsibility for his issue, thinking that she needs to dress more provocatively and keep him seduced just like the women at the strip clubs.

Do any of these mind states resonate with each of you? Which one seems to fit the best? ______________________________

____

____

____

____

Perhaps you both utilize several of these mind states. Spend some time reflecting on how they may have served you in the past. ______________________________

____

____

____

____

Why are they no longer helpful in creating a healthier you or relationship.

____

____

____

____

____

____

Share with each other how you see your old mind states compensating for the addiction, trauma and betrayal that occurred in your life.

Once you have identified your mind state you then can understand how you created a mind story to support it. The mind story "is a conscious or unconscious narrative created in relationship to your emotions, thoughts, and beliefs." In both addiction and betrayal, you tell yourself stories about why this has happened to you that correlate with the mind states. You do your best to understand all that has happened to you in your life and the things you tell yourself usually have a negative connotation as to the person that you have become.

Part of the grieving process for both of you is to refocus on creating new mind states and mind stories that support your new sense of self and they co-occur with intentional self care and compassion. Self-compassion is crucial for healing.

For the Partner: The addiction has naturally made you feel like you need to totally focus on him and his behaviors, but as you process the pain you need to focus on yourself and rebuild a self-intimacy that will rebuild your sense of trust and confidence in you.

Here is an illustration of what needs to happen after the betrayal:

FORD ISOMORPHIC PATH TO SELF-INTIMACY

It is imperative that you begin to refocus on you again, and yet your brain is screaming trauma. It is as if you do not have the capacity to quiet the mind to allow for that shift from him to you.

Darrin explains that to gain self-intimacy, you must practice distress tolerance and be present with the uncomfortable emotions because it is an inevitable outcome of partner betrayal and, on a larger level, our humanity.

1. He suggests that when you begin to feel the emotional flooding that accompanies partner betrayal, you reframe it as an awakening to what is occurring inside of you.

2. He then encourages you to identify the emotions to better understand their gifts.

3. He wants you to explore the questions “What might the mind stories be telling you about yourself?” and “What maladaptive thoughts are co-created out of the rejection you are understandably feeling right now?”

I am going to list some common mind stories that women express when sharing their grief about his addiction.

- Might you be saying to yourself that you must not have been good enough to keep him faithful?

- Or you are reminding yourself that you were not a good enough sexual partner to keep your husband satisfied?

- Or maybe you believe that something you did in your past caused this action against you, and you wonder if God might be punishing you for your promiscuity, abortion, or pre-marital sex.

4. As you think about the mind stories you may feel your body tensing up further and wonder if the trauma cycle is in full force. This is where you can take control and practice deep breathing with visualization or do a somatic experiencing exercise to refocus the mind onto another body experience. By practicing gentle compassion and changing your focus you will be better able to regulate those distressing feelings.

5. You can tell yourself other compassionate thoughts to remind yourself that you are good enough just the way you are and that your uniqueness has a special quality only you can harness. You could remind yourself that his addiction started way before he knew you and that there was nothing wrong about you. His addiction was caused by something deep inside him. Whatever compassionate thought you choose to use, make sure to say it gently to yourself.

6. When you practice constructive compassion, you begin to become aware of "a calming" which feels very different from your typical reactivity and activation.

7. You recognize that your relationship to self has shifted and there is no judgment in the response to yourself. It allows you to appreciate a new sense of self-intimacy that no longer requires another person to reinforce who you are.

The betrayal still hurts, but it is not who you are. You can separate yourself from his "addictive condition."

To the Addict, the pressure of participating in good recovery can feel overwhelming, and it might seem that you cannot get the relational piece down. You believe that you have come so far, and yet she seems to get so easily triggered. It leaves you wondering if there is ever going to be connection again. You question whether you are traumatizing her further by disappointing her at every juncture.

Mindfulness can help you to put into perspective what is happening in your environment. I am not talking yoga or meditation, although those are two great processes. I want you to go through a self-intimacy process that starts out by identifying your feelings.

1. A MBATT therapist suggests that when you begin to feel the emotional flooding that accompanies your partner's trauma, you reframe it as an awakening to what is occurring inside of you.

2. As you awaken to an awareness, identify the emotions to better understand their gifts.

3. What mind states naturally occur when she is discouraged by you? Do you step right into denial and pretend that nothing is wrong hoping that your choice keeps the environment more neutral? Or are you more likely to take on an aversive mind state where you can see the conflict, but you push it away? You may be exhibiting more of a delusional mind state and searching for a fantasy that will cover up the conflict and please you more.

4. Mind states are an invitation to explore what mind stories you might be telling yourself. What maladaptive thoughts are co-created out of the rejection that you are understandably feeling right now? Might you be saying to yourself that you are a perpetrator of pain and there is nothing that can change that? Or are you reminding yourself that you will never be a good enough partner to please her, and you might as well go back to using to numb the on-going trauma that keeps occurring?

5. As you think about the mind stories you may feel your body tensing up further and wonder if the sexually addictive cycle is in full force. This is where you can take control and practice deep breathing with visualization or do a somatic experiencing exercise to refocus the mind onto another body experience. By practicing gentle compassion and changing your focus you will be better able to regulate those distressing feelings. Your urges and cravings will be regulated in conjunction with the painful emotions that you are feeling.

6. You can tell yourself other compassionate thoughts to remind yourself that you are a work-in-progress and that your self-acceptance will help you to love yourself more so that you can love others.

7. When you practice constructive compassion, you begin to become aware of your "calm," which feels very different from your typical reactivity and activation.

8. You recognize that your relationship to self has shifted and there is no judgment in the response to the mind. Your mind is a sense organ that you can calibrate to work for you. It allows you to appreciate a new sense of self-intimacy that no longer requires another person to reinforce who you are.

This mindfulness-based process allows you to shift your thoughts because you are no longer attached to them!

I know that this chapter was new information for both of you. The good news is that when you delve into your commonly used mind states and mind stories, you can consciously reconstruct healthier ones that release you from your own trauma. And when you learn to use self intimacy and compassion, you repair the traumas that have occurred in your past.

Please don't underestimate how important it is to learn how to be constructively compassionate with yourself and with your partner.

For more information about mindfulness-based processes, go to sanopress.com where you will find by Darrin Ford, *Awakening from the Sexually Addicted Mind: A Guide to Compassionate Recovery* and *Transforming the Addictive Mind* by Darrin Ford and Christy Cosper.

Chapter 12

Relational Skills 101 to Rebuild Trust in the Relationship

Rebuilding the relationship will take time, and I am going to ask both of you to communicate differently when you are working together to reinforce the connection. Although this is a slow process, if you use the following guidelines, you will be more likely to expedite the work and make greater gains.

Some of the skills were addressed in *Help. Her. Heal.* I encouraged the addict to structure his communication based on the book. What I found is he either got complacent and stopped practicing them as instructed or did not realize the magnitude behind the recommendations. When I brought the partner in to do the work, the couple was much better at utilizing the directions that were given in *Help. Her. Heal.*

So even though, I thought my directions were a stand alone intervention and could be implemented by the addict, I found that encouraging the couple to learn them together in conjunction with a trained specialist who is familiar with the work expedited the process and reinforced the connection. When you work with a specialist who understands this work, you will have the added advantage of having a professional guide to support both of you as you gain these skills.

KNEES-TO-KNEES COMMUNICATION

The basis of empathy work is communication. That starts with following some basic foundational tools. Communication requires focus and listening.

THE SET-UP

When the two of you are talking, I want you to really work at facing each other directly and finding a safe way to physically touch. I recommend touching each other with your knees because it is a safe way to re-establish "safe touch." This is a difficult process for the typical couple, but it can be extremely challenging for a couple that has experienced so much pain.

In my book, *Help. Her. Heal*, I call that "knees-to-knees," where you are looking at each other knees-to-knees and are attending to each other's posture and facial expressions by looking at the left eye, the window to the soul. You may question what the "window to the soul" is, but research has shown that when you look at the left eye, you are much more able to understand the other person's position, as well as communication. Human beings have a subconscious agreement

to take notice of the personality in the left eye. Because of the crossover, our left eye imagery goes to our right brain and looks for a deeper sense of meaning.

William Henderson in his book, *The Science of Soulmates*, states, "The left eye is literally the window to the soul and the indicator of the hidden unmasked true self."

Most couples' therapists do not realize how contraindicated it is to sit side by side and communicate. I never let a couple sit on the couch where they cannot attune to each other's nonverbal skills. Much of the communication you do at home is done "on the fly." There is no deep focus. You are not reading each other. You both will be making a commitment to this work if you set up your communication by attending and attuning to each other before you speak.

DOING KNEES-TO-KNEES WHILE USING REFLECTIVE LISTENING

REFLECTIVE LISTENING

You have likely heard the adage; the best form of communication is not to communicate verbally but to listen. Reflective listening is the best way to do this because what you are doing is allowing each other to share one's beliefs, thoughts, and feelings. It is so important for a partner to have an uninterrupted voice. And, you are listening without any emphasis on explaining or defending your own position. It may be the first time you ever really heard your partner without feeling obligated or compelled to respond.

Women can typically be very wordy, and as a couple, the two of you will need to work diligently on keeping your communication clear, direct, and succinct. Partners know that it is difficult for addicts to communicate and listen without becoming defensive, and therefore, if you can keep your thoughts and beliefs short and under three minutes, he will do a better job of being able to hear and understand you. That is the goal of good communication. We want him to have a renewed sense of who you are, how you have been affected, and what you want for your future, so I want you to practice reflective listening daily.

This can be very difficult for men because they fear conflict, and therefore, they want to avoid communication because they know it could likely bring up more pain. Partners unequivocally yearn to know the man that had two dual lives, so increasing your communication as a couple will bring up conflict. But when the couple has worked on self-regulation and co-regulation, they will begin to appreciate the honesty in the share. Both of you will feel more gratified, and the connection will grow.

As an addict you are wondering what is the one thing you can do for the relationship? Know that the number one skill you can practice every day is empathy with focused communication. When you initiate communication and follow through with the commitments you have made to the relationship, it will exponentially provide the most emotional investment in your relationship.

Just know that as your relationship gets healthier, you will be able to experience conflict, and as the relationship becomes healthier, conflict will breed intimacy. I know that both of you are craving and longing for emotional intimacy in the relationship. We are not talking about physical intimacy. To have a close and physical relationship takes a lot of time and patience, and first there needs to be a solid foundation of emotional intimacy.

To the Addict: You must create that emotional bond of safety that she so desperately needs to redevelop the trust.

You are wanting to see her love you again. You are needing that from her, so as you practice empathy, be patient. Know that this is the emotional fuel that is going to fill her love tank. And do not forget to practice patience. She will require a lot of patience because she will test you every step of the way. Not only is she traumatized but she is angry that she must try this hard. When you repeat back the concerns she has, she feels heard and will automatically feel less defensive.

Reflective listening takes structure. The next time she makes an angry or defeated statement, I want you to calmly request for her to sit down at the kitchen or dining room table. Move the chairs out about two feet and have them face each other. Ask her to please sit down so you can share what you just heard. If she will allow it, ask her if you can sit knees-to-knees so that you can find a safe way to connect physically. If she will not let you, tell her that it makes sense to you why she would not want that closeness.

Proceed by sitting down and looking at her left eye, the window to the soul, and repeat back what she said verbatim.

WHAT MUST THEY THINK OF ME?

Here is what a couple I work with said their first experience with reflective listening was like.

"Crystal, I heard you say that you are exhausted, your mind is racing a mile a minute, and you can't stop thinking that you didn't sign up for this! Did I get that right?"

Crystal shook her head in agreement and said, "I just don't think you know how embarrassing this is. I cannot even walk into the grocery store without wondering who else might know. You have ruined every conceivable place in this town. Not only do I wonder who knows but I question what people must think of me. I am embarrassed for myself and for the kids. This is exactly what people love to gossip about, and when I walk into church, I can see the pity in their eyes. No one is asking us to do anything anymore, and I fear that I will live in isolation forever." She burst into tears.

Tom waited for her to stop crying, but his heart was aching because he wanted to hold her and have her sob into his chest. He knew that she would not be able to trust the man who caused her such great pain to be the source of comfort, so he just continued to silently wait for her to stop crying.

Once she started to stop crying, she looked at him and shook her head. She looked so alone, hurt, and discouraged.

Tom asked, "Can I share what I heard to make sure I heard it correctly?" She shrugged her shoulders in quiet resignation. He said, "I heard you say that you just didn't think I knew how embarrassing this has been for you, and you're embarrassed to even walk into the grocery store without wondering who else might know about the affairs I have had in the past 20 years. I have ruined every conceivable place in this town for you, and now you do not even want to face people because they are probably talking about you behind your back. You wonder who knows about the betrayal, and you question what people must think of you and think that they must see you as weak or afraid. You are not only embarrassed for yourself, but you are embarrassed for the kids because this is a small town and people talk about stuff like this. This is exactly what people love to gossip about and when you walk into church, you can see the pity in their eyes. Our relationships have changed, and no one calls anymore. No one is asking us to do anything with them and you fear that you will be alone forever. Did I get that right?"

She nodded her head in agreement as she looked down at the floor. Tom could see that she was not only defeated but devastated.

He said, "Well I want you to know that whatever you decide to do, I will help you every step of the way because you and the kids should not have to deal with this mess. I hate that I caused you this pain. I cannot take it away, but I am going to overcome this addiction, and I am going to do whatever it takes to prove that I am going to make a living amends to you whether we are together or apart."

As you can see, there are many great opportunities to use AVR and see if she feels heard and understood. It also gives you an opportunity to remind yourself of the hard work that you are putting into your individual and relational recovery.

To the Addict: Both of you find two chairs that allow you to touch knees as you both talk to each other.

1. Encourage her to speak about anything that has been bothering her. She will talk about a trigger, or she will share feelings about your inability to keep her abreast of your daytime events and business plans. She may want you to talk to her brother and sister-in-law about your infidelity so that they will understand her pain. She can bring up anything related to the sexual acting out and encourage her to begin to share. It helps if she speaks no longer than a couple of minutes so that you can use reflective listening to make sure you heard her thoughts and feelings.

2. Repeat back verbatim exactly what you heard her say. No need to respond to her because this is an exercise in listening.

3. Next, ask her, "Did I get that right?" so that you are assured that you heard her completely (This is an empathy exercise that lets her know that you want to hear her and understand her feelings, thoughts, and beliefs).

4. When you have completed this process, it becomes your turn to respond.

HE MUST BE ACTING OUT AGAIN: SCENARIOS THAT OCCURRED IN MY OFFICE

You have this gut feeling that something is not right between you and your husband. He takes an especially long shower and then reminds you right as he leaves for work, that he may be late due to a 4pm meeting. He wants to give you a "heads up" so you won't worry, but you think to yourself, I am not buying the "I may need to stay at work longer due to a meeting excuse."

You remain worked up all day, and when he calls you to check in, you are short with him. Your heart is pounding, and you are thinking about all sorts of scenarios. You cannot get your work done, and you are miserable questioning why you are staying in a marriage that causes you so much angst.

He gets home 25 minutes early. He explains that the meeting was shortened because the VP was ill. You are cold and distant with him. He asks you what is wrong, and you clam up and refuse to share your concerns. You tell yourself, "I am not going to be vulnerable and share my fears with him ever again."

He is confused, and his tendency is to avoid the conflict altogether. He leaves the room and considers going for a run to escape the tension, but he remembers last week's session where Carol had encouraged them to practice AVR in times of conflict. He takes a deep breath, goes back into the great room, and moves two chairs together facing each other.

Jason says, "Darlene, would you come over here so we can talk?"

She says, "I am not in the mood."

He says, "I promise this won't take long. I need to find out what is bothering you, and I suspect I've done something that has caused you pain."

She looks up and reluctantly sits down in the chair.

He asks her, "Can I practice some AVR with you like Carol encouraged us to do?"

She stares at him blankly, but he can see that behind the blank stare is a world of hurt.

He says, "Can we do a knees-to-knees?" She does not respond, so he moves closer to her and touches her knees with his.

He takes a deep breath and says, "I can see that I have done something today that has brought back the pain of my acting out"

(Acknowledging the pain).

"It seems to have caused you to be angry with me"

(He picked anger as the primary feeling that he was witnessing).

"And I want to reassure you that although I am not sure what happened today, I really do want to understand it because I don't ever want to cause you more pain. Will you please tell me what happened?" Reassurance.

She scooted her chair back, broke the knees-to-knees contact, and said, "I suspected that you had something going on today. You took an extra-long shower and then talked about being late due to a 4 o'clock meeting. You *never* have 4 o'clock meetings, and it felt very much like a flashback from your acting out days. I know you came home early, but I am wondering if you were even at work this afternoon...I just do not feel good about this at all!"

Jason knows that this is the time to practice empathy, although "the old Jason" would have tried to argue or talk her out of her feelings. He takes another deep breath, focuses on her eyes, and says, "It makes sense to me that you would worry that I was acting out, and I would only assume you felt scared and alone. Yet I want to reassure you that I never want to go back to being that guy again, and I like who I am now" (Later he told me that he wished he had focused more on her feelings when he reassured her).

AVR looks like a simple formula, but during the conflict, it can feel overwhelming. The men that use it admit that it feels foreign at first, but eventually it gets easier with practice.

THE WORST DAY OF HER LIFE BECOMES THE BEST

Will and Joanne have been in early recovery couples work for 1.5 years. Will acted out overseas with prostitutes, and he had created an entire action plan to make Joanne feel safe. After the formal therapeutic disclosure when she found out the entire truth, Joanne would feel nauseous and terrified when he was given overseas assignments. Will encouraged her to come with him and since the kids were grown, she agreed because she wanted a safeguard that he would not act out. There was still much trepidation about him being away from her, but she felt more assured when she accompanied him on his trips.

Then COVID hit, and it prevented Will from traveling at all. Joanne was thrilled because she got a rest from the nagging fear that he would someday have to walk into the "devil's den" without her. COVID gave her extra time to work on her trauma and see a Brainspotting and EMDR therapist to work on the target behind the triggers. And then the inevitable happened when Will was told he would need to resume his traveling. Joanne had found out the night before and had not slept at all. She came in anxious and extremely triggered.

I had the couple sit down to discuss their fears.

Joanne said that she knew it was going to happen, and she feared that Will would not have enough support overseas to fortify his recovery. She stated somewhat angrily, "You won't have access to your sponsor, meetings, or fellowship. And those guys have been a strong team for you. You have been doing so well, and now I am afraid that it will all be for nothing." Then she started to cry.

Will looked at his activated wife and said, "I see that you are in so much turmoil about me going back to my old behaviors. That has to make you feel so scared, reminding you of those gut wrenching days after discovery, but I want to reassure you that I have already put a plan into place to use the app "WhatsApp" to have free international calls. I have four guys lined up who work second shift so that I can have around-the-clock support if I need it, and I am willing to take a poly to help you feel safe...We are going to get through this together."

Joanne looked up at him with a tear-stained face and said, "You've already developed a fire drill with your buddies in preparation for this day? Are you afraid of your own impulses, urges, and cravings?"

He looked at her, shook his head, and said, "Well it's always good to have a backup plan. I feel strong in my recovery, but I know that I should never take my recovery for granted and that I would need a plan for you. I hurt you terribly and I want to make sure your brain is protected, so I got back up for when this day would eventually come."

Joanne told both of us that something lifted that day, and she realized that she would need to trust his wisdom and move away from her fear to see if he could maintain his good recovery.

That day was a turning point for them, and she later would say, "How could the worst day of my life turn out to be the turnaround for us?"

That is how ERCEM works—the empathy he used became the glue for rebuilding the relationship!

ASSERTIVENESS—DEVELOP YOUR COMMUNICATION BACKBONE

Will was being authentic and honest and showing Joanne that he took his recovery seriously. He was clear and direct about his feelings and his recovery. Unfortunately, most couples have not been taught how to express themselves, so they relate to conflict by being passive, aggressive, or passive-aggressive.

Let's take a look at the three types of maladaptive but commonly used forms of communication, and then we can talk about assertiveness. As you both read these definitions of communication and relational styles, think about which style you predominantly use.

PASSIVE COMMUNICATION

Are you or is your spouse passive? People who are passive are easily overlooked or walked on. This allows others to control them or not understand what is going on in their lives. If you are passive, you probably present with poor self-esteem. Deep down, you feel that your opinion does not count.

If you are the addict, you might experience so much shame wrapped up in what you have done, and you do not feel you deserve to stand up for what you feel or believe. John Gottman calls this "stonewalling" and says when you walk away from conflict, nothing can get resolved and that you are contributing to further problems in the relationship.

If that sounds like you, it can be helpful to take time out to assess your feelings or gather your thoughts, but not to walk out permanently from the conflict or communication.

If you are the partner, you may be so saddened by the betrayal that you have no energy to think through your situation and stand up for yourself. You resign yourself that this is as good as it will get, and you are so afraid of what the future might bring that you do nothing and assume a passive role.

Passivity can be genetic or a learned response to your childhood or other primary relationships. Think back over your lifetime and list three times in your past that you exhibited passive communication and let things happen because it was easier or safer than working it out.

The Addict's response:

1. ______________________________

2. ______________________________

3. ______________________________

The Partner's response to times you used a passive style of communication:

1. ______________________________

2. ______________________________

3. ______________________________

AGGRESSIVE COMMUNICATION

People who communicate aggressively are trying to communicate by intimidation. You may have witnessed this in your own family of origin. You watched how one of your parents aggressed against the other to keep them in a "one down position."

As the addict, you may have become increasingly more aggressive to shut her down and protect your addiction. Many addicts have confessed that they communicated aggressively to stop their spouse from figuring out about the addiction. When the addict uses aggressiveness, there is an element of gaslighting that occurs. The spouse, who is trying to figure out what is really going on, ends up feeling crazy because the addict is attacking her for her vigilance. It ends up being a double betrayal.

Aggressive personality types attack the character of others and appear very demanding. People who communicate aggressively typically want to control and dominate others. They may try to intimidate a person into doing it “their way.”

For the Partner: Although women are less likely to be aggressive, it can be a trauma response to partner betrayal. Have you found yourself communicating much more angrily and aggressively to your spouse? Are you lashing out at him? Are you feeling uncontrollable amounts of rage?

Your amygdala may be activated, and you are fighting as a response to trauma. Both you and your husband are wondering what is happening to you because you have never shown this aggressiveness before. If this sounds like you, know that you do not possess an “aggressive personality.” Your aggressive style of communication will subside when your trauma gets better; however, you will need a clinical specialist to help you interrupt your reactivity so that you feel better.

I often hear partners accusing their husbands of gaslighting them. I may get criticism for saying this, but many addicts are accused of using gaslighting when it really is using another form of addict manipulation called DARVO. DARVO is intended to keep the wife from knowing about his addiction (which will be further explained in the next section under passive-aggressive communication).

Gaslighting is a serious, abusive form of manipulation where the addict is intentionally and purposely wanting his wife to question her own reality.

In the field of sex addiction, you will hear a term called "gaslighting" used to depict what can happen when an addict purposely belittles and manipulates a partner and intentionally tries to make her feel crazy for suspecting that something is going on. He is purposely trying to manipulate her into questioning her own sanity and reality.

An example of this would be a wife who notices that her husband looks like he is spending hundreds of dollars a month. She will challenge him by saying, "Rob, there are hundreds of dollars that are missing out of our account, and I want us to sit down and compare last year's finances to this year's balance."

Rob knows good and well that she is on to him. He immediately goes into defense mode and not only denies the reality, but he will put her down in the process by telling her she is crazy, making her doubt her financial abilities, and bringing up past situations where she may have made financial mistakes. The partner will start to doubt herself and her abilities. It seems like he is being abusive, but he denies it and leaves her feeling like she is going crazy. She will doubt her own perceptions to the degree that she also questions if he could be right. Again, gaslighting is a serious, abusive form of manipulation where the addict is intentionally and purposely wanting his wife to question her sanity.

To the Partner: I want you to understand gaslighting so that you can protect yourself from it if it occurs.

To the Addict: List three ways you have related to your wife aggressively or have shown aggressiveness in your past to keep her from finding out about your addiction.

1.

2.

3.

To the Partner: Do you believe that you react with aggressiveness? List the ways you have reacted aggressively in your past. Is this normal for you to react aggressively or do you believe this is a trauma response?

1.

2.

3.

PASSIVE-AGGRESSIVE COMMUNICATION

People who use a passive-aggressive style do not feel comfortable with their own conflict within relationships and choose to retaliate secretly to externalize their anger. They cannot express themselves directly, but their anger is so intense that they make the choice to be angry without owning it.

Many partners complained that when their spouse was in full addiction, he was very passive-aggressive. Addicts would leave for work and not come home on time. They would not answer their phone for hours. They would use DARVO techniques on the partner.

DARVO

DARVO, which was mentioned earlier, is a type of communication addicts might use when they are being held accountable for their behavior. It was coined by Jennifer Freyd and stands for "deny, attack, reverse victim and offender."

Addicts at the height of their addiction will do anything they can to keep their spouse from discovering their addiction. When a partner intuitively senses that something may be wrong, she might ask inquiring questions to try to understand what is situationally happening. As she begins the inquiry, he will:

Deny that he has done anything wrong.

Attack her by becoming defensive and blaming her for her inquisition.

Reverse the roles.

The addict will take on the role of ***victim*** and try to convince her that she is "picking on him" for no reason.

The addict calls her *the* ***offender*** and wants her to believe that she is being unfair to him.

This scenario might look like when an addict does not come home after work because he was acting out, he might deny his actions, attack the partner for confronting him, tell her that she was controlling, and reverse the scenario to make her feel that she was constantly discouraging, blaming, and angry. He would accuse her of sending him the message that he could not do anything right. He would manipulate the situation so that he would appear to be the victim and she the offender.

Addicts who are passive-aggressive are angry and will get even with people behind their backs. People who forget appointments that they do not want to attend or do not answer a question because they do not want to talk about things may be relating in a passive-aggressive manner. Addicts who want to do what they want to do will disappear, do what they want, and then act innocent, denying their behavior.

Again, men in full addiction will do anything to protect their addiction including sacrificing their wives sanity.

Can you think of times that you used DARVO?

Can you think of times that you used passive-aggressive behaviors to hide your acting out?

1.

2.

Women too, have used passive-aggressive behaviors in retaliation for how they were treated. I worked with a woman who was regularly beaten by her husband for not cleaning the house properly. Each week, she would come in with a defeated reaction to her life. Her bruises were visible, and she hung her head in discouragement.

Week after week, I would talk with her about her options. I knew that I had to be careful with my advice because if this woman was too forceful or assertive, her life could be in danger.

Then one afternoon, she walked into my office with a totally liberated look on her face. She sat cross-legged on my couch and was animated.

I secretly was cheering because I sensed she had left him. I was already thinking about safety plans to make sure that her separation went smoothly. I asked her how her week had been, and she said it was normal. I repeated her statement and said, "So you had a normal week?" She nodded her head and said "Yes."

I told her that she looked different and that I noticed less bruising, and she coyly smiled in response.

I asked her what was different, and she told me that she had finally cleaned the house to her husband's satisfaction.

My heart sank as I thought she had acquiesced to his brutality. I said that I was surprised that she had walked in so gleefully. None of this was making sense to me. She smiled again and replied, "I am now cleaning the toilets with his toothbrush!"

My client had learned how to passive-aggressively get her husband back without his knowing and seemed to find great satisfaction from her new cleaning venture. I of course worried that if or when he discovered her retaliation, he might kill her. I worked with her for many more months creating a safe exit plan so that she could leave him and not fear for her life.

My client did not feel safe to assert herself, so she used passive-aggressiveness instead.

ASSERTIVENESS IS THE BACKBONE FOR GOOD COMMUNICATION

Assertiveness is standing up for your beliefs. It is being clear about what you think and how you feel. When you are assertive, you let each other know the real you, and you stay true to yourself so that you can achieve your goals and move closer to what you need. Assertiveness is conveying a direct message about your needs. It is proactive, and it empowers you to share your feelings so that you can eventually ask for a behavioral change.

This means that you are being clear and direct about what you need and want. It does not mean you will get what you want; it means you have stated your feelings and facts clearly.

When you assert yourself, your loved ones or coworkers will know where you stand. It does not mean that you get your way, but it does send a clear message of how you feel, what you believe, and what you may need.

It is the first step to creating other forms of healthy behaviors, like increasing your communication, setting up boundaries that would keep you both safe, or developing consequences with others if they violate your boundaries. It enables you to set limits so that others will not walk all over you. It creates healthy boundaries and enables you to accomplish goals because it reinforces what is important to you.

As you move towards healthier forms of relating to each other, you will need to practice different types of assertiveness. Most couples do not know what assertiveness is, let alone know how to practice it with each other. Are you one of those couples? Are either of you good at being clear and direct in your communication? If so, maybe you saw an important person in your life assert himself or herself on a regular basis.

To the Addict: It can be daunting to practice assertiveness because you feel shame and guilt for what you have done. However, when you avoid assertiveness, it can propel you into the other negative types of behaviors.

As an example, it may be common for you to get discouraged when she does not trust your new recovery, and you may want to lash out at her (aggressive style). At other times, you may want to say, "Oh forget it" and walk away (passive or passive-aggressive) which does not resolve the situation. When you resort to passivity, you miss the chance to be your authentic self and let her know what you need or want. The following information will be especially helpful in breaking old maladaptive behaviors that keep you from working on connection and intimacy.

As the Partner: You may also have had trouble expressing assertiveness and sharing your feelings and thoughts. Although women are inherently better communicators, they may have kept some of their feelings to themselves to avoid conflict or to promote harmony. Does that sound like you?

Many of my partners have spent so much time attending to the needs of others that they rob themselves of the satisfaction of achieving their own goals. If self-esteem is solely based on doing for others, the person will not have the opportunity to know what he or she wants. Learning assertiveness will bring clarity to your own needs.

What is your definition of assertiveness?

Addict: ______________________________

____

____

Partner: ______________________________

____

____

What communication style are you most likely to exhibit?

Addict: ______________________________

Partner: ______________________________

What situations have both of you experienced where you could have been assertive?

Addict: ______________________________

____

____

Partner: ______________________________

____

____

It is important as your relationship heals that you both practice being direct with each other. It does not mean that you get what you need, but it does mean that you are clear and direct about how you feel, what you think, and what you would like in the relationship. If you want to have a connection with each other, you will need to get better about communicating your thoughts in a safe way. In *Help. Her. Heal.* I encouraged the men to look at the predominant type of communication they used.

I know that it will feel scary, but I would encourage both of you to spend some time talking about how you have communicated in the past. As your relationship gets healthier, you will want to share your thoughts and feelings with each other, which requires vulnerability and trust.

A secondary gain of assertiveness is that it creates better self-esteem and helps you to know yourself better. We call it developing your backbone—the backbone of self-esteem.

I would like each of you to ask yourself which profile fits your style of communication.

Which person are you?

- Do you assert yourself with others?
- Do people know how you feel and what you think?
- Do you speak about what is on your mind in a direct, concise manner?
- Do people know the real you and what you stand for?

or:

- Are you afraid to share feelings for fear of hurting others or retaliation?
- Do you squelch your opinions because you think they are not important, or you are afraid they will be shot down?
- Do you feel like you do not have the right to share your feelings because of what you have done in the past?
- Are you afraid to speak your mind because if you do, your needs may not be met, and you will feel that double rejection?
- Are you fearful to speak your mind because you fear another's anger or wrath?

So, which person sounds more like you? Maybe you are a mix of both types. It is important to be honest so that you can make needed changes. Are you the first one or the second one? Circle the descriptions that most emulate you and then share it with each other so that your spouse knows how you see yourself.

Most people have never received any formal assertiveness training. This workbook will help you to polish your assertiveness skills, which is crucial to improve your communication with each other and form better connections.

Oftentimes people who do not assert themselves get walked on or they find themselves putting their needs on the back burner. Assertiveness keeps you out of the victim role. It lets people know where you stand.

Many life strategists stress that you teach people how to treat you. When you assert yourself, you teach others about your feelings, limits, and boundaries. You no longer can get walked on because you have changed your behavior.

There are two basic formulas you can use to assert yourself. Both involve using "I" messages. Begin by thinking about something you have kept to yourself, and then practice using one of these sentences to share your thoughts. Take a moment now to fill in the blanks below:

USING THE BASIC ASSERTIVENESS FORMULA (WITHOUT CONSEQUENCES)

As an experiment, think of one thing that has to do with your feelings that you have kept inside and not shared with your spouse or others. Using the assertiveness formula, practice filling in the blanks and imagine yourself saying that statement to the other person. Be sure to write the statement down, which will make you more likely to use it in your daily life.

For the Addict:

1. ____________________, when you __________________________________,
(Name) (Specific Behavior)

I feel ____
(Feeling Word)

because ____
(The message it sends me, or the message I hear is)

2. ____________________, when you __________________________________,
(Name) (Specific Behavior)

I feel ____
(Feeling Word)

because ____
(The message it sends me, or the message I hear is)

3. ____________________, when you __________________________________,
(Name) (Specific Behavior)

I feel ____
(Feeling Word)

because ____
(The message it sends me, or the message I hear is)

For the Partner:

1. ______________________, when you ____,
(Name) (Specific Behavior)

I feel ____
(Feeling Word)

because ____
(The message it sends me, or the message I hear is)

2. ______________________, when you ____,
(Name) (Specific Behavior)

I feel ____
(Feeling Word)

because ____
(The message it sends me, or the message I hear is)

3. ______________________, when you ____,
(Name) (Specific Behavior)

I feel ____
(Feeling Word)

because ____
(The message it sends me, or the message I hear is)

ASSERTIVENESS STATEMENTS WITH A CONSEQUENCE

1. ______________________, when you ______________________________,
(Name) *(Specific Behavior)*

I feel ____
(Feeling Word)

because ____
(The message it sends me, or the message I hear is)

****THE SECOND PART OF ASSERTIVENESS IS TO SET A CONSEQUENCE IF YOU FEEL MISTREATED****

I do not like ____,
(The Behavior)

And this is what I'm going to do about it if it occurs again: ______________________

____
(Statement of action you will take)

HERE ARE SOME EXAMPLES OF ASSERTIVENESS:

1. In the past, Randy had left work to visit prostitutes on his way home. Now that he is in recovery, his wife had requested that Randy call her and share a picture of himself leaving the office when he was going to be late. When he would forget to notify her that he would be late she would say: "Randy, when you forget to text me that you will be late, I feel afraid, and the message it sends me is that you don't value the need for me to feel safe. Since this is my interpretation of your actions, I am going to ask you to sleep in the guest room because I need to have more space from you when you disregard my feelings."

2. When Sybil gets triggered, she tends to rage at her husband, calling him names and physically pushing and smacking him. In a check-in, Chris revealed, "Sybil, I know that I caused you all of this pain, but when you get triggered, become physical, and start raging at me, I feel angry because the message it sends me is that you are going to punish me for my past and that I deserve this abuse."

   "We have been working on this in Couples Work, and I need to remind you that I really do want to hear why you are angry. But when it becomes abusive, I will be forced to take a time out and come back when you have gotten control of your feelings and can share them calmly.

3. Peggy, a mother of three, is dealing with her husband who frequently slips and relapses. She knows that she can't control him, but she wants to be clear and direct about how his inability to work a healthy program affects her. She tells Pat, "When you slip and act out, I feel angry because the message it sends me is that you are not willing to do the hard recovery work to stay sober." She did not feel that she had any true consequences for him, so she decided that she was going to start going to SANON to get more coping skills.

   Side note: She decided to go to counseling, and after three more years of his on-going slips, she decided she was strong enough to live on her own and live a life free from his addiction.

Many couples complain that their assertiveness will not get their spouses to change. That is exactly right—being assertive is simply about letting your spouse or another know how their behavior affects you and is one step closer to you changing yourself. Nor does being assertive guarantee that the other person will hear you, it means that you are being strong and direct about how you think and feel.

The exciting part of assertiveness is that once you are clear with others, you feel better about you. Consequently, you work on doing things that will move you closer to getting your needs met.

The important thing to remember about assertiveness is that it is about you being clear and direct about what you think, feel, and believe. It is not used to change others. When there are consequences, they are there to provide safety for you.

YOUR ASSERTIVENESS HISTORY

Review your history and describe times when you were assertive.

To the Addict: Think of three times you were clear and direct about how you felt or what you wanted:

1. ______________________________

   ____

   ____

2. ______________________________

   ____

   ____

3. ______________________________

   ____

   ____

To the Partner: Think of three times you were clear and direct about how you felt or what you wanted:

1. ______________________________

____

____

2. ______________________________

____

____

3. ______________________________

____

____

To the Addict: As you can see, out of the four types of behaviors, assertiveness is the goal. Since the discovery, it may seem difficult to use assertiveness because you feel you have no right to share your true feelings and thoughts. But a relationship cannot heal unless there is honesty between both people.

You may need to journal to encourage yourself to decide what is the best way to honestly share your thoughts.

It is important to be gentle because she is highly dysregulated and will not know if she can trust your honesty and assertiveness.

I typically teach couples to practice the following formula to use assertiveness because it includes an explanation of your own personal perceptions of what you believe is going on.

THE GENTLE ASSERTIVENESS FORMULA

Assertiveness helps you own your perceptions. It may create some conflict, but know that if you are being honest with each other, you must face the conflict. That way, your spouse can know where you stand and understand your feelings and truth. It will be important to use a gentle tone as you share your thoughts and feelings to decrease the possibility of triggering your spouse.

To the Addict: As you share your thoughts, it will take her to a place where she initially feels the need to remind you that you betrayed her and did not allow her to have a voice. This is true. Your addiction robbed her of a safe place to have an honest, authentic connection, so make sure to validate her experience before you proceed to assertiveness.

The formula below will help you to identify situations that you would like to be vulnerable about and share what comes up for you when you see her reactions. It is easy to use and begins with addressing what you have put her through and normalizing her behaviors. I have listed in bold font the acknowledgement of the damage you have caused which makes this a gentle assertiveness statement.

"Pauline, **I spent a lot of time acting out before I came home.** But now that I am in good recovery, when you get frustrated with me for being late, I feel sad because the message it sends me is that you are sure that I am still acting out again."

"Emily, **I want you to know that I absolutely understand why you would question my integrity,** however when you go through my texts and demand to know who this person is, I feel irritated because the message it sends me is that you still think I am keeping things from you."

"Tiffany, **I have caused you lots of reasons to be angry with me** and when you talk about our problems in front of the kids, I feel scared because the message it sends me is that I will never be able to redeem myself in their eyes."

The reality of your assertiveness statement is that she will confirm that she does fear that you are acting out or she is afraid that you are keeping things from her.

You may want to alter the sentence with, "What I fear most is ____________________

____."

"Pauline, when you get frustrated with me for being late, I feel sad ***because what I fear most*** is that you will never believe that I am in good recovery and not acting out anymore." And then you might add with a question, "What else can I do to show you that I am taking my recovery seriously?

"Emily, when you go through my texts and demand to know who this person is, I fear that you will not believe that I truly do not know, and you will understandably go to the fear that I am acting out." And then you might add with a question, "What can we do together to find out who the person is behind this unknown text?"

"Tiffany, when you talk about our problems in front of the kids, I feel scared ***because what I fear most is*** that the kids will be confused and not be able to process our adult conversation." And then you might add with a question, "Can we figure out where we can talk in privacy?"

THE GENTLE ASSERTIVENESS FORMULA

____________________ (acknowledgement of reasons for their behavior), however when you
(Name)

____________________ I feel ____________________
(Behavior) *(Feeling Word)*

because the message it sends me is ____________________

Or:

____________________, I know that my past actions caused you this pain, however,
(Name)

when you ____________________
(Name the specific behavior)

I feel or felt ____________________
(Pick a specific feeling)

because what I fear most is ____________________

This type of communication will take both of you some time to learn. It takes practice, but the more you both practice, the easier it will be to create and use assertiveness statements. When you concentrate on changing yourself and not others, you speed up the process of getting what you want and need.

THE CONNECTION-SHARE: A TIME TO CONNECT AND SHARE

Checking in with each other is crucial in developing safety and promoting the teamwork that it takes to rebuild your relationship. Check-ins allow both of you to hear about the progress each of you are making, and it is the building block to committing to a time for on-going communication. Once addiction has been discovered, it is natural to want to hide what you are feeling because it feels too vulnerable for both of you. Check-ins provide that safe place and accountability to talk about the hard subjects.

It is a formal process to access information to develop more empathy. For the addict, developing empathy requires that you must know how to put yourself in your wife's shoes. Addicts do not necessarily know how to do this naturally. For many addicts, they need to practice developing the art of empathy. Even if they were able to guess what was on her mind, it would be dangerous to do so because they might get it wrong and miss the opportunity of truly knowing what she thinks or feels. As a couple, you need more opportunities to check in with each other to find out what is going on in the head and heart of each other. Your relationship requires a lot of repair, and check-ins are another way to reassure your wife of your progress. When you both develop and create the daily ritual of spending five to 15 minutes sharing your highlights and struggles with each other for that day, you are investing in the connection necessary to develop trust.

Check-ins have been used for decades by the addiction community to hold the addict accountable with his sponsor or fellowship. There are various check-ins that you can follow, but I advocate for a check in that I call "The Connection-Share."

The format for The Connection-Share is simple. It is important for you to customize it for your comfort level as a couple. Most partners want to know what their husbands are struggling with so that they will stay aware of his issues. However, if the partner feels this is too activating, she may ask him to share this daily with his sponsor, and she may choose some alternative "connection statements" that are equally disclosing and connecting.

It is important to create a structure that enhances good communication. Whenever you are communicating, it is important to sit and watch each other to pick up nonverbal signs and cues that will enhance communication. You both sit down face-to-face, and you check in with these five points:

- Your primary feeling that you experienced today
- A struggle/concern that you encountered
- An appreciation for your recovery
- An appreciation for your relationship
- What you would like to work on for tomorrow's recovery

This format would entail the SA looking at his wife—facing her and looking into her eyes—as he shared his thoughts for the day:

MY PRIMARY FEELING THAT I EXPERIENCED TODAY:

- "Overall, I feel glad that my recovery and our relationship recovery is a stabilizing factor in my life. I feel happy that you have stayed with me and that we are working on our marriage together."

A STRUGGLE/CONCERN THAT I ENCOUNTERED:

- "Even though I felt happy, I struggled with feeling edgy today and was not able to pinpoint why I was emotionally out of sorts. I realize that once my recovery is rock solid, I will need to focus on how I can give back and pay it forward."

AN APPRECIATION FOR MY RECOVERY:

- "I could not wait to get to my meeting today as I could sense that I was edgy, and I just knew that if I had a chance to listen to others and check-in I would feel better. My fellowship allows me to know that we are all struggling, and it gives me hope that we can get through this together. I wish that we had a way to grow together in a recovery program. I mentioned that to my sponsor, and he talked to me about a group called Recovering Couples Anonymous. The group is for couples who want to work on themselves to improve the recovery for the coupleship. I would love to explore that with you to see if that is something that you might want to do too."

AN APPRECIATION FOR OUR RELATIONSHIP:

- "I know this is going to sound silly, but it felt deceiving that I didn't let you know that I was having an off day. I didn't want to worry you because I worried that it might trigger you, and I sometimes avoid a conflictual interaction because I hurt so badly when I watch you struggle. And yet something kept saying that Tami would want to know. I guess I was hoping that you would see that something was wrong and would ask, and then I would share and be able to get some reassurance from you. But I avoided that because I did not want to trigger you, even though my therapist has told me to start sharing my emotional self with you. I guess what I am saying here is that I appreciated that we are still together, that I thought about texting you, and that I am sharing it now."

WHAT WOULD I LIKE TO WORK ON FOR TOMORROW'S RECOVERY?

- "I am going to spend more time journaling about what is going on with me internally so that I can connect to you more fully and be more vulnerable. I will reread *Help. Her. Heal* and remind myself that I need to be more vulnerable. Guess I need to read more Brené Brown, huh?"

HERE IS AN EXCERPT FROM A PARTNER'S CONNECTION-SHARE:

MY PRIMARY FEELING THAT I EXPERIENCED TODAY:

- "I felt anxious today. In two weeks it will be a year since discovery, and even though I know we are doing well it feels scary. I don't know if I can trust it."

A STRUGGLE/CONCERN THAT I ENCOUNTERED:

- "I had to meet with my boss, and since I have not been on my game for months since our disclosure, I wondered if she sensed that I am not running on all cylinders. I hate that my mental state has been compromised. I end up feeling resentful because I think to myself, 'I didn't do anything to deserve this, but it feels like I am the one who is most affected." And then I get mad, and I want to pull away from you. I feel so conflicted because I can tell that you are working a strong recovery program, but I wonder why I have to suffer so much. I am an innocent bystander, and I am the most impacted!"

AN APPRECIATION FOR YOUR RECOVERY:

- "I can tell that I am slowly getting better. Sometimes I feel like I am going crazy because I want to be close and share my real feelings, but I fear that if I do you might get lazy and stop doing all the hard work that you have been doing. I also have mixed feelings, and I hesitate to tell you this because I do not want you to think that you are off the hook. But I am forcing myself to be honest so that we can get better quicker, and I know that means that I must be vulnerable and trust you again. I am glad that I am taking that risk. Please do not let me down."

AN APPRECIATION FOR OUR RELATIONSHIP:

- "I appreciate that we are talking more than we ever have for years. For so long I felt shut out of your life, and I could not figure out why, and now I can tell that you are working hard to make things right."

WHAT WOULD I LIKE TO WORK ON FOR TOMORROW'S RECOVERY?

- "I would like to learn how to reach out for help. I hate that I need to call my SANON sponsor when I feel triggered because I want to try to handle it myself, which invariably adds to the anger I feel towards you for causing the trigger in the first place. I think there's a part of me that doesn't want to let you off the hook. There is a part of me that wants you to suffer like I have to because sometimes the pain is unbearable."

CHECK-INS REQUIRE THAT YOU BE VULNERABLE, OPEN, AND NON-DEFENSIVE

It is important to do check-ins with an open heart. You must be able to hear what each other says and stay open to the feelings and thoughts of your spouse without going into the natural by-product of the trauma.

As an addict your tendency is to move into a shame spiral. Remind yourself that when you hear her concerns, fears, and progress you must be able to contain her pain. That will assist you in being better able to move forward, put yourself in her shoes, and even anticipate what she feels. Over time, this will build on itself, and your empathy will be a natural byproduct of who you are! Of course, it is always good to check in with her emotions and thoughts to see if you are on target. Do these exercises daily so that you are available to connect and share. At first, it might feel like you are inviting conflict into your life because it may feel like another opportunity for your partner to vent about her pain. Remind yourself that conflict is normal and natural, and as you get healthier you will move through it and may even feel closer as a result.

As a partner, your job is to stay as open as you can to his changes and also take his improvements slowly because you need to protect yourself until he has proven himself to you. You will know when you can begin to let your guard down. Your intuition will tell you when it is time to enjoy the changes. And when it does, you will recognize that you deserve to be able to trust again!

BOUNDARIES AS A COUPLE

There is no doubt that you both have boundaries that will need to be respected. As you begin to do your early recovery couples work it will be important to remind each other of your boundaries. Most sex addicts in early recovery are willing to forego their boundaries to allow their partner a sense of safety and certainty. This is advisable because when he puts you and your needs first, it helps to recalibrate your sense of stability.

Occasionally, there can be understandable pushback, especially if the addiction novice gets "traditional" advice from his support group or sponsor. It is not uncommon for a wife to ask for recovery details as she attempts to decide how safe she feels. A partner will ask for her husband to share his recovery goals or will ask him to change one. The old recovery might look like this:

Susan asks Tom, "What are your current recovery goals, and have you set up time with your sponsor to regularly review them?"

Tom declares a boundary and says, "Susan, in all due respect, I share that stuff with my SAA group, and I am not privy to giving you that information."

Susan becomes disgusted and says, "I'm not sure what you are saying, what do you mean that you can't share where you are at in your recovery plan? Tom, this is important for my safety!"

Tom reiterates that his recovery is between him and his fellowship. The fellowship has warned him that too much information is triggering, and it is best that he maintains his boundaries "for her protection."

He says, "This information would only keep you activated. I am not going to share that with you as that is a recovery boundary that I will not violate."

That is the "Old School Way."

Tom does not know that he has been advised from the old model of support. There are still groups out there that do not understand that sex addiction is a relational problem in addition to being a sobriety/recovery problem. He has clearly set a boundary based on the advice of his fellowship, but he needs to review his early recovery couples work because the premise of ERCEM is total honesty and transparency with massive amounts of empathy. He has spent so long deceiving her that now it is time to step up and share anything for which she has questions.

Besides, why would he not share his recovery goals with his partner? He should be proud of the work he is doing, and his first goal in conjunction with his own recovery is to help her feel safe. Tom got bad advice, and he did not know what he did not know, just like his support group. The good news is more and more sponsors *are* being partner sensitive. And men like Tom are going back to their 12-step meetings and are sharing the partner-sensitive perspective. Other men in the fellowship are wanting the same thing too because they know how distraught their wives are from the addiction. This field is changing quickly, and you both can help further the change by sharing ERCEM and partner sensitivity.

Tom practiced boundaries that he hoped would keep Susan safe, but he was trumping what Susan needed and putting the advice of his support group first.

Boundaries create safety, and Susan needed to know that her husband was using his accountability partner—his sponsor—to maximize his recovery team. Since Susan is also on his team, she had the right to make a recovery request.

THE PREMISE OF ERCEM IS TOTAL HONESTY AND TRANSPARENCY WITH MASSIVE AMOUNTS OF EMPATHY.

Sometimes boundaries can feel like punishment, and although they should never be used for punishment, it is true that there will be times when her requests limit your choices and freedoms.

Chris and Tina came into my office with a look of closeness as they sat down to talk. Chris was proud of the progress they were making, and Tina reported that Chris was a better husband than he had ever been.

I was pleased that this couple had made so much progress in the two and half years they had worked with me. Chris had several years of recovery, and he had wanted to go back to concerts to practice what he called "outer circle behaviors."

In Sex Addicts Anonymous, addicts develop a "Circle Plan." Chris had shared that he really had been craving music, and he knew that music was a healthy behavior that could produce dopamine in a legitimate way (as opposed to acting out).

Tina expressed in the session that something did not feel right to her. She thought long and hard about it for several days. She figured out that she was not opposed to him going to concerts, but she was concerned that he might drink too much when he went to the shows and that drinking was a contributor to his acting out.

Chris has abstained from drinking for the first two years of his sobriety and slowly added it to social events, like a couple of glasses of wine at a fine restaurant or a couple of beers at a party. He had been successful for over a year with his controlled drinking, but going to a concert might be too much for him.

She decided to use reflective listening and share her concerns, so she asked him if they could talk after dinner and of course he agreed. He sat down on the couch and asked her to join him, but she grabbed two kitchen chairs, moved them facing each other and asked him to join her instead.

She started by asking him to stay open to a fear she had and not to get defensive with her. He looked dumbfounded and said he would not.

She said, “Chris, I don’t want you to think I am being irrational, but I have a lot of fears about some things you were talking about the other day. I have been thinking about how much you want to return to the concert scene, and I know I will be with you at most of them. But you love hanging out with your buddies, and my fear is that it will prompt you to drink too much and get inebriated, which might cause you to go back to your old ways and look at porn. Then the whole cycle will begin again.”

Chris was shocked. He did not see this coming! He immediately felt a pang of anger because he was working a solid recovery program, and he felt it was time to resume some old activities that he loved. He thought “I can’t believe she is going to try to restrict me after all the hard work I have done! It’s like she is punishing me for good behavior!”

He tried to breathe through it, and he reminded himself that he needed to use his 4-7-8 breathing technique to manage the increased adrenaline he was feeling. He took four deep breaths in through his nose, held it in his belly for seven seconds, and released it for eight seconds straight. He felt better and was ready to rationally discuss her concerns.

He used some reflective listening and repeated back exactly what he heard.

He said, “I heard you say that you don’t want me to think that you are being irrational, but you have a lot of fears about me going to concerts because you think I might drink too much, especially if I am spending time together with my buddies. Your fear is that it will trigger me to drink too much and get inebriated which may start me thinking about acting out. And because I have been drinking, I will have less inhibitions, won’t work my recovery tools, and will be more likely to act out.”

Tina looked at him and said, "Well I didn't say all that, but you definitely got my point." She started to defend herself, but Chris interrupted her and said, "Can I AVR you?"

She shook her head in agreement, and he said, "I can really see why you have concerns, and that must make you feel scared as hell, but I want you to know that I am willing to be alcohol-free at these concerts. I am missing the music, and I know why you would worry about that combination because to be truthful I had not even thought about it. But I think it would be a deadly combination too!"

We talked about what a good job both had done.

Tina had listened to her intuition and spent some time processing it before coming to Chris.

She set them up psychologically to do good communication.

She started off with sharing her fears that he might think she was irrational (Sharing a fear will usually bring down defensiveness).

Chris felt angry but did some breathing exercises to resource and ground himself.

He used reflective listening, and then followed it up with AVR so that she felt heard and understood.

Now that is good relational recovery!

I told them that I wanted to do cartwheels, and they both laughed. We talked about all the healthy choices and changes that they were making (I also asked them if they would write up to the best of their ability the events that occurred at home so I could include it in the book).

I often ask clients to be videotaped so that I can teach ERCEM Specialists how to do this work. I am amazed at how generous they are with their lives.

Now that you have heard Chris and Tina's story, I would like to talk about the three circles because I would like for you as a couple to discuss what could be in each circle.

THE THREE CIRCLES EXERCISE

The Three Circles Exercise was developed by Sex Addicts Anonymous to define what behaviors and boundaries increase abstinence. They were often done in conjunction with the work the sex addict may be doing with his sponsor in SAA. This work helps the addict to clearly understand and define his own boundaries. His work is to create healthy expectations for his recovery.

1. His assignment is to draw three circles. He is to label each circle with relapse behaviors, gateway behaviors, and healthy behaviors.
2. The inner circle is called "relapse or bottom-line behaviors," and men are expected to define what deal-breaking sexual addictive behaviors fed his addiction. They are commonly pornography, prostitution, massage parlors, escorts, sexting, webcams, adult hook-up sites, etc. He puts those behaviors in his inner circle as a declaration that he will stay away from those bottom-line behaviors.
3. The middle circle behaviors are activities or behaviors that could prove dangerous. Watching R-rated movies, looking at social media, drinking, browsing a lingerie magazine, or going to the beach could potentially trigger an addict, depending on his arousal template, and cause the urges and cravings to feel uncontrollable. These behaviors should be avoided at all cost, as to not set the addict up for a slip or a relapse.

4. The outside circle known as the outer circle should include healthy behaviors that might produce dopamine, reinforce good values, or increase connection. This circle teaches men the importance of balancing their lives with healthy behaviors as well.

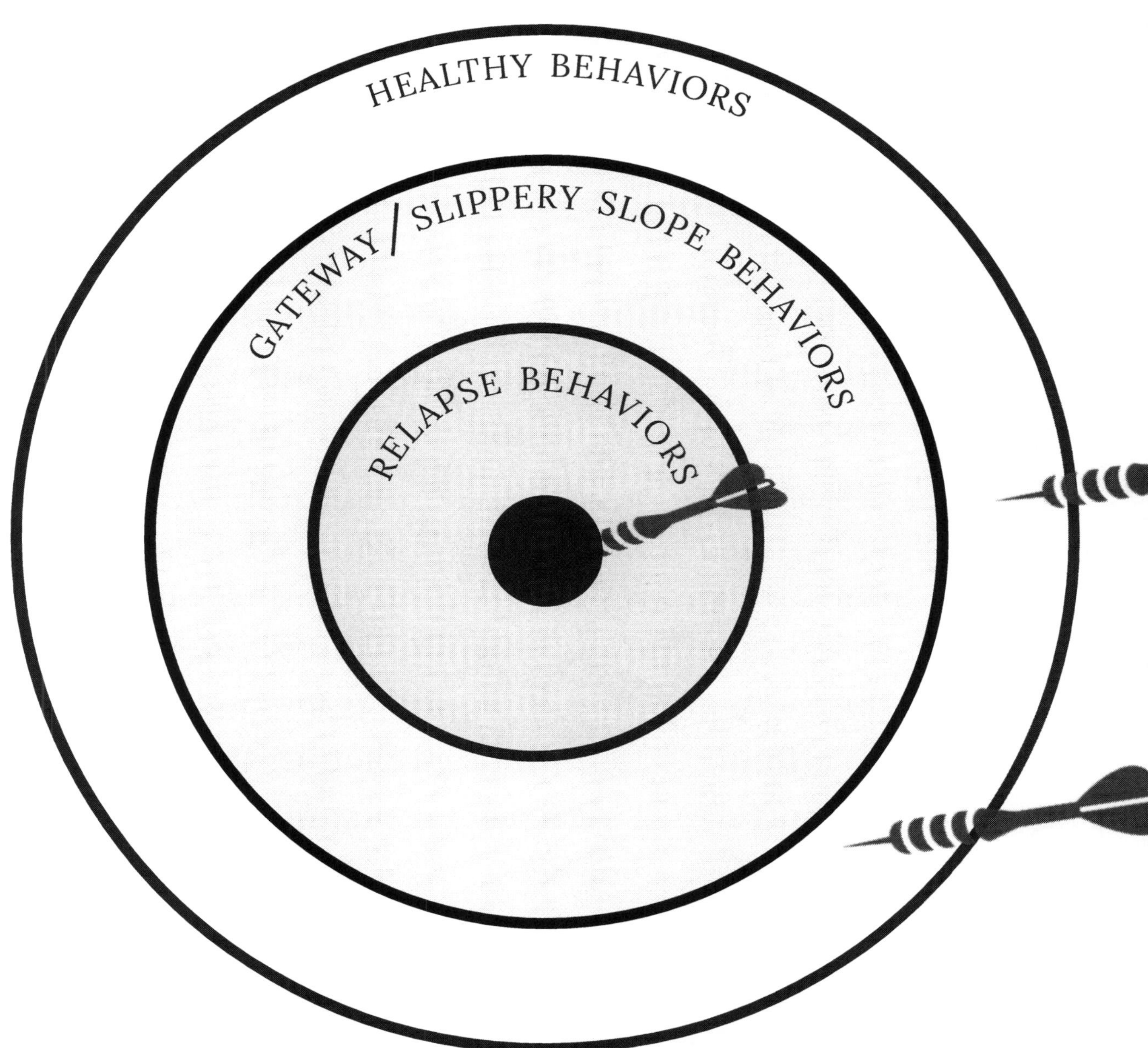

It is important for addicts to share their three circles to help their wives know his potential triggers. She may want more clarification as to why something is, or is not, in one of the circles.

She may want him to add something to the circle that he had not thought was potentially dangerous. Since she can frequently go into hyper alert, she may have access to knowing what could be triggering for him.

She also may want to contribute to the healthy behaviors circle and make suggestions that he might enjoy with or without her.

This is his recovery, and it should be done initially by him. You would not want to do it for him and rob him of the opportunity to evaluate his own boundaries, but as a partner-sensitive ERCEM Specialist, I believe that working on his Three Circles template together allows both of you to design a recovery program that is relationally smart for both of you.

Knowing the three circles allows her (if she chooses) to support him by reviewing movies, finding the safest tables at restaurants, or researching vacation spots that are less triggering in the early stages of recovery.

Women react very differently to monitoring the sex addict's environment. Some women want to jump in and get involved as it makes them feel like they are doing recovery as a partnership. It is also an opportunity for her to give him some feedback on things he may not have thought about so that his recovery becomes more comprehensive and relational.

Some women want to take the reins and make *all* the decisions, which is never advised. In part because it is exhausting, and it also cheats him out of figuring out and being responsible for his own program.

Other women do not want to be involved at all. They explain that this is their husband's journey to navigate, and they want to steer as far away as possible.

To the Partner: Which partner profile most resonates with you?

List five reasons you feel that way.

1.

2.

3.

4.

5.

WHAT DO YOU THINK YOUR HUSBAND MIGHT NEED FROM YOU MOST?

Practice doing a knees-to-knees and encourage your husband to share with you what his thoughts and feelings are about you being, or not being, an active part of recovery. Listen intently so that you can focus on the main points in his communication.

When he is finished, use your reflective listening and repeat back what you heard him say.

After you are finished, ask him if you got it right.

Listen for his response and then repeat it again.

BOUNDARY STRENGTHENING FOR THE PARTNER

Now, a partner may have very distinct boundaries so that she can begin to feel that her life is within her control.

Again, my colleague Dorit Reichental shared how she does boundary work with couples, and I thought it had a lot of value, so I included it here.

Reichental works from the premise that:

1. Sex addiction is a violation of a partner's rights on all the multidimensional spheres, and there needs to be discussion about the previous violations in terms of the traumatic impact of sex addiction on the partner.
2. There are several areas that need to be explored to restore safety and trust. Learning to respect a partner's boundaries is the foundation of a sex addicts' recovery. When that foundation is clear, other safety building areas can be developed or redesigned, such as empathy building, intimacy, and sexual healing.

3. Therefore the boundary must be relational, written by the partner and then jointly completed by the couple.

She goes through all the usual boundary categories using this format and illuminates assertiveness, which we will discuss in this chapter. The boundary always begins with these words: "In order to keep the relationship safe..."

BOUNDARY ASSERTIVENESS

The assertiveness statement starts like this:

"In order to keep the relationship safe...
when you say/do: ______________________, it makes me feel ____________________________."

i.e.: "*When you forget to call me to inform me that you will be late, it makes me feel:*

- *"scared that you are acting out again,"* or
- *"It impacts me and makes me feel like you do not prioritize me,"* or
- *"It impacts me and my sense of security and confidence in our relationship."*

Until you can demonstrate an understanding of the impact on me, I will:

____

(This should be something that protects you or increases your intentional self-care)

On the following page is a written contract completed by the couple after they had both weighed in on how things could go smoother for the future.

THE COUPLESHIP CONTRACT

FOR THE ADDICT

1. We have agreed that I will make consistent and predictable changes in my words/ actions by: ______________________________

____

(i.e. "Setting a regular alarm on my phone five minutes before my target time to leave so that I no longer forget how important it is to hold true to my commitments.")

2. By when: ______________________________

(i.e. "I will do this right now as we are sitting here.")

3. I recognize that it has violated your sense of safety when I ______________________________

____

(i.e. "Forget how much you need consistency from me.")

FOR THE PARTNER

4. She then shares with you that it will help her to feel ______________________________

____

(i.e. loved, cared for, respected, valued, etc.)

when you change the offending words/behaviors ______________________________

____

(i.e. being late)

5. As a result of the changes you make, I (the partner) will ______________________________

____

(words/actions)

in order to demonstrate to you that I now feel heard, safer, more trusting, and willing to ______________________________

(action)

As a result of the changes you make, I will be vulnerable enough to recognize those changes and lean into them to demonstrate to you that I now feel heard, safer, more trusting, and willing to look for ways to be closer.

To show appreciation because of your ______________________________
(loving, thoughtful, empathetic, healing)

I will ______________________________
(actions/plans)

FOR THE PARTNER, CONT.

DORIT EXPLAINS:

1. The boundary is now a coupleship contract, signed and agreed to by both. It is an instrument used to change offending behavior into respectful, empathic behaviors over time, consistently and predictably, to heal a damaged relationship.

2. This is very different from a punishing wife overseeing and controlling (willing or not) her husband's recovery.

3. The consequence is not meant to be punitive; it is meant to take whatever actions or words necessary to create relational safety. It allows him to make a living amend for violating and offending his/her partner when breaking an agreed boundary.

4. He is accountable and takes full responsibility for his actions by making physical, emotional, sexual, relational, spiritual, or relational restitution. When this process is done with intention and integrity the responsibility for keeping the relationship safe becomes a shared responsibility.

5. This can also be used in a constructive way to safely allow a partner to express her anger, minimize the addict's overwhelm, and to help her heal. When a boundary around anger, rage, fear, is negotiated and established ahead of time, the couple knows exactly what to do and can safely express negative emotions, in the hopes of avoiding a triggering cycle.

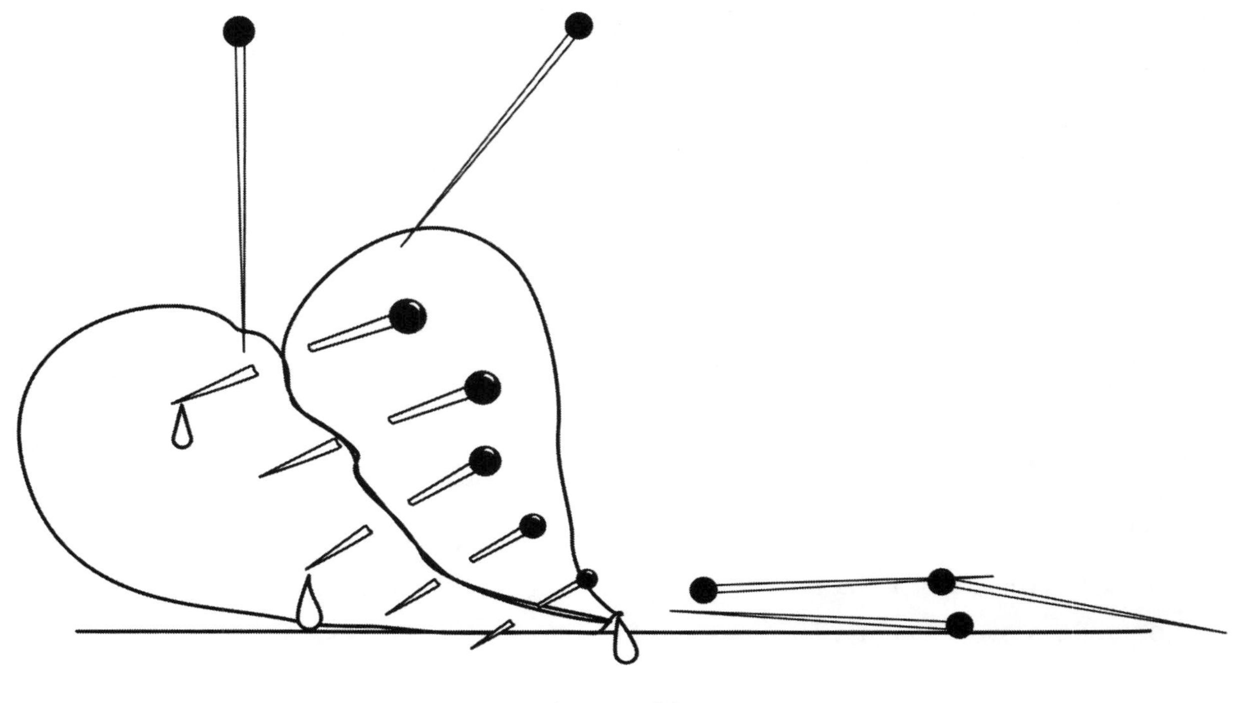

Chapter 13

Moving Into the Conflict—Using the 7 Principles of Conflict to Decrease Shame

All couples experience conflict. In fact, conflict is normal, natural, and necessary. Conflict in healthy relationships breeds intimacy, and yet the two of you have faced what may seem like insurmountable conflict. Your conflict will take real focus, patience, and perseverance to overcome.

I have seen many couples overcome the anger, sadness, and fear that betrayal trauma has caused, but both people in the coupleship must want to heal from the broken relationship.

To the Partner: The process of working through the anger you feel towards him and the addiction requires that you work through the feelings while simultaneously feeling vulnerable. To do this kind of work, you must have a clear vision in sight, and you must fully express yourself so that you can get the negativity out of you and leave space to accept his recovery and his journey. As a betrayed partner, are you able to move in and out of the pain, vulnerability, sadness, and anger? Can you let your guard down and be vulnerable again? It is important to know what you need from him to feel the anger, express it, and then to surrender to it so that you can release it to rebuild the relationship stronger. You will learn more about this in Chapter 16.

DO NOT TAKE THINGS PERSONALLY

Don Miguel Ruiz in *The Four Agreements: A Practical Guide to Personal Freedom* says that 95% of the beliefs we store in our mind are nothing more than lies, and we suffer because we believe our lies.

One of his guidelines is to not take things personally. It is so important for you to remember that his addiction had nothing to do with who you are, what you looked like, how you related as a couple, or how good you were sexually. His addiction started before he even knew you.

We know that it greatly affected you, but you did not contribute to his addiction.

When Don Miguel Ruiz says "Do not take anything personally," he is suggesting that when others do things to us that are abusive, conflictual, or injurious, we should never internalize the message and believe we are at fault. What others think and do are a projection of their own reality. When you are immune to the opinions and actions of others, you will not be the victim of needless suffering.

I want you to feel the pain the addiction has caused, but I *never* want you to feel that you were responsible for your husband's addiction. Unfortunately many women do wonder what they could have done to prevent it!

As a partner you have wondered what might have been wrong with you that could have spurred or contributed to his infidelity. Nothing could be further from the truth. His addiction had nothing to do with you. And in some ways the whole concept of addiction mirrors what Ruiz says about "not taking things personally." I understand that you are screaming at me saying that your husband betrayed and cheated on you—how can I tell you not to take that personally? Well, of course you would have those thoughts, but if you believe that your husband had a compulsion that was uncontrollable and hijacked his brain, then you understand that his addiction was about him. It was not because you were not worthy. And when you have that thought you are less likely to personalize the thought.

When you question whether you could ever compete with the women he watched in porn, you can remind yourself that those women were objects that fueled his addiction. Now that he is in recovery, he has very different views of how he exploited and objectified women. It makes him sick to know that he did that, and he knows that those women exploited him! He also should feel compassion for them and wonder what led them to their choices. We know that most of those women he betrayed you with, whether they were prostitutes, escorts, masseuses, pornography actresses, or any other sex worker, were abused in their childhoods and now are reenacting their trauma and exploiting others.

To the Addict: As the addict in good recovery, you have been sober long enough to have come out of the fog and learn the recovery skills to manage your life. This means that you are also recognizing that you cannot change your past, although I am sure that you wish that you could.

In *Help. Her. Heal.*, I wrote about the Seven Principles of Dealing with Conflict that your actions caused. I would like for you to read each one of them within the context of your relationship and answer two questions.

Which principle of the seven most replicates the "Don't take things personally" message that Ruiz wants you as a recovering addict to remember from *The Four Agreements*? And which principle provides the most comfort to you?

THE SEVEN PRINCIPLES OF DEALING WITH CONFLICT

1. When you experience conflict ask yourself, "How has my past contributed to the present-day conflict?" Recognize that 90% of the conflict is about your past and not who you are today.
2. Hold yourself accountable for causing the pain while not going into shame mode.
3. Know that although her pain is a direct response to your past actions, it is not in response to who you are today.
4. Recognize that you are strong enough to be a container for her pain. You can help her work through her own trauma and move beyond it, while working on your own solid recovery.
5. Tell yourself the issue is not about you, but about a trauma response from your acting out in the past.
6. Practice saying, "This is not who I am today. This is about the consequences of my past actions." Know that your addiction was your kryptonite and your recovery is your superpower!
7. Tell yourself, "I won't give my past guilt and shame the power to make me feel ____."

   (*Sad, shameful, inadequate, unworthy, angry*)

The principle that most encourages me to persevere and stay in good recovery is:

____

I know that I should recognize that I need to acknowledge her pain and stay out of the cycle of shame. I do this by practicing the principle that helps me to "not take it personally," which is principle # ____________________________

As a couple review them again together and decide which principle you think will keep you, as a recovering sex addict, in the here and now working a good recovery program and investing everything you have in the relationship.

We would choose principle #__________ because it would benefit our coupleship by

____

____

____

If you were to apply these 7 principles to the relationship, they might look like this:

1. When you experience conflict with each other and it is directly related to the past, ask yourself, "How has my past contributed to my present-day conflict?" If there have been significant changes in safety and stability, each of you should recognize that the other 90% is about your past pain and not about what is going on today.

For the Partner: This will keep you from going into your pain from the past cycle and will help you stay in the present.

For the Addict: This will keep you from spiraling into the shame cycle when she is triggered about the past, and it will help you to stay strong. When you stay out of the shame cycle you avoid "making it all about you" when it should remain "all about her."

2. Each of you should hold yourself accountable for staying in the present.

3. Each of you should know that although the pain is a direct response to past actions, it is not in response to how you are developing as a couple today. Both of you are working hard to get "past your past." It takes constant focus to stay cognizant of all the work both of you have done.

Note to the SA: If you are subject to occasional slips, you need to tighten up your program because she must see that you are 100% devoted to your addiction program. You cannot afford to let a poor recovery program interfere with keeping her safe.

4. Recognize that you are both becoming stronger and that together you can acknowledge each other's pain. As a couple, you can work together to see the growth in each of you separately and as a couple. You can move beyond it together if you are both willing to acknowledge the changes.

5. Practice saying, "This is not who we are today. Our work is creating a new relationship which is honest, transparent, and real."

6. When either of us is feeling unworthy, we will take the risk to share it with each other so that the other person can see and know the understandable vulnerability that accompanies doing this work. Each one of us can use a mantra that fits the trauma response. The partner can say, "I won't give my past pain the power to make me feel:

   ______________________________."

   (Sad, scared anxious, inadequate, unworthy, angry)

7. And the addict can say, "I won't give my past behaviors the power to make me feel: ______________________________."

   (Shameful, hopeless, unworthy)

These principles will help you both cope with the natural feelings that come up as you both heal. When you use these statements, you will be, as Brené Brown says, "armouring up" to keep you in the present, stay protected, hold yourselves accountable, and put things in perspective. Make sure to make a conscious effort to practice these principles once a week and then check in with each other to report how it improved your functioning. You will be amazed at how it changes your perspective, and you no longer take conflict so personally. (It might be something to report in your check-ins.)

"ACTING AS IF" CAN MOVE YOU FORWARD

To the Partner: There is no doubt that there is going to be a natural resistance to being this proactive about your relationship. You are reading this book to create a "new" marriage that will stand the test of time. I am not asking you to be all in, but I am suggesting that you begin to practice the art of "Acting as If."

"Acting as If" originated from the recovery movement. When an addict did not believe he was capable of sobriety or getting a job, finding a relationship, or changing immature behaviors, his sponsor would validate his fears and then encourage him to practice the behavior and "act as if" he could do it anyway. The premise was that if someone practices something long enough, it becomes a habit, and over time they found that they did indeed acquire the skill.

As he repairs the relationship, empathizes with you about the pain he has caused, and shows willingness to rebuild your trust, there comes a time when you must trust your gut to continue to do the hard work and lean into the premise that change is occurring. You will know if he is worthy of your trust, although it is normal to second guess yourself. When you act as if you can trust the new relationship that you are building, you will be more likely to enjoy and lean into it.

AS HE REPAIRS THE RELATIONSHIP, EMPATHIZES WITH YOU ABOUT THE PAIN HE HAS CAUSED, AND SHOWS WILLINGNESS TO REBUILD YOUR TRUST, THERE COMES A TIME WHEN YOU MUST TRUST YOUR GUT TO CONTINUE TO DO THE HARD WORK AND LEAN INTO THE PREMISE THAT CHANGE IS OCCURRING.

"Acting as if" will move you forward! We will talk more about the concept in chapter 18 as you move into Post-Traumatic Growth.

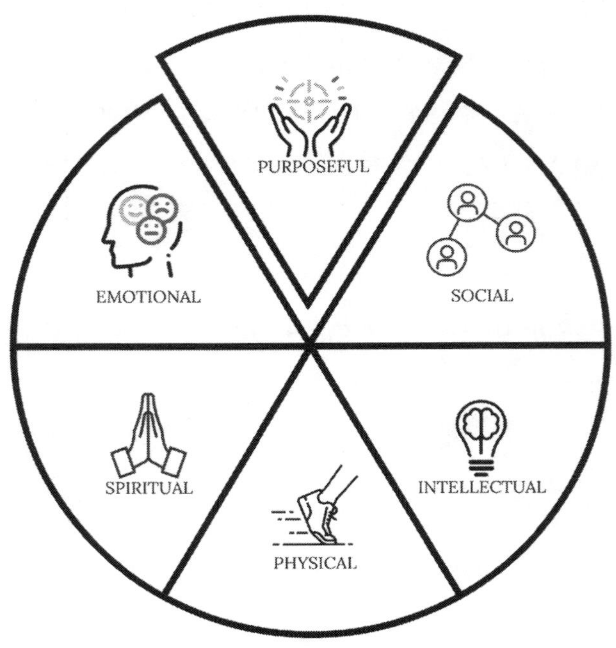

Chapter 14

Your Needs Individually and as a Couple (The Pie Theory)

It is so important for couples to know what they need in the relationship, and I typically have the couples I work with break down their needs into six segments. Imagine a pie-shaped diagram with the pieces of that pie including physical, intellectual, social, emotional, spiritual, and purposeful needs. When you think about your life as a couple, how might you deepen the all-important need quotient in the relationship?

PHYSICAL NEEDS

What do you need physically from each other? That might look like "I would like my spouse to work out with me," "I need more non-sexual touch," "I need more sex," "I need my partner to rub my feet," or "I need more hand holding." "I need my husband to stop expecting sex." You get the drift. It is so important to think about your physical needs and know that there are many ways to deepen or enrich them.

Men are afraid to talk about their needs because they do not believe they deserve to express them. You said to yourself, "I have ruined her life with my addiction and self-absorbed behavior, and I want her to know that I have changed. So I will not express my needs, and maybe she will know that I have changed."

To the Partner: Women in the safety and stabilization stage are not ready to trust him with her needs. All partners relate differently and may challenge the SA to meet many needs individually. You fall somewhere on that continuum because you want to see where you stand with him.

Are there some physical needs you might be willing to express and test the waters for some level of comfort? Could you tolerate sitting next to him on the couch, sleeping in the same bed, or having your feet rubbed? If he is maintaining recovery and is working his program, I would encourage you to stretch out of your comfort zone and scan your body for what you might need from him physically. When women have triggers, they often want to have the back of their head or neck rubbed to feel the natural self-soothing that can occur from that.

It does require that you stretch yourself to allow him to give to you again, so you may need to look for other forms of connection first before you tackle your physical needs. The most important thing is to really check-in with yourself to determine what you might let back into the relationship. This may mean that you specifically journal your thoughts and your feelings because quiet contemplation is the precursor to your own need for connection.

INTELLECTUAL NEEDS

When you think about intellectual needs as a couple, you may decide that you would like to take a cooking course together or want to buy a new computer and work on learning the techniques you need to master using that computer. Many people choose to go back to school, but they do not necessarily choose to do that together. Are there classes, book clubs, or Bible studies that you could participate in that would stimulate you intellectually? As the addict moves out of his addiction, he needs to create new neuropathways where he can find stimulation and build substituting behaviors. After partner betrayal occurs, a partner needs to be thinking about ways of enriching her life that are separate from partner betrayal.

There is no doubt that partners are walking encyclopedias on sexual betrayal. You have read everything there is to read, and you have looked up YouTube videos and podcasts to understand what has happened to your husband and what has happened to you. This kind of intellectual stimulation helps you feel safe and provides some form of stabilization. But as a couple who is investing in their relationship, it is so important to renew the relationship by finding stimuli that takes you both away from the addiction and the betrayal and creates a new sense of connection for you both. This assessment of your needs is a good place to start the connection process. As you surveil your life together, can you imagine taking on a new hobby that required that you learned it together? Would it feel safe for you both to try something new like golf, tango lessons, woodworking, or skydiving?

SOCIAL NEEDS

As you look at your social needs, there is a good chance that you both have made fellowship connections, and you now have a group of people who understand what you have been through and do not judge you for it. This fellowship is crucial to your sobriety and even your sense of sanity, but what you need to focus on now in addition to that rich fellowship are opportunities to create social relationships that no longer define you as an addict or as a partner.

When you think about your life, you more than likely have put your social relationships on the back burner because you were not sure who you could trust to share what you had been through. You did not want to engage in what would seem like superficial connections with people who did not understand what you were going through.

Now as you look at your life and are assessing your needs, how might you add social diversity to your well-being? Would you like to combine the physical and social needs together and take a tennis class? Would you be up to learning pickle ball with a group of people together? Are you able to imagine taking a dance course or joining a meet-up for people who like to hike? You have always enjoyed cards but never pursued joining a card club and meeting new people. Think about branching out socially and ask yourself, if you had all the time in the world, what would you like to learn as a couple that would increase your skills and your social network?

Redefining yourself as a couple means developing some new relationships in addition to the old so that you can create a new life together separate from your past. I can forecast that you may be afraid to seek out new ventures because you do not trust him to *not* have a wandering eye. Yet, he has been learning skills that he has been putting into place when you are not around, and it is important to assess how he is doing. I always tell my partners that if they cannot trust their spouse to be respectful and exclusive, they obviously need to depend on him less for connection. But that moves us into the emotional needs.

EMOTIONAL NEEDS

What do you need emotionally? We have talked before about needing safety and stabilization so that you can move forward in the relationship. What might you need to get you through the anger, mourning, grief, and loss that you have experienced from this whole ordeal? What do you need to validate your feelings? Oftentimes many couples work through my book, *Help. Her. Heal.*, because it helps to reinforce the work the addict needs to do to help his partner heal. If you are having trouble really separating yourself from what you have been through, you might want to take an intensive course with other couples to work through any emotional residue that is left from the betrayal.

On the flip side, what would you like to gain emotionally from your relationship? If you could envision your relationship five years from now, what would you like it to look like? Would you like to buy that lake home where you could invite friends over, swim, paddle-board, and enjoy the serenity that the water can bring? Would you like to move to a new location where you could emotionally get a new start, perhaps changing your lifestyle, raising goats, planting gardens, or becoming missionaries and helping people in other countries? When you are looking at your emotional needs, I want you to dream big. The truth of the matter is that you can accomplish anything as a couple if you work on processing your emotions and are vulnerable enough to begin to reinvest in what you need from each other emotionally. John Gottman, author of *The Seven Principles of Making a Marriage Work*, says that every couple needs a vision, and I know that you would love to be in the place where you could dream about that again.

I know one couple who has made it their mission to experience the United States, so they bought an RV and travel from destination to destination in it. What they have found is that they are making new memories and having fun again, and it has moved them through the agony of the past.

YOUR SPIRITUAL NEEDS

SAs in recovery typically struggle with two simultaneous thoughts and feelings. As their recovery strengthens, they want to find ways to connect again. But as they work on their empathy, they know that this can take three to five years, and they patiently wait for the cues. Their program tells them to give it to God, and that also means to surrender control.

Partners are typically questioning where God was when he was acting out. How could a loving God have allowed him to hurt her so much? Have you wondered where God was as his acting out became so out of control? How can you get this need met when you have so many questions and doubts? Have you been able to reckon with the injustice of having to hurt this much? Have you questioned why God had seemed to forsake you?

CAN YOU EVER TRUST GOD AGAIN?

It is likely that as you look at your spiritual needs, you will have to do the hard work of processing why this happened to you. Many men and women wonder how God could have allowed addiction to have occurred in their lives.

For the Addict: You must reckon with the fact that you continually tried to do it yourself and did not ask for help. Many of the recovery programs and the 12-step movement suggest that you must surrender the need to control the acting out behaviors to your higher power. It is only after you surrender spiritually and rely on your higher power that you can find the recovery you deserve.

For partners, it is a bit different. Frequently I hear partners wonder how God could have let this happen to them. They ask themselves what they did to deserve the sexual betrayal, and if there are things in their life that they feel ashamed or guilty of, they wonder if it is God's retribution upon them to have allowed addiction to fracture their lives.

Strengthening your spirituality is imperative for finding recovery and mental health. I know that I do not have the answers, but I frequently tell people that God gave all of us predetermination. That means that bad things can happen to good people, and it is your ability to lean on your belief in good and in your higher power that will carry you through the worst of life's circumstances.

What can you do as a couple to strengthen your spiritual knowing? Would you benefit from attending a new church, temple or mosque, participating in a Bible study, or reading that new book on spirituality together? Would you like to increase your sense of the spiritual world by studying Buddhism, Taoism, or some other form of religious teaching? Would renewing your faith comfort you?

I would encourage you to identify what your primary feeling is regarding your partner betrayal and your relationship with *your* Higher Power. What I believe to be true is that God understands your anger, sadness, and despair at your husband and with God himself.

You might need to write out your conversations with God to get clearer on how you have been affected by His inability to have protected you.

And more importantly, you may want to ask Him how He might use you to help others who are hurting.

Exercise: Individually, but together as a couple, commit to spending ten minutes a day *everyday* for one month sharing your innermost feeling with God.

As an Addict: Have some deep conversations, asking Him why you had the childhood that led up to your compulsive behavior. If there was any form of trauma in your childhood, make sure to ask Him how he could have left you in your darkest hour.

Undoubtedly, there were hundreds of times when you asked Him to take this addiction away from you, and yet He never seemed to answer any of your prayers. And now you have watched your wife become a shell of a woman, doubting every inch of herself and her existence. You have begged God to take her pain, and again, He has ignored your pleas for help.

Each day spend ten minutes asking God what you can do to feel better, help your wife heal, and bring her back to life. Ask Him what you need to get closer to Him and renew that spiritual connection. Write down what He tells you.

To the Partner: Share your real feelings with your higher power. Do not hold back. Get angry, cry, share your feelings of abandonment. God can handle your genuine feelings. You need to confront them so that you can learn from them. God is there to hold your anger and grief.

Ask God what He would like you to know. Be open and receptive to what you need to learn. I am sure He will reassure you that you never deserved this, and you may need to strengthen the bond with Him to move forward in your life.

If you are a couple who does not believe in a spiritual practice, I would encourage you to spend time out in nature observing the miracles of life. A blooming flower, a plane overhead, a mountain urging you both to climb it together. The couples that I work with that are Atheist, or Agnostic report a sense of awe and wonder noticing how nature reminds them of something bigger than themselves. They don't necessarily believe that there is a higher power but they are reminded that life is not all about them.

PURPOSEFUL NEEDS

After you have worked through the trauma, you make a conscious choice to find some purpose out of the chaos. You either make the decision to contribute to the lives of others and focus on giving of yourself to improve the lives of others or you ask yourself, what can you do from all that you have learned about addiction and partner betrayal.

For many people, this involves being there for others. You may choose to watch your grandkids twice a week, or volunteer at the local elementary school, or help seniors with their taxes, or become a boy scout leader.

Or you may decide to become a sponsor in SA or SANON. You may decide to become a counselor to help others with sex addiction or partner betrayal.

The ultimate goal is to do something together that has meaning and purpose. It doesn't have to be a huge goal but together you ask yourselves how can we find more purpose in our lives together? I have an 83 year old couple who both sponsor in their S-groups, watch their grand-dog together, and allow me to video tape them for the trainings I do to help professionals to learn ERCEM. They inspire me in everything they do!

I have 2 colleagues that went through sex addiction and partner betrayal and decided to help other couples work through this ordeal. They wanted to do more so they went back to graduate school and got their degrees and got their Sexual Addiction Certification (CSAT) and started a counseling practice. They knew they had more to give so they wrote a book on helping couples work through the chaos of sexual betrayal and are living out their passion together.

What might you do as a couple to find more purpose in your life? We will explore this in the post-traumatic growth section in Phase 3.

Chapter 15

Your Sexual Relationship

There is no doubt that your relationship has been affected by the sexual infidelity of your partner. Yet, many couples restore their sexuality at different times in their relationship. For some couples, they immediately have sex after the discovery because that is the number one thing that felt most jeopardized and therefore, they go right for working on that. Partner-sensitive therapists do not necessarily recommend that because that can be what I call a reactivity response to the intense reaction of feeling rejected. Partners may desperately need to feel affirmed, so they immediately seek affirmation and approval by initiating sex to see if they are still desired. Did that sound like you? Did you immediately question whether he loved and desired you, so you initiated sex to see if he was still desirous of you?

Other couples have had sexually barren lives for one to three years after discovery because it feels too vulnerable and scary to give this special connection to him after he violated the sanctity of your marriage. What started as confusion about your sexual life after betrayal developed into a "No Sexual Intimacy Zone" because it just did not feel safe. It is something that easily got put on the back burner to deal with another day, and then it got ignored for days, weeks, months, and years after discovery. The addict is walking on fragile territory because he knows that he caused the pain, and when he has hinted or brought it up, it has caused so much distress that it was not worth the fight. But, it created lots of fears for the relationship. She thinks, "What happens if we do not rekindle this part of our lives?" and he fears "What happens if we never have sex again?"

On a rare occasion I have seen partners who are so devastated and angry they have decided that they will never have sex again. It can be a way of punishing the acting out partner. Have those thoughts crossed your mind?

In the beginning after discovery, we oftentimes recommend that couples do not have sex for 30-90 days so that his reward center can be calmed down and he can dim the images from the sexual addiction.

Many a partner has said that this is not fair that her sexual life must be compromised because he needs to alter his arousal template. And it is true, your sexuality should not have to be compromised because he needs to recalibrate his, but the truth is, if he had cancer or surgery that required total recuperation time, you would not resent him for his illness.

This is one of the toughest dilemmas to face. It feels like what happened to you was his fault, so it is hard to support his need for a healthy recovery if you are also having to pay the price. You have been reckoning with his consequences, and it is infuriating when you must experience a loss as a result.

Sex can be challenging for all couples and you as a couple are especially vulnerable after sexual betrayal. It is important for couples to know that the biggest sex organ is the brain, and communication is the key to working through sexual issues. I also want to encourage you to work on developing other types of closeness, connection, and intimacy, especially if sex has been put on hold.

Unfortunately, for lots of couples there was sexual anorexia anyway, in part because the addict knew he was living a dual life and was unable to perform. For other men, they had trained their brains to like pornographic images or partners, and they were no longer stimulated by the loving, caring relationship of a spouse. For a variety of reasons, it is imperative that you get with a good therapist who deals with sexual addiction and partner betrayal, who can help you work through these issues and begin to restore the physical and emotional sense of safety that occurs in sex.

Couples who are working towards post-traumatic growth want to restore their sexual relationship, but they are not sure how to go about doing that because they fear it will be too vulnerable for their partner. It is important to talk about the fears for both the addict and his spouse so you can negotiate what does feel safe. Oftentimes that will be experimenting with very simple touching experiences that involve non-sexual body parts and positions. My colleagues Dr. Bill and Dr. Ginger Bercaw have a wonderful sexual reintegration program for couples after sexual betrayal. Their books help guide you through the process, even if you are not sure that you are ready to take the leap to physical intimacy.

Talking about sex requires a lot of emotional maturity, and this means that it is important for each of you to spend some time sharing your fears, concerns, and hopes. Sometimes partners can talk about what would need to happen before sexual activity could be resumed. What do you both need to feel safe? What would you like in your relationship with each other? Has there been irreparable damage done, and therefore sex is not discussed?

Men in the program are oftentimes told that sex is not necessarily part of the equation after deception. This means that their sponsors and other people in the fellowship may be telling them to take sex off the table permanently. A couple can live a healthy and happy life without sexual activity, and but it is such a physical and spiritual aspect of the relationship that ignoring or denying it would mean you would have to really increase your other needs as a coupleship.

SEXUAL INTIMACY

In most cases, sexual intimacy is something that you learn as you navigate through life with your partner. Many people are uncomfortable with talking about sex, and therefore, sexual intimacy is learned without communication and is based on trial and error. There is no doubt that when sexual addiction and partner betrayal occurs, that intimacy was fractured, and your fear as a couple is that it may never be rebuilt again.

To the Addict: If you are an addict who is in good recovery and is seeking to develop a closer relationship with your partner, it can feel intrusive to want to work on your sexual intimacy because of the damage that you have caused. Sexual intimacy requires that you look for ways to be close and develop trust in many different areas. It will be necessary for you to check on the temperature of your wife's sexual comfort level. This means that you will need to check in with her frequently to find out how she is doing, what she is thinking, and what she needs to feel safe.

When you nurture your wife inside and outside of the bedroom, you are more likely to build trust, dependability, and empathy in your sexual relationship. Most men have heard the adage "foreplay begins outside of the bedroom," and it is about your ability to care for the kids, do your fair share of household chores and duties, and seek closeness without sexuality. Since this relationship has been so damaged, it can be especially helpful to find ways of restoring her trust by asking her what she would like most in your relationship.

THE FIVE LANGUAGES OF LOVE

The 5 Love Languages by Dr. Gary Chapman is a simple read based on the concept that we all have a primary love language that increases marital satisfaction, compatibility, and security. You may have already gone to Dr. Chapman's site to assess what is both your love language and what your spouse desires most.

Now as the betrayed, you may be fearful to enter this arena. It may feel too soon, too scary, too hopeful, too positive, and too vulnerable after such a violation of your relationship.

That is why we are leaving sexuality last—we know that you must build on the communication and your basic needs for safety first. I understand why you need to go through safety and stabilization and the grief and mourning stages to feel like you are ready to take your coupleship to the next level.

Many couples had poor sexual relations from the beginning of their relationship. You may not have talked about sexual pleasure; therefore, neither of you knew what to do to please each other. Sexual needs could be compromised because you both have different sexual preferences, which results in a stalemate in the bedroom. To complicate things further, sexual addiction interferes with healthy sexual functioning and skews how a couple feels about their own needs and arousal template.

The arousal template is the part of the brain that signals when you are turned on or aroused. It tells you what you like sexually, whether that is being cuddled and caressed while being pleasured or having the lights on high as you view your partner's body and expressions. Sometimes it is a certain act or position that is especially appealing.

Everyone has an arousal template that started early in childhood and was a co-creation from your own chemicals and hormones. It also includes the teachings that occurred from your parents, the church, and important people in your childhood. Lastly, it is based on experiences that occurred in your lifetime that were both good and bad, including trauma like sexual molestation and exploitation, and pleasurable sexual activity that solidified your desires and needs.

It is important to talk with each other about how you are feeling about yourself sexually and what you need from each other since sexual addiction has made itself known. Talking about sex can often be a vulnerable experience for any couple, let alone for the couple who has experienced betrayal. You may want to get some specialized help by going to a professional who understands sexual betrayal, sexual addiction, and sexuality. It is my experience that a normal counselor does not possess the sensitivity to help a couple that has experienced this type of trauma. Make sure you research your professional for sensitivity to this topic.

Let's take this slow and get some understanding of where you are today if you are ready to go back to the basics and examine how you might redevelop your love life and your sex life. I recommend that you both go to Dr. Gary Chapman's website (the5lovelanguages.com), and even if you did this before, I would like you both to see where your style for love is now that betrayal has occurred.

I would like you to use it during your next check-in and for both of you to share what is most important to you. As you reconsider rebuilding your relationship, allow this book to guide you to the safe ways you can show each other love. It will absolutely take courage on both of your parts to be vulnerable and share how you might work on loving each other again.

THE LOVE LANGUAGE CHECK-IN

Bring your assessment to the check-in and share the ranking of the 5 languages of love.

1. Sit knees-to-knees and explain why you feel the assessment was valid or did not apply to your relationship.

2. Share any surprises that came from taking the test.

3. Share one "safe" way you might be able to get your needs met, make a behavioral request, and share why you are afraid to ask for what you would like or need.

4. Get your spouse's feedback about the request.

Tom and Nancy took the test. Tom was sure that when he and Nancy had done this previously, his love language had been physical touch, but today it had changed to words of affirmation.

When he sat down with Nancy, they had the following dialogue:

"Nancy, my scores showed that I ranked a nine for words of affirmation, a seven for physical touch, gifts and acts of service were both a four, and quality time was a three."

"I was not surprised by the shift because I found that on the test I could not even acknowledge my physical needs. I felt so much shame about what I have done to you and to us. I think there is something wrong with me because I have lost my sex drive, and I believe it is because I have so much guilt and shame."

"I know that I am starving to be the man that you can trust again, and when you smile at me or say something nice, I melt inside."

As you can see, sexual intimacy starts with good communication. If you can start with sharing your vulnerabilities, and the basics with your partner, you can establish more intimacy which is a precursor for better sex.

EMOTIONAL INTIMACY

Laura Dawn Lewis coined the concept of the Eight Stages of Intimacy (copyright 2004, The Couples Company). One of the eight stages is emotional intimacy, which covers feelings, trust, security, and safety in a relationship. Many couples never achieve emotional intimacy because you must accept your partner for who he or she is without reservation. At this level of intimacy, the couple feels comfortable sharing anger, happiness, secrets, sensual, and sexual feelings. Each of you know that you are loved and you deeply love your partner, no matter how either of you feel or act.

That is the goal for this book and your life. In post-traumatic growth, you have a rock-solid relationship whereby you can trust that your spouse has learned the emotional skills to love and support you.

My colleague and co-author of the "Intimacy" chapter in *Help. Her. Heal*, Allan J. Katz LPC, CSAT, believes that in sexual and porn addiction, there is so much wounding that the emotional intimacy is diminished, and it becomes difficult for the wounded partner to feel comfortable enough to share anger, happiness, and erotic feelings. Some spouses call for a sexual cooling-off period of celibacy, so the addict can heal the addiction's damage to the brain. They also don't feel safe enough to engage in sexual activity until they can trust their partner once again.

To build intimacy and empathy, the wounded partner needs to know that the addict understands the pain is due to the addict's poor choices and is not the wounded partner's fault.

Emotional intimacy is achieved when trust is established again and the couple can speak about sensitive topics without constantly bringing up past indiscretions.

We have asked some sensitive questions around intimacy that really involve vulnerability. Please look at the following continuum and see where you land so that you can look for ways to strengthen your intimacy quotient. This will likely require you to go to an ERCEM Specialist who can help you develop more intimacy.

As a couple I would like you to sit together and rate each area from 1 to 10. One represents that you are not currently able to achieve the goal and ten represents that you master it regularly.

THE INTIMACY ASSESSMENT

1. In a state of fear, uncertainty, or danger, your partner is the person you turn to for comfort.

1 2 3 4 5 6 7 8 9 10

NOT GOOD WORKING ON IT CLOSE TO MASTERY

2. Crying, showing frustration, sadness, or anger in front of your partner is healthy. You know he/she will not see you as weak, psychotic, crazy, or out of control.

1 2 3 4 5 6 7 8 9 10

NOT GOOD WORKING ON IT CLOSE TO MASTERY

3. You can speak about sex, secrets, and your feelings without a fear of being betrayed, ridiculed, or compromised.

1 2 3 4 5 6 7 8 9 10

NOT GOOD WORKING ON IT CLOSE TO MASTERY

4. No matter what happens, you know your partner loves you and will not abandon you during a state of crisis, ill health, or financial difficulty.

1 2 3 4 5 6 7 8 9 10

NOT GOOD WORKING ON IT CLOSE TO MASTERY

5. You often show or tell each other, through words and actions, that you love and respect each other.

1 2 3 4 5 6 7 8 9 10

NOT GOOD — WORKING ON IT — CLOSE TO MASTERY

6. Past wrongs are not dredged up in arguments to get even with each other. The past is discussed, forgiven, and left there. This may take some time recovering from sexual betrayal, but when both partners work on healing themselves, the chances of recapturing the intimacy can be achieved through empathy for each other.

1 2 3 4 5 6 7 8 9 10

NOT GOOD — WORKING ON IT — CLOSE TO MASTERY

7. Passive-aggressive behavior and name calling does not exist in your relationship.

1 2 3 4 5 6 7 8 9 10

NOT GOOD — WORKING ON IT — CLOSE TO MASTERY

Use this to identify areas you want to work on as a couple and discuss them with your partner.

Questions to determine emotional intimacy for both the addict and partner:

1. What will it take for you to feel safe in this relationship?

2. What will it take for you to want to build trust within this relationship?

3. It is likely that you can show empathy when your partner respects and admires you, but how do you build intimacy amidst conflict?

4. Have you showed vulnerable feelings like sadness or even tears in front of your spouse?

If not, what is your fear about being this vulnerable?

What's the worst that can happen?

Has that ever happened? ______________________________

____

____

____

____

If yes, did your partner react with empathy or with scorn? __________

____

____

____

____

This assessment was created to help both of you begin to think about the many forms of intimacy that you can strengthen in your marriage. I want you to go back to the "Pie Diagram" and refer to those six needs to determine what would enhance his or her intimacy quotient and to check on the temperature of each other's comfort level sexually.

You need safety in the relationship to build intimacy. You both are doing a good job of making that a priority by learning all the relational skills in this book. Couples who are practicing the skills of good recovery and are seeking to develop a closer relationship with each other will automatically feel closer and more connected, but they need to assess whether they want to work harder on the sexual intimacy part of their relationship.

For addicts, it can feel intrusive to want to work on your sexual intimacy because of the damage that has been caused. Be sure to share that vulnerability so that she knows that this is not easy for either one of you.

There are two simple but not easy to use "pieces of advice" that you can begin immediately as you reintegrate into the bedroom together.

1. Practice "Open Eyes Sex" or "Open Eyes Physical Contact." As uncomfortable as it may be for both of you to open your eyes during sex or physical contact, it is the number one key to restoring safety in a physical or sexual relationship. Dr. David Schnarch runs webinars all over the world to improve sexual performance. He found after surveying thousands of people that: 7.5% of couples never have sex; 32% never make eye contact during sex; 42% sometimes make eye contact during sex; 18.5% have orgasms while looking into each others eyes. When his eyes are open, he can admire the closeness within the relationship. It is a testament to the fact that you, the partner, are allowing him to connect so intimately. It is a real gift for both, and it certainly reaffirms that the relationship is sacred and special. It also keeps him focused on the present and assures you that he is not deep in fantasy somewhere else.

2. The second request I have for you both is to practice being verbally vulnerable with each other. Despite the tendency to want to stay in your own heads while making love or physically connecting, you both can enhance the connection by commenting on how the experience feels and how grateful you both are that you are relearning how to share this with each other. Talking while touching each other can be a roadmap for what you both need. If it feels inconceivable that you would talk during sex or after touching each other, make sure to spend some time after you finish holding each other to talk about what you liked or didn't like.

Again my colleagues Drs. Bill and Ginger Bercaw have devoted their lives to improving the sexual lives of couples who have experienced partner betrayal. Their books are guides that will walk you through the steps. I highly recommend *The Couples Guide to Intimacy: How Sexual Reintegration Can Help Your Relationship Heal* as it is respectful of the small changes you will need to make to build more trust and intimacy.

LIVING WITHOUT SEX

The truth of the matter is that you can both live without sex and increase other forms of connection. That being said, I don't advise it. I would recommend that if you want a sex life, you should build it slowly. This guidebook is here to help you get all six of your primary needs met, and that includes your sexual coupleship.

Your sexuality is most dependent on your ability to communicate with each other and to develop emotional intimacy. This means that you need to be honest, open, and forthright. I know that both of you will have times when there is a pit in your stomach because you do not want to talk about your fears or be honest about your inadequacies, but having a solid sexual relationship involves authenticity, transparency, and honesty. Even though this part of your relationship has been so badly ruptured, it requires that you begin to find the building blocks to share yourselves totally with each other.

What are your fears about being more honest about your sexual self and your couple's sexuality?

For men, that might include worrying about sexual performance or being too sexually assertive or needy. It may be that you as a man have never really communicated about sex, so this is completely new to you. And anything that is new feels uncomfortable and unfamiliar, as if it was unchartered territory.

For the Partner: Your sexuality has been affected by the rejection you feel and general feelings of inadequacy. You may be worried that you are not enough and can no longer give him what he needs. You may have thought you had a good sexual relationship prior to discovery, or you may have known that something was off. He may not have been a good lover from the start of your sexual relationship, but you never shared that with him because you did not know how to be honest. For that reason, I want you to sit down and write about your fears. Write about what sexuality was like for you before, what it is like currently, and what you would like it to be in the future. Both of you need to be honest with yourselves before you can be honest with each other.

What has happened to you has been so devastating, and you do not know how to navigate the pain. You are afraid that if you don't have sex, you will lose him completely, but you don't feel ready. It doesn't feel safe, but the last thing you want to do is reject him sexually because your fear is he will cheat on you again, whether that be with pornography, or with another woman. It has left you in a very fragile state and more than likely it doesn't feel safe to talk to others about what you should do because sex is a private, sacred experience. Instead you say nothing, and you certainly don't share your vulnerability with him because you're not sure that you can do that or if he will be honest.

Sexuality is about being vulnerable! You both need to practice being honest and up your transparency. You both deserve to know the inner thoughts of each other. I implore you both to take the risk and share your fears. I can assure you that it will increase your intimacy.

Chapter 16

Getting Through Phase 2 of Partner Betrayal: Anger, Grief, Loss, and Mourning

Now that you are through the shock of what has happened and understand that it was his addiction that created this chaos, you can begin to deal with all the underlying feelings that keep hijacking you both. It is important to identify and honor those horrible feelings because they are the pain that you both carry around with you.

This will require that you work through the grief, sadness, anger and mourning for what has happened to you both. Sexual betrayal has damaged your sense of self, and no one can know how that feels. But I promise that your husband is experiencing trauma because now that he is in good recovery, he cannot believe that he has done this to the woman he loves. Although you can do this work on your own, using the ERCEM method suggests that he should be the person to help you go through these emotions. It is important to address these feelings so that you can externalize and release them in order to move on.

As a partner, it would make sense to me that you are reading this and thinking, "Why in the heck would I need to work through these horrendous feelings? I did not cause this, but I have been devastated by it. I don't want to spend another second on it!'

That is your prerogative. However, at some point you will need to process the feelings and pain so that they do not sit inside of you and cause bodily damage. I promise you, as Bessel Van der Kolk wrote, "the body keeps the score." If you try to ignore the anger, sadness, and grief of what happened to you it will show up psychologically and/or physically. There are many autonomic responses to trauma that manifest as conditions and illnesses, and processing them is the only way to heal from the damage it has caused. It is not fair that you must go through this, but you will grow through it if you do the work.

COMMON SYMPTOMS OF TRAUMA

As you look at this illustration, are you able to see how this trauma may be showing up in other areas of your life?

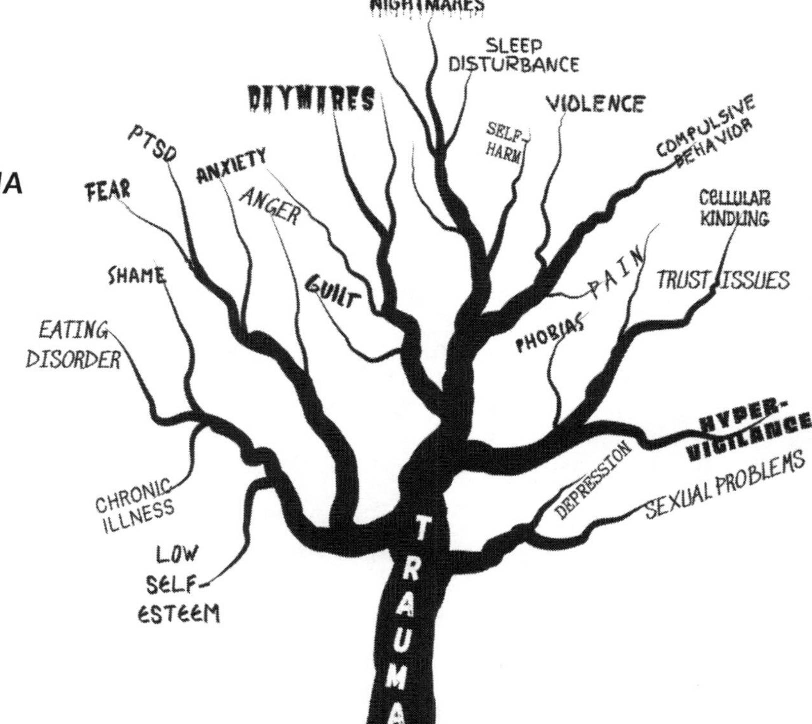

As the addict, I want you to help her with this work because she should not have to do this alone. I know that this will bring out painful feelings for you too. You are not your addiction, and now that you are in good recovery, you are sickened by all the devastation that sex addiction has caused both to her and your relationship. You might tend to want to avoid doing the hard work, but I assure you that by going through it together you will help her heal.

To the Partner: Where do you begin? Doing a feeling check-in as we discussed in Chapter 7 is the place to start. Initially, the best way to recognize feelings and how to deal with them is to write about and verbalize them to others who understand their magnitude in your life.

Do you feel stuck in betrayal? Are you having difficulty detaching from the trauma and moving on? It may be that you have not worked through your feelings. They may have immobilized you and kept you tethered to him and the pain.

Since he has caused you to feel these feelings, it can expedite your healing if he helps you process them. After many years of working in this field, I discovered that if he could be there and contain your pain while you externalized it, it assists you in working through it and healing faster.

Initially, assessing how you feel in a daily check-in helps both of you because it allows you to monitor your feelings and helps him to know what is going on inside of you. You will want to practice this daily to prepare you for Phase 2. In a couples check-in you will be appraising the following questions:

Have you given yourself enough time to be angry and grieve the losses this has caused? Does he know what the losses are and how they have affected you?

In your check-in or with your therapist, both of you should write down what losses you have experienced. How did it make you feel? How might you process them?

MY LOSSES

TYPES OF LOSSES	PRIMARY FEELING	PROCESS WORK TO BE DONE
I no longer can count on you for security.	*Angry and Cheated.*	*Write an anger letter to the addiction raging at the injustice that has resulted.*
We are 100K in debt for your treatment.	*Sad and Fearful.*	*I will have to keep telling myself that I would have spent any amount of money for treatment for cancer and stand convicted that I (we) did the right thing to get you the help you needed.*
I have lost confidence in myself.	*Scared.*	*An ERCEM assignment is to write out 25 examples of my strengths as I have weathered this horrible ordeal.*
I have lost the assurance of your recovery.	*Angry and Fearful.*	*He should track all daily recovery activities that he is doing as a reassurance reminder.*
I have lost my connection to God.	*Sad.*	*Write a letter to God and read it to my husband so that I can grieve the huge sadness I feel inside.*
The loss of a normal life.	*Anger and Sadness.*	*There are several anger exercises to externalize the anger in Carol's book "Unleashing Your Power: Moving Beyond Sexual Betrayal." When I feel this way, I can beat pillows with a racket. I can do a Vesuvius with my husband where he hears all the pain inside. I can write out 50 reasons for feeling angry and read them to my husband.*
The preoccupation with your sex addiction robbed me from quality time with our kids.	*Angry and Sad.*	*Write a letter to my children expressing how sorry I am that I lost such precious time with them. This letter should be read to your husband and not read or given to the kids.*

This chart is a reminder of the ways you can feel, process, and express the pain. If you are fearful, do it with your husband, or if that does not feel safe, I would ask you to find an ERCEM Specialist who can walk you through this grief work.

Are there areas of your life that stay the same despite your desire to change?

TYPES OF LOSSES/FEARS	PRIMARY FEELING	PROCESS WORK TO BE DONE TOGETHER
Loss of self-esteem.	*Sadness*	*Both SA/PA create reality affirmation to remind her of her strength.*
Loss of security in self.	*Anger or Sadness*	*Have him write and read 50 ways he has hurt me.*
Loss of self-esteem.	*Anger or Sadness*	*Have him read those to me. "I took away your self-esteem when..."*
Loss of relationship.	*Anger*	*Do a "Vesuvius" and/or write a "venomous letter to the addiction" (see format at end of chapter).*
Inability to trust.	*Fear*	*Write out 25 "What I fear most about my life" statements.*
I cannot trust that you will stay sober.	*Loneliness*	*Regular polygraph tests/He sets up quarterly tests.*
I fear that you will be tempted to cheat.	*Fear*	*SA sets up AVR daily on this issue.*
I fear that you will not maintain rigorous honesty.	*Fear*	*Participate in Omar Minwelas' course on "Integrity Abuse."*

VESUVIUS: EXTERNALIZATION OF ANGER AND DEVELOPMENT OF PERSONAL BOUNDARIES

"Vesuvius" is an exercise developed for couples. It has been adapted from "PAIRS." It is a tremendous exercise for a woman because it allows you to release your anger and experience the support from your husband who initially caused you the issues. You can do this by yourself as a couple, but I recommend that you do this with a partner sensitive therapist due to the strong emotional component in the work.

It helps to have a third person who can sit with both of you to help process your feelings after you are finished. Show this exercise to your therapist and ask him/her if they would be willing to guide you through this. If they are not comfortable with Gestalt work, contact an ERCEM Specialist as they have had training in this exercise.

This exercise encourages you to get in touch with suppressed or repressed anger. Women are often taught that they should not have ugly, angry thoughts and feelings. You have been surprised at how angry, rageful, and out of control you have been since discovery, and you likely have thought that you are going crazy because this is not who you are. So much of this is trauma brain, and when you do these cathartic exercises with your husband you feel supported and can make a conscious choice to release them to be able to move on.

They also clarify boundaries, which is helpful as the two of you continue this journey. Couples who have done this exercise find that her anger helps her feel empowered because she had permission to use her voice. The addict is there to hold her anger as she experiences the externalization of it, which will give her a sense of serenity and calm.

Not only will she get to spew her feelings, but she will also get uninterrupted time to say whatever is locked inside of her. This exercise gives women permission to identify their feelings and erupt like the ancient volcano, Vesuvius.

PURPOSE OF THE VESUVIUS

This ritual allows for the emotional purging and spewing that needs to occur when your anger has been suppressed and repressed for months, years or even decades. If you are tired, frustrated, and enraged, you will find this tool a safe way to unload, uncork, explode, and erupt. It is done with permission and for an allotted amount of time. The following steps outline the Vesuvius process.

THE PROCESS

Step 1: You request a certain amount of time to vent your anger, frustration, and rage. In most cases, this exercise requires three, five, or ten minutes (You will likely find that when you have uninterrupted time to say what is really on your mind, you will not need as much time as you would think to find your voice).

Your husband will silently hold your anger. He is called the "container," because he metaphorically holds and contains your anger. You share how much time you will need, and he will tell you when your time to vent is up.

Step 2: He will be learning and practicing how to contain your anger without internalizing it. He needs to visualize a Plexiglas shield, Teflon coating, wall, or any other protective mechanism that prevents him from internalizing the anger that is spewing forth. It may be beneficial to internally speak a mantra such as, "This is not about me."

Step 3: As the partner, you begin by verbalizing your anger regarding a core issue. Here you emote your dark, ugly, and judgmental feelings. Nothing you say during this period has to be true, fair, or politically correct. Yelling, screaming, and even cussing (if you are so inclined) are common, expected, and encouraged.

Many times, as you share your anger, your issue will deepen, or your focus will shift to another person who has betrayed you in the past. Many women have experienced that as they are yelling, their anger shifted from their unfaithful husband to their mother or father because of trauma experienced in childhood (Please note that this is natural and does not take away from the anger you feel towards your spouse, but it does link together the on-going trauma that you may have felt your whole life).

Step 4: Once you have emotionally purged or after time has run out, you thank your husband for safely containing your anger. Then, it is vital to "de-role," acknowledging that your husband was there to witness and contain your anger. You were not yelling at him; you were emoting about the pain. He then uses reflective listening to acknowledge that he was there as a support person to help you externalize all the feelings locked inside of you.

Step 5: After you and your husband debrief, you can do a knees-to-knees and share with each other what it was like to be in this exercise.

Again, I recommend that you have a specialist present for this specific exercise.

EXTERNALIZE YOUR FEELINGS THROUGH LETTER WRITING

If you are a survivor of sexual betrayal, sexual abuse, or other forms of trauma, this exercise can feel frightening, yet freeing, because you can use it to say whatever you want to the perpetrator(s) in your past, no matter how violent or graphic.

Anger and grieving need to be released. These feelings are on a continuum and require a multitude of ways to be expressed. Many partners report much relief from writing out their feelings because they get to decide how much anger, sadness, and grief they want to emote. It is important for you to write all three letters to begin the process for healing.

To the Addict: Remember, as her husband, you will be supporting her by sitting with her as she reads her letters. You are not there to console or shut down her feelings. You are there to "contain" the emotions—nothing more and nothing less! You will be

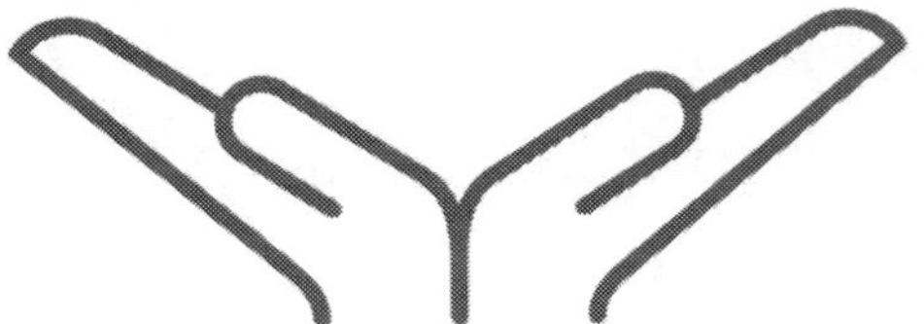

helping her by being brave enough to see all those strong emotions that have come from the trauma and to support her in holding the pain.

THE VENOMOUS LETTERS

LETTER 1.A.: THE VENOMOUS LETTER IS A LETTER WRITTEN TO THE ADDICTION, NOT THE ADDICT

The venomous letter is an opportunity to describe the sexual betrayal that the addiction has caused and its effects that have permeated every cell of your body.

1. Describe in detail the pain the addiction has caused you. Let the addiction know what parts of your life have been impacted and the hell you have been through because of its power over your husband. You are encouraged to let your "shadow side" take over. The important thing for cathartic purposes is to acknowledge all the thoughts and feelings you have had in the past about how this addiction has affected you and how it has robbed you of the relationship.

2. Next, find a special time to read the letter to your husband so that he can be a witness to your past pain. It is important that you do not share the letter as you are writing it, as you want to deliver the full, completed letter to him at one time.

3. The best way to read it is when you are assured total privacy and can sit before him, face-to-face, but not touching. You will slowly read to your husband your feelings about the addiction, looking up at him every two or three sentences. Some women prefer to stand about one to two feet

away and read their letters because they say it feels like a different continuation of the Vesuvius.

4. After you have read the letter, take some deep breaths and debrief from the exercise. Thank him for being there to see the wreckage. He may look visibly upset because he can relate to how the addiction has robbed him of precious time. Remind him that you know he is not the addiction itself, and that he is there to provide support to you as you share your feelings.

5. You as her husband are to say nothing unless she asks for your observations, feedback, or feelings.

To the Addict: As in the Vesuvius, you are witnessing and holding her pain. Make sure to prep by imagining your forcefield to protect yourself and recognize that you are there to support her and help her heal.

Note: You may find that you want to address past abuse you have experienced as a child. These 3 letters can be used for sexual abuse, molestation and sexual assault. You will find them therapeutic in addressing childhood trauma.

LETTER 1.B.: THE VENOMOUS LETTER IS FOR PAST TRAUMA AND ABUSE

The venomous letter is an opportunity to describe the past trauma and its effects that have impacted your ability to trust.

1. Describe in detail the pain you have experienced, and do not hold back from writing about the torture you have felt. You may tell the perpetrator that you wished the same thing could happen to him. That there are times that you have thought about doing the same thing so he could feel the anguish and despair. You are encouraged to let your "shadow side" take over. The important thing for cathartic purposes is to acknowledge all the thoughts and feelings you have had in the past.

2. Next, find a special time to read the letter to your husband so that he can be a witness to your past pain. It is important that you do not share the letter as you are writing it, as you want to maximize the impact of the past trauma and abuse.

3. The best way to read it is when you are assured total privacy and can sit before him, face-to-face, but not touching. You will slowly read to your husband your feelings about the abuse, looking up at him every two or three sentences. Some women prefer to stand about one to two feet away and read their letters because they say it feels like a different continuation of the Vesuvius.

4. To the Addict: As in the Vesuvius, you are witnessing and holding her pain. Make sure to prep by imagining your forcefield to protect yourself and recognize that you are there to support her and help her heal.

5. After you have read the letter, take some deep breaths and debrief from the exercise. Thank him for being there to see the wreckage, and if you talked about anyone else in the letter let him know that you are suffering from many layers of trauma. Remind him that you know he is not the perpetrator, and that he is there to provide support to you as you share your feelings.

6. As her husband, say nothing unless she asks for observations, feedback, or feelings. You are witnessing childhood or past trauma.

My colleague and I have done this work with 1000's of women and have seen the experience as cathartic and extremely beneficial in releasing the suppressed feelings from sexual abuse.

Again, this is a very liberating experience, releasing the pent-up feelings you have been feeling your whole life.

LETTER 2: THE SURVIVOR LETTER

The Survivor Letter is the second letter you read to your spouse, as he sits in silence until you are finished. Again, you decide whether you want to sit face-to-face or stand.

The Survivor Letter is a rational, direct, assertive letter telling the perpetrator your feelings and the consequences of his actions. This helps reclaim your strength and move on from the event. You will want to include the boundaries you may be enforcing for your children or grandchildren to keep them safe from the perpetrator or other potential perpetrators.

Finishing with this rational letter helps you reclaim yourself as a strong survivor and provides closure. It further allows you an extra opportunity to regain composure. You can ask your husband for feedback/observations, or you can let him know that you would prefer to end in silence.

The work will be completed when you finish this activity with the resilience letter below.

To the Addict: You will sit silently as she reads the letter. Your responsibility is to witness and contain her pain.

LETTER 3: THE RESILIENCE LETTER

To the Partner: The third letter highlights what you have learned and what has carried you through as you talk to your past-self from the perspective of your present-day self. The truth is that you already have wisdom to share about what has carried you this far in life. This may be a tough letter for you to share with your husband because you do not want to sanction what the abuser has done in any way, and talking about your resilience may feel like it is "letting the abuser off the hook."

This may be the first time you have contemplated how you have found strength amidst the trauma, and quite frankly, it feels like a foreign concept to wonder how all this wounding as a child might have served you and made you stronger. There can be a tendency to not own your strength because you do not want to legitimize what he has done. We understand your possible hesitance, but acknowledgement of your resilience is necessary to move forward and set limits that keep you safe from anyone else in your future. It can also lead you closer to post-traumatic growth, which will free you from much of this bondage.

To the Partner: Devote some time to writing and responding to the following: I am stronger now, and this is what I appreciate about my resiliency:

____

____

____

____

To the Addict: I would like for you to write a paragraph about what you noticed about her as she read her resiliency letter. Share with her how you feel about her finding some strength amidst all this trauma.

This might look like: "What I noticed about your declaration of strength was..."

____

____

____

____

GRIEF WORK

Do you wonder why you both cannot get over the hurdles and make your life different? It is impossible to move on when you have not grieved as a couple about how the addiction robbed you of what you had built together. The grief may be holding you back from becoming the couple you really want to be.

It is important to honor the grief. Betrayal trauma is so complex and overwhelming that it can seem insurmountable to get through it. It comes and goes like waves in the ocean, and that is a natural process. But partner betrayal requires a more structured approach to moving through all the losses that result from it.

The format is quite simple and follows on the next page.

To the Addict: Please be sensitive to all the losses she is experiencing. She is having to deal with layers and layers of losses, and this is another loss in her day-to-day functioning.

GRIEF EXERCISE

Let's look at the many losses she has experienced. I would like you to list 25 losses she has suffered because of the addiction.

The immediate losses:

1. My wife has lost her trust in me.
2. My wife has lost her faith in God.
3. My wife has lost her sense of self.
4. My wife has lost her ability to trust herself.
5. My wife has lost her sense of safety.

6. My wife has lost ____________________

7. My wife has lost ____________________

8. My wife has lost ____________________

9. My wife has lost ____________________

10. My wife has lost ____________________

11. My wife has lost ____________________

12. My wife has lost ____________________

13. My wife has lost ____________________

14. My wife has lost ____________________

15. My wife has lost ____________________

16. My wife has lost ____________________

17. My wife has lost ____________________

18. My wife has lost ____________________

19. My wife has lost ____________________

20. My wife has lost ____________________

21. My wife has lost ____________________

22. My wife has lost ____________________

23. My wife has lost ____________________

24. My wife has lost ____________________

25. My wife has lost ____________________

Now think about all the losses she is experiencing when she thinks of rebuilding a future together. Think about growing together as a couple and imagine the feelings she might be having as she contemplates what your relationship might look like together.

For the Addict: Write out ten additional statements that might describe your wife's fears, concerns, and issues about the future.

1. My wife fears that her life will never be normal again.
2. She has lost her ability to see a future for us.
3. My wife has lost her ability to have faith in my recovery and consistently minimizes the recovery process.
4. She is afraid to talk about growing old with me.
5. She does not want to talk about creating a vision with me, like having a lake place when we retire.
6. My wife ____
7. My wife ____
8. My wife ____
9. My wife ____
10. My wife ____
11. My wife ____
12. My wife ____
13. My wife ____
14. My wife ____
15. My wife ____

Now as painful as this exercise is, I would like you to ask her if you can review this list together and if she could add 5 more immediate losses to your list. The Partner adds her losses to your list:

1. A loss I am experiencing today is ______________________________
____
2. A loss we are experiencing today is ______________________________
____
3. A loss I am experiencing today is ______________________________
____
4. A loss we are experiencing today is ______________________________
____
5. A loss I am experiencing today is ______________________________
____

Next, I would like her to review your list of losses for the future and then add five more losses of what she fears will never be.

For the Partner:

1. A fear I have for my future is ______________________________
____

2. A fear I have for our future is ______________________________

____

3. A fear I have for my future is ______________________________

____

4. A fear I have for our future is ______________________________

____

5. A fear I have for my future is ______________________________

____

Next, I would like you to write five losses you have experienced because of your past.

To the Addict:

1. A personal loss I have experienced because of the betrayal that I caused you is:

____

____

2. A personal loss I have experienced because of the betrayal that I caused us is:

____

____

3. A personal loss I have experienced because of the betrayal that I caused you is:

____

____

4. A personal loss I have experienced because of the betrayal that I caused us is:

____

____

5. A personal loss I have experienced because of the betrayal that I caused you is:

____

____

To the Addict: List five losses that you fear for the future. I would like you to use this list to help her understand that you have fears that have robbed the relationship of a potential future.

1. I am worried that I have caused irreparable damage for our future, and a fear that I have today about our future is ____

____

____

2. I am worried that I have caused irreparable damage for our future, and a fear that I have today about our future is ____

____

____

3. I am worried that I have caused irreparable damage for our future, and a fear that I have today about our future is ____

____

____

4. I am worried that I have caused irreparable damage for our future, and a fear that I have today about our future is ____

____

5. I am worried that I have caused irreparable damage for our future, and a fear that I have today about our future is____

____

____

This is an opportunity for you both to grieve what the addiction has stolen from your relationship.

These dark, deep, and sad feelings are inside of both of you and need to be acknowledged and released.

You may feel like you need the support of a partner-sensitive therapist to help you name and claim your losses. Grieving what you lost will allow you to decide that the old marriage is gone and that you want to rebuild a stronger addiction-free marriage that will honor the love that you feel together as you move towards restoration of a new marriage.

It is a commitment, but you have both already put in so much time and effort that it certainly can help to look towards the future and live the life you both deserve.

A LETTER TO THE ADDICTION

Sometimes it can be helpful for you the addict to write a letter to the addiction saying anything that you would like to express—naming all the anger, sadness, grief, guilt, shame, and loss that is deep inside of you. You then read it to your wife so she will know your despair.

When you externalize the feelings together you can decide how to process them and what to do with the letters. Some couples like to burn them, some like to bury them, some like to rip them to shreds and state the mantra, “I won’t give my feelings the power to stop me from making space for the hope and commitment that I feel.”

Grief is a process and it needs to be acknowledged and expressed. You can’t immerse yourself into the future until you have done your anger, grief, and mourning work. Doing this work decreases the intensity and frequency of the feelings. It does not eliminate the anger and sadness, but it makes feelings more manageable.

I know that men are not encouraged to express feelings. Historically, men have been seen as weak and vulnerable if feelings were acknowledged. They had it wrong! It is good to externalize feelings and let your wife see your understandable feelings and how you have been impacted by them. There is no shame in sharing your feelings. Expressing vulnerability increases connection.

To the Partner: I know that you are incredibly tired and exhausted by partner betrayal. It can be easy to ignore this second phase because there is a part of you that is undoubtedly depressed and it is hard to muster up the energy to this “Grief and Anger Work” but you need to mourn what you had or thought you had. You need to grieve what you will never have to move you into a new acceptance of what you can have.This work frees you up to begin to find yourself and find a new coupleship and you both definitely deserve that!

Chapter 17

What Happens If She Is Not Getting Better?

You may be a couple that is really struggling. You just cannot seem to get past the impasse of his acting out. I meet many couples where the addict has done a great job of getting into recovery treatment and is doing well and proving himself, but she has difficulty accepting the concept of his addiction and is struggling with being hurt again.

Understandably, when a couple experiences betrayal, each person goes through many changes. As the partner unravels what has happened to her, she typically feels it is incomprehensible that he could have done this to her, and she wants so badly to understand so that she can put her own reality together.

For many women in the relationship, the acting out is so unfathomable that it takes months or years of watching the addict maintain good recovery before she can trust the new reality.

This can be frustrating and discouraging for an addict who is doing well in his own recovery because he thinks, “Nothing I’m doing is working.” He wonders if his wife will *ever* get better and questions whether his presence may be causing her more harm.

What I love so much about sex addict group therapy is that the members I work with will remind the addict, “Dude, you acted out for twenty-one years and you think she can just ‘just get over it’ in eighteen months? You don’t have the right to even think about giving up until you put the same amount of time into the relationship that you did in your addiction!”

It is such a powerful reality call when addicts can help other addicts to put her resistance back in perspective. Although I know it is hard to watch your wife be in trauma, I can assure you that the level of anger, disconnection, sadness, and doubt that she is experiencing is in direct proportion to the trauma she is experiencing in her brain.

To the Addict: If this sounds like your scenario, I urge you to understand that your spouse is not holding the acting out over your head to punish you. She is dealing with so much anger, sadness, grief, and trauma that it is preventing her from being able to let her defenses down.

She is in survival mode, and although this book is going to help her be more present with her uncertainty and work towards healing her brain, it takes time for the brain to heal. She is doing whatever she can to find safety in her present-day life. Doing these grief exercises together will help her process the grief and anguish that she feels. Your journey will be to contain her pain as you walk through the grief and mourning together.

It is an interesting phenomenon that sometimes when there seems to be a real impasse in your relationship, it may be necessary to stop, take a pause, and recalibrate your focus. You both may be concentrating on fear as opposed to growth and change.

ARE THERE TIMES WHEN NO MATTER HOW MUCH WE TRY THERE IS TOO MUCH DAMAGE TO MAKE IT WORK?

Jill discovered her husband was looking at gay porn. This had left her questioning his sexuality and his desire for her. He adamantly denied any homosexual or bisexual tendencies.

He had done a deep dive into his fascination with gay porn, and we had hypothesized that he may have been curious because he was molested by an older neighbor when he was ages 8-10. He had many mixed feelings about this teenager who showed real interest in him. Their sex play was scary and exciting both at the same time. He felt intense shame and desire for what naturally felt good. He feared that they would be discovered, and the last thing he wanted anyone to think was that he might be gay.

Tim and I talked about "the sex play" that was really molestation due to the age differentiation. Tim said, "It never felt like he was taking advantage of me. He never forced me into anything or coerced me or threatened me. He would make suggestions, and I would follow his lead. I know it screwed me up and created a desire to experiment more, but I would never have done anything with anyone else but him. It sounds weird, but it felt safe with him.

He told me, "I don't know when I learned the concept of homosexuality, but I knew that I would be made fun of and ostracized if anyone knew of our experimentation." Regardless of his fears, this behavior continued until his friend found a girlfriend and moved on. Strangely, he felt abandoned, and although he was relieved that he did not have to worry about being discovered, he missed the special attention and the physical attention he received.

About that time the internet came on the scene, and as a tween he and his friends would attempt to look at internet porn. It was tough to scout out because there was only one computer in his house, but he still took that "familiar risk" and was able to share sites with his friends. He reported that he looked at typical porn and found it stimulating and curious. He could not wait to share what he had seen with a girl, but he was too shy to ask out any girls. At about seventeen, he discovered gay porn, which took him back to his younger days. It was like he was addicted to those sites, although he reassured himself that he was not interested in males. His fetish would turn into an addiction in college, and he spent most of his evenings after studying looking at gay porn.

He met Jill at the Union, a hangout for college students. She initiated the conversation and their first date. Jill made it so easy to be together, and he remembered thinking that he needed this type of girl if he was ever going to get on with his life. The truth is that he never dated anyone else. He and Jill were so compatible that when she suggested that they get married, he was "all in."

Jill had no idea of his secret life. She did not know that he was looking at gay porn, nor did he talk about his molestation. It was not until a decade into their marriage that she discovered his addiction for gay porn.

One afternoon when he was at work and she was home sick, her computer had crashed, and she decided to use his computer to Google her flu-like symptoms. Although password protected, she opened it up, played around with conceivable passwords, and quickly got past the password protection. "That was easy," she thought as she congratulated herself on knowing him so well that she could guess his password.

But then the unimaginable happened, and it opened to the last site he had been on. She was looking at gay pornography. At first, she thought it was a mistake. She was horrified to see what he had been viewing! She did a browsing history and saw hundreds of gay sites. She was in a state of shock as she opened each site under his browsing history. She thought she was going to throw up on the spot. Her husband was gay. What did this mean?

Her thoughts started to race. Was she married to a latent homosexual? What was going on? She called him immediately, told him what she had found, and insisted that he come home.

As she waited for his arrival, she wondered who this man was that she had married. She was in shock. She kept asking herself "What does this mean?" repeatedly. When he got home, he looked as shell shocked as she felt. He kept trying to reassure her that he was not gay, but he could not explain his fixation with gay men. If he was telling her the truth, then what did that mean for their marriage?

For days she questioned her reality and whether he was ever really attracted to her. Could they ever find that attraction to each other? Could she be attracted to him now that she discovered his secret?

As they consulted with me, they both felt defeated. She admitted that she did not know whether their marriage could be repaired. Every time she looked at him, she questioned his sexuality. He consistently stated that he loved her and was attracted to her, but that never really convinced her because she had all those images in her head of gay men having sex, which absolutely repulsed her.

She cried in her session, "That is not my life, and I can't make the images stop. I love the husband that I knew, but I can't find it in my heart to love this man I suspect is hiding from himself."

Much of our work together was educating both as to how a fixation can move into a compulsion.

Although she understood about trauma reenactment and how he could have developed this compulsion, she was not able to reinvest in the relationship. Her brain had seen images that she would never have allowed into her world. They synched to who he was, and she could never uncouple them.

For months, she told herself that if he had cancer, she would stay with him because she would *never* leave him because of an illness. She tried to apply the same rationale to his sex addiction, but there was so much damage done that she could not recover. She did not want a divorce, but staying with him would have meant living a lie. She wanted to honor her true self.

Together, both her husband and I validated her feelings and encouraged her to start a new life. She admitted that this was not what she wanted, but she knew that she could not live with him, even though he had faithfully worked a good recovery program and was willing to do anything that would make her feel safe. He slept in another room, took three polygraph tests to prove he was not gay, and used AVR to acknowledge the pain.

He reported to me that if the roles were reversed, he would have the same trauma, and he loved her so much that all he wanted was for her to be happy again. And that meant with or without him.

They had the hard conversations and decided on a therapeutic formal separation. Jill felt so relieved to have time to herself and quickly knew that she needed to divorce to regain her serenity. During their last session with me, she described to both of us that her decision to leave allowed her to truly accept that he did have an illness, but she could not be with him as he worked on his recovery.

They divorced in integrity, and she moved on with her life.

For some couples, there is nothing that can change the impact of the sexual acting out that has devastated their lives.

WHAT IF HE IS CONSTANTLY SLIPPING?

Unfortunately, there are addicts who cannot maintain and sustain their sobriety. They want the relationship and the sobriety, but they do not work a strong enough program to fortify their relational and sobriety recovery.

Some partners get so healthy that they detach themselves from his slips and relapses, accept his struggles, continue to enrich their lives, and focus on connecting with others in healthy ways.

Others cannot tolerate only having lapses of good recovery and decide to move forward in divorce.

If you decide to leave him, I encourage you to get a partner-sensitive specialist as they know all the hard work you have put into healing this relationship and they will be able to coach you through the transformation that needs to take place as you continue to rebuild your own life apart from him. It is important for you to get the support you deserve as you decide how to proceed with your life.

Many women have put into place a post-disclosure or postnuptial agreement to acquire 75% of the assets, or sell the house and receive 80% of the equity, etc.

A man in good recovery agrees to this because he wants to prove to you that you deserve extra compensation for the pain he has caused you and that he is sincere and unwilling to hurt you again.

Regardless, there are no right or wrong choices. You decide what you need for your own emotional health and sanity.

But, if he is working good recovery, and you are not ready to walk, I would ask you to participate in the next phase of partner betrayal.

Phase 3 can help you to move into a space where you decide to try on the possibility of a new life together. You both have worked hard on accepting the past, and you feel better about you. You have more energy now that you are in that state of acceptance, and you are no longer fighting the past.

You have *surrendered* to what you had, what you thought you had, and what you will never have under the old marriage. It can open doors to making the decision to create a new marriage, if you are so inclined.

Suddenly, the Serenity Prayer has new meaning to you, and you recognize its true meaning.

"God grant me the serenity to accept the things I cannot change,
the courage to change the things I can,
and the wisdom to know the difference." ~ Reinhold Niebuhr

Side Note: If you have done all this grief and anger work, and you absolutely are still reeling in the pain of what has been taken from you, then consider it may be time to take a different direction.

If you have done this hard work and still cannot get to Post-Traumatic Growth, I would encourage you to check in with your intuition. Sex addiction interrupts and interferes with your ability to make decisions. Consider taking the pressure off of yourself and to "sit with the confusion and the pain, and trust that as you become still...the answer will come."

No matter what you decide, you always have a choice. I am confident that you will make the right one for you. Some women require a network of people who understand sex addiction, partner betrayal, and the many facets of feelings and emotions that accompany it. They find it essential to process their feelings with the supportive community such as their support group, therapy group, or partner sensitive specialist who has been trained to know your pain and your brain. Your community will be able to walk you through this process so that you can work through the trauma of partner betrayal, feel your feelings, grieve the deception, find a sense of restoration for yourself, and decide how you want to proceed with your life.

If you do not have this kind of team, I would encourage you to build it so that your experience can be validated by the women in your support group and the professionals in your network. It can expedite your healing on this arduous journey.

Other women prefer to work things out by themselves using podcasts, books, and workshops to assist them in the education they need to make difficult decisions.

If you feel that things are not getting better, a therapeutic separation may give you the space to decide what is in your best interest. There is no shame in your choices.

Of course, I lean towards support and connection in validating your confusion and doubt. But everyone is diverse and has unique needs.

One woman came in after many months of agonizing and said, "Carol, I am paralyzed in fear! Part of me wants to stay and settle into what we can potentially be as a couple. But my gut says that despite his changes, I will never be able to trust him again. There has been too much damage, and I need to move on. The other part says that I have invested too much energy in repairing this relationship, and he is showing me he is in good recovery. Why can't I get past the impasse? When will I ever be able to make a decision?"

I recommended a therapeutic separation so she could have quiet time to come to her own decision. After eight months she knew what she needed to do. This addiction had taken too much of her serenity, and she needed to create a new environment that allowed her a life free from those memories.

There is no shame in needing that new life because she left knowing she had tried everything, and she left honoring her emotions. She was then able to move into Post-Traumatic Growth.

There is no shame in you both trying to make things work and then deciding that it is time for you both to take a different path. Not every couple will make it to the other side together so if you need to separate and divorce, I encourage you to keep using your relational skills with empathy as you move on in your lives. These skills can be used anytime, in any situation with anyone. Even if you can't make the relationship work you can still work on getting to Post-Traumatic Growth.

Chapter 18

The Third Phase of Partner Betrayal: Post-Traumatic Growth

All the work that you have been doing has been hard. The first phase, Safety and Stabilization and Security, was the hardest because you both had to stay in the relationship even though it had been shattered by the addiction.

The second phase was about processing what had been done to the relationship. It was the death of the relationship as you both knew it. Together as a couple, you had to decide how to help her through her grief, anger, sadness, and excruciating pain. You, the partner, had to go through the pain, and your spouse had to walk with you through it. "The old way" would have expected the partner to walk through it herself, but the new way is for him to not only walk with you but watch your agonizing pain as he holds it for you. You both do the work together. This is tough for him because he *must* contain your pain—his addiction caused this. His active participation helps become the antidote for recovery from the devastation of sexual addiction.

You have now arrived at the third phase of partner betrayal. It is known as restoration of the self, relationship, and connection to the world. In this phase you have surrendered to the past, and you recognize that you are no longer going to be held hostage by it. I use the word "surrender" because it is not only an acknowledgement of what happened but also a decision to recreate a new relationship. It creates a new space to allow you both as a couple to consciously decide how you can renew your connection and build something different that has purpose. It also requires a belief or faith that you both are going to walk this journey together. No matter what happens, you are strong enough to stand firm in your own self-worth.

This is known as the Post-Traumatic Growth Phase because it allows both of you to make a choice to live your life with a new realization that a purpose can come out of this tragedy.

Even if you haven't finished Phase 2, I would like for you to read this entire section so you will have something to look forward to for your future. It will give you a taste of what is possible even when it doesn't seem probable.

In my sessions with couples, I will utilize some of these exercises as early as Phase 1 and then thread them in parts of Phase 2 because you both are working so hard at recognizing and facing the pain. The addict is fervently using his skills and you are able to see much growth in both his recognition and accountability for the pain in the relationship. Reading this section and finding opportunities to practice Phase 3 work preps you for the gifts in PTG!

This is always a sensitive subject to discuss with couples who have been through the trauma of partner betrayal. No one would ever want a couple to go through this, and yet we know that this ordeal and the experience you have garnered from it has taught you great things individually and as a couple. You may be curious or even confused as to what I am referencing, but I assure you that as you move forward on this journey, you will be able to ascertain how you are stronger and what you have both learned from it.

First we need to understand what post-traumatic growth is and what criteria defines it.

THE FIVE INDICATORS OF POST-TRAUMATIC GROWTH

Post-Traumatic Growth (PTG) was developed by psychologists Richard Tedeschi, PhD, and Lawrence Calhoun, PhD, in the mid-1990s. They had done research on people who had experienced great trauma, and as they interviewed them they found that this group of people also expressed that they had gained a "strength from the trauma." Much to the researchers' surprise, they found out that the traumatized population who had endured so much psychological struggle—from being in combat or torture camps to catastrophic events like tsunamis, hurricanes, or accidents—described that following their adversity they were often able to see positive growth afterward.

Their research showed that when you have experienced trauma, you can get stronger from the wreckage. They were so intrigued by this phenomena that they interviewed thousands of trauma survivors. They concluded that many people who have experienced tragedy underwent a positive change because of the struggle. They grew stronger and had a renewed sense of self where they felt stronger and more alive. Their relationship with others took on a new meaning, and it seemed to deepen as a result of the trauma. They were also surprised to see that trauma survivors looked at life differently and seemed to search for new possibilities. It helped survivors find, as Victor Frankl coined it, "a search for meaning."

As a result, people increased or strengthened their spiritual growth. Thus the five domains of Post-Traumatic Growth were born and included:

1. A richer appreciation of life
2. A deepened sense of relating to others
3. A better understanding of one's own personal strength
4. A new sense of possibilities for one's self and/or the world
5. An emotional connection & appreciation for their own spiritual growth

According to researchers who studied Tedeschi and Calhoun's work, the idea that human beings can be changed by their encounters with life challenges, sometimes in radically positive ways, is not new. The theme is present in ancient spiritual and religious traditions, literature, and philosophy. What is reasonably new is the systematic study of this phenomenon by professionals and how they work with trauma survivors like you.

The researchers defined post-trauma as an extended period that can last from days to years, in which people develop new ways of thinking, feeling, and behaving because the events they have experienced do not permit a return to baseline functioning. This is a crucial way that PTG is also distinguished from "resilience," which is a return to baseline or resistance to trauma, and "recovery," which has similar connotations. In PTG, a new baseline is created.

As both of you enter this third phase, you may notice that you take on these traits as you move closer together as a couple. Both of you may read these and begin to recognize that understanding the criteria helps you to identify your personal strengths individually and as a couple.

Are both of you able to identify how you are stronger? Are you both able to have a new appreciation for life?

When you know your strength and have a new appreciation for what is before you, you might notice that the universe puts new opportunities before you both. It might be as simple as getting to watch your grandchild on Wednesdays, your pastor asking you to mentor new members at church, or you being compelled to sponsor people in your 12-Step group. There may even be a part of you that would like to help other addicts, partners and couples.

The possibilities are endless because you are ready. It may not feel like you are truly in PTG, but when you make the decision to let go of the pain and the fear, you automatically shift to a place of empowerment.

To the Partner: Your brain is back online, and you are aware of increased grace and compassion for him as you practice intentional self-compassion. You are standing strong in your convictions and are exercising your boundaries, even though you are feeling less likely to use them.

To the Addict: You may feel more accomplished because you learned how to help with her triggers. You know what empathy is, and you practice it daily. You are less defensive and reactive. You are practicing skills like mindfulness, and your focus is on healthy things like the family, your church, or your 12-step group.

THE 5 INDICATORS OF PTG	PARTNER BEGINNING TO ENDORSE?	S.A. BEGINNING TO ENDORSE?
A richer appreciation of life.		
A deepened sense of relating to others.		
A better understanding of one's own personal strength		
A new sense of possibilities for one's self and/or the world.		
An emotional connection & appreciation for their own spiritual growth.		

Both of you look at this chart above and check each of the five indicators that you believe you are beginning to endorse. Acknowledging the small changes helps to reinforce ownership. As you move into this phase, notice the shift in your perspective.

You might want to incorporate the five PTG indicators above into your Connection-Shares and let your spouse know what you appreciated about how he or she handled a certain situation. In PTG you may notice that you have less judgment or are focused on the small things, like your son playing with a dandelion. You look for opportunities to start a new program at work, and you are open to the possibility of mentoring employees to actualize their potential.

You might share with your spouse how you have recognized the deeper level of connection with him or her and with others.

To the Partner: By entering that third phase, you have decided that you cannot live under that cloud of fear and doubt. You are strong and wise, and you know that you are willing to live your best life with him.

In other words, you both as a couple decide what needs to be implemented to be able to enter the new and exciting phase of restoration, which I call PTG.

There are many factors that come into play when you enter this phase because you get to decide how you would like to play out your vision. What would you like your new relationship to look like? What would you like to add into the marriage that would make it more connected, richer in meaning, and focused on the best version of you as a couple?

In the beginning it may feel like a daunting venture, but there is also great security in creating a life together that brings closeness back into the relationship.

As the Addict, I know how exciting this is because your fear was that you would always have to live in a state of purgatory for what you had done. You feared that you would never be forgiven for your betrayals. You have worked hard to get here, and you will never take it for granted again.

Now you can really see that there is light at the end of the tunnel, but you are scared to believe it because you do not ever want to go through this pain again. You were betrayed by your addiction, and now that you are in solid recovery, you are so grateful for this second chance. You are scared to believe it because you could not endure the pain it would cause if the rug were pulled out from underneath you. There is still a part of you that fears that she will change her mind.

You cannot believe she has offered this grace. You tell yourself that this is a miracle, and it is...It is the miracle of recovery.

THIS IS THE MIRACLE OF RECOVERY!

CREATING A VISION

As difficult as it sounds, it can be a healthy and helpful exercise to think about what you might want your future to look like now that you both have moved through this crisis and reestablished your own growth.

I know that it might not feel like it is time to begin this process, and your trepidation is normal. But many couples need to start reaching for a new beginning. In her TED Talk on shame, Ester Perel said, "Many people will be married two or three times, and some will do that in the same marriage." Well, this is your chance as a couple to devote your time to rebuilding a rock-solid marriage that will be more committed and laced in healthy values. It will be the foundation for the love you feel towards each other for the rest of your lives. When you make the decision to do this, you begin the process of restoration.

You both have really hung in there to support each other. Deciding what you need and want in the future will fortify the changes that you have made and the changes you will make in the future.

What is your vision for the future? As you do the exercises in this chapter, I will ask you this question again so you both can declare an intention for how you would like the next chapter of your life to play out. This time, you will make conscious decisions about your relationship that will bring meaning and purpose to your lives as a couple!

MIND STATES AND MIND STORIES THAT WILL TRANSFORM YOU AND THE RELATIONSHIP

A NEW PLAN FOR CONNECTION

It is important for you both to change your focus and spend one day a week reconstructing how you want your life to be.

It can be helpful for couples to place themselves in that imaginary place of seeing the good in each other and reconstructing a belief that they can be on the other side of partner betrayal. To do this, I encourage you both to do what may have seemed in Phase 1 like an insurmountable and overwhelming exercise. But now that you are entering Phase 3, you recognize that much has changed.

For some of you, it may feel a bit fake and disingenuous, but I am asking you to do it anyway with as much energy as you can muster.

I created this exercise to help neutralize the fear that accompanies growth and change. You have lived with fear for so long that it feels foreign to walk away from it. You are making a conscious choice to shift your focus and live the live you deserve. You can use this exercise when you identify that you are doing better and need a little reminder that you are doing well.

THE CHANGES HE HAS MADE (EVEN IF THERE ARE STILL SOME DOUBTS THAT IT WILL NOT BE PERMANENT)

To the Partner: It will help you to write out ten examples of how he is showing you he is different. As your brain has gotten clearer and your executive functioning has come back online, it will be necessary to remind yourself of his progress and acknowledge it to yourself.

You may say that there is no way you could ever think of ten positive changes that he is making, but I will tell you that if you stretch yourself and look for small changes, you will be able to acknowledge the small changes that show you that he is willing to do what it takes to be the man you have always wanted him to be.

1. I can tell that you are different because ____________________

____

2. I can tell that you are different because ____________________

____

3. I can tell that you are different because ____________________

____

4. I can tell that you are different because ____________________

____

5. I can hear that you are different when ____________________

____

6. I can see that you are different when ____________________

____

7. I noticed you were different when ____________________

____

8. I appreciated that you were different when ______________________________
____

9. I can hear that you are different when ______________________________
____

10. I can tell that you are different because ______________________________
____

WHAT YOU APPRECIATE, APPRECIATES

The Addict: In this third phase you will need to work on the concept of appreciation for self and the changes you have made in the relationship. Most recovery programs will stress the importance of being humble, and although it is important for you to show humility, it is also important that you appreciate what is working for you personally and in your marriage.

When a man in recovery can remember who he was in addiction and "own" the things he has accomplished to be a better man, he will have a better sense of the direction he is going, no matter what anyone thinks of him. He will gain a true sense of appreciation for how recovery has changed him.

Your wife needs to know that you believe in yourself and your relational recovery. You have worked hard in this book and on yourself. It is time to acknowledge the changes that you have made.

Write out ten things that you have changed or are working on that are an investment in the coupleship. How are you showing appreciation for your relational changes?

There is likely a tendency to not want to identify your changes for fear that the changes may be put down or that you do not deserve to have them acknowledged, but it is important for you to stay abreast of your progress.

Although "Openness, Brokenness, and Humility" are signs of good spiritual recovery, it is absolutely essential to know and appreciate the changes you are making.

EXERCISE: WHAT YOU APPRECIATE, APPRECIATES

Write out at least ten things you are doing to invest in and appreciate your own personal recovery.

RECOVERY CHANGES	**RELATIONAL CHANGES**
1. *I appreciate my sobriety.*	1. *I appreciate what recovery has taught me about myself.*
2. *I appreciate my fellowship.*	2. *I appreciate the hard work I have done.*
3. *I appreciate my readings.*	3. *I appreciate what I have learned in* Help. Her. Heal.
4. *I appreciate...*	4. *I appreciate...*
5. *I appreciate...*	5. *I appreciate...*
6. *I appreciate...*	6. *I appreciate...*
7. *I appreciate...*	7. *I appreciate...*
8. *I appreciate...*	8. *I appreciate...*
9. *I appreciate...*	9. *I appreciate...*
10. *I appreciate...*	10. *I appreciate...*

As the Partner, Post-Traumatic Growth does not just happen. You have made a choice to take the next step in your healing. He is noticeably different, and you have appreciated his growth and effort. His skills are far from perfect, but there has been great improvement. You more than likely have assessed that his recovery is strong—not perfect but solid enough to invest in him again.

It is time to consciously appreciate his sobriety and recovery so that you can share this with him. Write ten recovery changes that he has made or sobriety skills that you have noticed him practicing.

HIS RECOVERY/SOBRIETY SKILLS AND CHANGES

HIS SOBRIETY/RECOVERY SKILLS & CHANGES	RELATIONAL CHANGES
1. I *appreciate his on-going discipline to practice good sobriety tools.*	1. I *appreciate that he initiates Connection-Shares.*
2. I *appreciate the way he mentors others.*	2. I *appreciate that he has not pressured me for sex.*
3. I *appreciate that he has become a sponsor.*	3. I *appreciate that he started his Help. Her. Heal Class.*
4. I *appreciate...*	4. I *appreciate...*
5. I *appreciate...*	5. I *appreciate...*
6. I *appreciate...*	6. I *appreciate...*

HIS SOBRIETY/RECOVERY SKILLS & CHANGES	RELATIONAL CHANGES
7. I *appreciate...*	7. I *appreciate...*
8. I *appreciate...*	8. I *appreciate...*
9. I *appreciate...*	9. I *appreciate...*
10. I *appreciate...*	10. I *appreciate...*

To the Partner: When you choose to focus on the positive changes, you are in a state of PTG. You have made the conscious choice to stop living the way you were living. You choose PTG for yourself because you want to detach from the anger, fear, and sadness you have felt for so long. You want to take a deep dive into finding yourself again. You no longer want to be defined by partner betrayal. You want to create a new normal, and you have decided to do that with him.

YOU NO LONGER WANT TO BE DEFINED BY PARTNER BETRAYAL.

He has not been able to do this because he needed to walk beside you in your pain, but now the time has come to reinvest in the relationship. With some trepidation, you start this journey together. It is normal to question whether this is really the right time, but when a woman has done all the hard work that you have and begins to wonder if there is more out there for her, she is ready.

In my online course, Partners Find Your Post-Traumatic Growth (on sexhelpwithcarolthecoach.com), I interview eight women partners, one male partner, and a couple who are working together in the field of sexual addiction and partner betrayal. They talk about how they made the decision to move into PTG. They discuss what motivated them and the new mind states that occurred that freed them from their fears and anxieties. They also identified what resources they used to help them make the choice to move on. All but one partner in the course stayed in the marriage and worked on personally getting stronger and owning her strength. When they acknowledged their strengths and changes, everything around them changed. This an incredibly inspirational course for partners, but I would encourage you both to watch it together so your husband can reinforce the changes he has seen in you!

There is no doubt that you have extra skin in the game because as you are recognizing and acknowledging your changes, it is validating the hope you have for the relationship.

To the Partner: To help women get to the place of PTG, I wrote *Unleashing Your Power Moving Through the Trauma of Partner Betrayal*. It is a book written just for you that goes over many of the concepts that we have talked about in this book, and it gives you empowering exercises to strengthen your sense of self. It can be a helpful resource to do the work you are doing with your husband because it is all about empowering you as you walk this journey.

You are in a place where you are noticing your own strength and wisdom while simultaneously focusing on changes you have seen in his individual recovery and within your relationship. Your ability to do both simultaneously creates an environment for growth. Recognizing the changes and admitting them aloud validates the change you both are making. Although there are no guarantees that it will change permanently, your new sense of empowerment reinforces that you will be ok no matter what the outcome.

As you do this next exercise, know that I understand how vulnerable you are being because I am asking you to trust me. I know that you may need to recalibrate your energy and focus on what is working or is different in the relationship. You may have a natural resistance to this because you do not want to set yourself up to be hurt again.

But I have worked with hundreds of partners, and sometimes they must put themselves in that "imaginary place" that allows them to "act" as if these changes are real to move forward and begin to build upon them. And when they do, a natural shift occurs where they feel better and safer. They become ready to move into the journey of restoration of self, the relationship, and the relationship you have with the world.

ACKNOWLEDGING THE CHANGES IN MY LIFE

This exercise will help validate your decision to do all that hard work you did with your husband in Phase 2. You needed to do the work so that you could move out of fear, anger, and grief and begin to trust both him and the relationship again.

Think about all the ways that you have grown in your own healing. Write out ten ways that you have grown in your own recovery or healing.

1. ______________________________

____

2. ______________________________

____

3. ______________________________

____

4. ______________________________

____

5. ______________________________

____

6. ______________________________

____

7. ______________________________

____

8. ______________________________

____

9. ______________________________

____

10. ______________________________

____

IDENTIFYING THE PROGRESS IN YOUR RELATIONSHIP

For the Partner: After discovery, you questioned if you would ever have a healthy relationship again. And as with most couples, his recovery has not been seamless, and he has had to learn what he should do to protect his brain from potential triggers. Every time he made a poor choice, it affected your ability to trust. But now, you have seen enough growth that you are willing to support the relationship by acknowledging the positive changes in your relationship.

ACKNOWLEDGING OUR CHANGES AS A COUPLE

As a Couple: Together, write out ten indicators that you have increased your skills as a couple. How has your relationship grown? Are you talking more, spending more time walking, going to groups together, practicing check-ins, reading this book together, praying with each other?

List those changes here to reinforce the concept "what you appreciate...appreciates."

1. ______________________________

   ____

2. ______________________________

   ____

3. ______________________________

   ____

4. ______________________________

   ____

5. ______________________________

   ____

6. ____

____

7. ____

____

8. ____

____

9. ____

____

10. ____

____

"ACTING AS IF" TO GET PAST YOUR PAST.

Addicts and partners are often stuck in the cycle of refusing to acknowledge his changes because they are protecting themselves. Even though I said very few partners are punitive, I have known it to happen. Could that be you? Is there any part of you that has wanted to stay in the punishing mode because of all the pain he has caused?

I had a partner tell me that her heart had ached for so long with excruciating pain that she just wanted to hurt him for the rest of his life. It kept her feeling safe and in a one-up position in the relationship, and he seemed comfortable being in that position. She remarked, "I know that it's bad to want him to remain my whipping boy, but I literally cannot fathom letting my defenses down and appreciating the changes he has made without reminding him of what a loser I think he is."

She said "Carol, what is wrong with me? I know that I love him, but I just cannot stop hating him. I am tired of this merry-go-round, but I can't get off. We have a couple of good days, but then when he does something that irritates or hurts me I am off to the races with rage again."

I praised her for her insight and desire to change. She did not like how she was showing up in the relationship, but she did not know how to get out of those destructive patterns. There was a part of her that did not want to stop punishing him because her brain was still in the fight mode of partner betrayal.

The second thing I did was AVRed her. I said, "Nora, I want to acknowledge that you are going back and forth with two very real feelings that are a part of you. That must make you fearful because it can be exhausting to treat him so differently based on your internal fears. But I want to reassure you that with that kind of awareness, you are on the brink of tempering those feelings.

I would like to share a technique that both of you should practice for 24 hours. It is like you are trying on a new behavior to see if it makes you feel safer and works towards the goal of becoming closer again. This is all about you Nora, so I would like you to try it to see if it gives you some relief."

We invited Sam back in the session, and I gave the couple the following assignment:

"Sam and Nora, I would like you to practice some behaviors that will move you forward towards healing. This may be the hardest assignment you have ever done because I am going to ask you to participate in an activity that was developed in the world of addiction recovery.

When recovering alcoholics were struggling with their sobriety, they would complain to their sponsor, 'I have no confidence. I have spent the last twenty-two years screwing up my life. I have two failed marriages, I have lost four jobs, I cannot even muster up the courage to call my kids, let alone have the self-assurance to find a job!'

This man was too afraid to put himself in a situation where he would need to show up and face rejection or a hard fall. The sponsor listened to his woes and then gave him the following advice:

'I realize that you lack the confidence to move forward in your life, but I want you to act as if you are playing the part of someone who does know what they want. This means you act as if you can call the potential employer and ask him where to submit your resume or grab the phone and act as if you not only want to call the kids but that you want to hear how their lives are going. When you act as if, you put one foot in front of the other, just taking one step at a time but all the while walking towards your destination.'

Nora and Sam, I want you to spend twenty-four hours letting go of the pain and the resentment and acting as if you could really appreciate each other for who you both are today. I recognize that this can feel like a daunting task because Nora, you are probably fearful that if you 'act as if' he will think that you have forgotten what he did to you in your past. And Sam, you may want to do this, but you fear what Nora's reactions might be and that fear of the unknown may keep you in the state of uncertainty and fear of rejection.

However, you both have been working hard, and you deserve to have a respite from your history. You are two people who want to rebuild your relationship, but to do that requires that you move forward in a well thought out, measured way. This twenty-four-hour exercise will help you to rekindle or build on a new relationship. It is based on the premise that *you can be happy* again. So why don't you give it a shot and agree to take the next twenty-four hours to be the couple that you really would like to develop into?" That includes no talking about betrayal, addiction *or* recovery.

YOU DESERVE TO BE HAPPY—ACT AS IF

Now when I ask couples to do this, they feel shaky because when they go for their walk or drive to the grocery store, they are not sure what to talk about. They say it was as if they needed to retrain their brain to bond without trauma.

But you deserve to be happy! You have done all this hard work, and now it is time to decide how you are going to proceed in your new couple's identity. You have risen from the ashes, and you are stronger. How can you move on with your life and create a new identity that follows those five indicators of PTG?

You might want to use the time to talk about creating an activity that is forward-thinking, like going out on a date, planning a family activity, or working on your next project or vacation. Since you will not be talking about recovery, you might want to share appreciation for each other or things that you are grateful for, like the beautiful clouds in the sky, your exercise program, or the friendships you want to cultivate from church. This may include things you have talked about early in the relationship or the small desires you have had inside of you that have been put on the back burner.

Use your Connection-Share to talk about your vision in the here and now. What can you do in your daily routine that would reinforce your new, healthy, and happy relationship together?

Would you be willing to do the "Act as If" Exercise and spend 24 hours interacting with absolutely no reference to recovery or betrayal? This is tougher than you think. If you do fall back to an old conversation or routine, just acknowledge it together and then proceed as if nothing happened to reinforce the concept that you can move on in your lives, feel close, and relate like a couple who did not carry this baggage.

THE POST-TRAUMATIC GROWTH INDICATORS

Take another look at the five indicators of PTG and ask yourself:

How can we as couple stay cognizant of our strengths that we listed above?

____

____

____

____

What are we appreciating today that we no longer take for granted?

____

____

____

____

What opportunities can we find today that open the door to new possibilities with ourselves, our family, our friends, our community, our church, and our work?

____

____

____

____

How can we show more empathy and compassion to others?

And how can we make the world a better place?

> **"WHEN YOU CHANGE THE WAY YOU LOOK AT THINGS, THE THINGS AROUND YOU CHANGE." ~ WAYNE DYER**

As you are doing the hard work to restore the relationship, it is important to stay as balanced as possible regarding what you need to do to focus on yourself. As a couple, you are going to be working diligently on restoring the relationship, but what is truly necessary is that you continue to develop a mindset where you can appreciate the changes you both have made in the coupleship and in yourselves.

One of the things that therapists and coaches know is how important it is to have a healthy mindset. That means that you must remain positive despite your history.

You were not aware of how your mind can create your reality and that what you project out in the world will persist. If you were to stay focused on the chaos, devastation, and trauma that has been caused by this partner betrayal you will be chained to that history. If you have done your work in Phases 1 and 2 you can choose to unlock the chains and focus on happiness instead.

One of the easiest formulas that we use in coaching is to look at three areas of your life that have to do with happiness. In Marci Shimoff's book, *Happiness for No Reason*, she discusses three fundamental principles that create happiness, and these tools are excellent strategies for dealing with addiction and betrayal.

HAPPINESS PRINCIPLES TO RESTORE THE HOMEOSTASIS OF YOUR RELATIONSHIP

Stay in the Moment.

What you have been through as a couple has been very difficult, so it will be necessary for both of you to stay in the moment and celebrate the subtle changes that you both are making. This means that as you think about your past, you shift your perspective and make a concerted effort to train yourself to stay present and focused on one day at a time.

For the Addict: Addicts naturally want to stop reliving the past since that keeps them in a state of despair, self-loathing, and shame. You will need to remind yourself that you are not an addict—you are an addict in recovery. You are learning skills in your recovery that will make you healthier and more relational. Addicts in recovery have both interpersonal skills and relational skills that contribute to their success as a person.

You may have occasional compulsions, urges, and cravings, but work those recovery skills because they will move you into healthy introspection, connection, and utilization of your skills. The addicts I work with ask themselves, "Are my thoughts and behaviors moving me forward towards healthier recovery or further away?"

Staying in the moment helps you to appreciate what is occurring right before you. As Darrin Ford states, focusing on the moment or the present state "gives you a greater propensity to manifest choices that are more skillfully related to a life in recovery." Your program supports that thinking when it encourages you to work it "one day at a time."

As the addict, it is important to stay out of that shame cycle. If you keep ruminating and reliving the trauma of the past, you will stay in that cycle of shame, which absolutely does nothing for who you were meant to be. Staying in the moment requires that you ask yourself, "What can I do today to help restore the relationship, and what do I need to do to make things better—one day at a time?"

Staying in the moment and living in the present is tougher for partners due to their innate trauma response. Although, a partner in Post-Traumatic Growth will be moving away from frequent or severe trauma reactions.

To the Partner: Your natural inclination is to relive the past or predict the future. When you do that, you ensure that you will not be duped again and that you will remain safe. Your reaction is understandable, yet staying in the past or ruminating about the past will keep you in an activated state of trauma.

Holding yourself accountable for your own mental health and learning how you can rebuild a new life with your spouse (or without him) requires that you stay in the moment. When doing so you look at what is occurring in your life and with your husband, and you stay focused on what is in your present-day experience.

There is no doubt that you are also worried about the future, which makes staying in the moment difficult. Staying in the moment keeps you in a reality state and is imperative for feeling ongoing safety and stabilization.

STAYING IN THE MOMENT

For the Partner:

1. One thing that I fear is that if I let my guard down and stay in the moment, he will hurt me again.
2. I fear that if I stay in the moment, I will not stay one step ahead of him, and he will be more likely to make the wrong choices.
3. If I stay in the moment, he will sense that I have let my guard down and he will take advantage of the situation.

NEXT

1. If I stay in the moment, I can enjoy the things that are working in my life.
2. If I stay in the moment, I can stop trying to control things, which depletes me and makes me feel exhausted.
3. If I stay in the moment, I will be better able to take control of my own life and detach from him.

1. If I remind myself to stay in the moment I can appreciate

____

____

2. If I work on staying in the moment I can remind myself that

____

____

3. If I stay in the moment I will

____

____

For the Addict:

It will be easier for you to stay in the moment because your program has taught you to live one day at a time. But, you also have fears that the PTG you are currently experiencing is too good to be true, and you fear that you will not trust its reliability. But when you stay in the moment, you are more likely to enjoy "what is" and be more present to her needs and yours.

1. What I fear most about living in the moment is that I will not be able to do it, and I will let myself and my wife down.
2. I am afraid to trust staying in the moment because I fear that I will get too comfortable with my recovery.
3. I am not very good at living in the moment because I constantly fear that my addiction will hijack my brain.

NEXT

1. Even though I fear living in the moment, I will be more successful on a day-to-day basis.

2. Even though I fear staying in the moment, I know it will decrease my urges and cravings because it will be more manageable.

3. Even though I fear having my brain hijacked, staying in the moment will teach me to appreciate "what is."

Now it is your turn. Write out three of your fears about staying in the moment. After writing those fears add a more realistic statement that reinforces why living in the now can help your sense of stability and serenity and move you closer to that mind state of happiness.

1. What I'm afraid of if I stay in the moment is

____

____

2. What I fear most about staying in the moment is

____

____

3. What I fear most about living in the present is

____

____

STAYING IN THE MOMENT

Now honor the fear but strengthen the thought by making it more realistic and pro-recovery.

1. If I stay in the moment I will

____

____

2. If I stay in the moment I can

____

____

3. Staying in the moment will benefit me because

____

____

STAYING IN THE MOMENT—PRESENCE—REQUIRES PRACTICE

It is normal for you both to move back and forth as you work this concept. As a result of the trauma, you have trained yourself to watch the past and be weary of what the future could bring. Of course, living in the moment would feel counterintuitive and not natural, but the more you practice the "power of now," as Eckhart Tolle would call it, the more you will be able to appreciate what is right before you in your daily living.

To the Partner: What do you do when you are working so hard on staying in the moment, but those thoughts get interrupted by your fears?

You are supposed to be in Post-Traumatic Growth, but your brain just got hijacked. You continue to agonize over the fear because you go back to an old thought that seems locked into the mind. The thought reminds you that it is difficult to believe that he could have had this addiction, lived a double life, and not thought about the collateral damage that he was causing in the relationship.

What does that mean for your future if he did have an addiction? If he was that sick, can he really stay sober? Can his new behavior be real? Will it really last? And then your mind is off to the races.

You want to live in PTG, but it can feel discouraging when something activates you and sends you back to that old mind state. Just allow the feeling and then use a reality statement that reminds you of what is in the moment.

This is where you have a choice:

You can push away the thought that "staying in the moment can restore your life to sanity."

Or you can be gentle with yourself and tell yourself that of course you would understandably get scared and go back to the past to protect yourself. However, that thought sends you right back into ruminating about your past and fearing for the future, which creates an auto-exacerbating cycle of agonizing for you.

When you are in PTG, you take back your thoughts and you utilize your choices. You decide what thoughts you are going to let go of and what thoughts you are choosing to store in that precious space called the mind.

Remember: Mindfulness reminds you that you are not your thoughts and that you can choose the thought that works for you and liberates you from your fears. You are not your mind!

Staying in the moment allows you to free yourself from those thoughts and live today, noticing what is working and feeling content for what is before you. Remember, where your attention goes, energy flows!

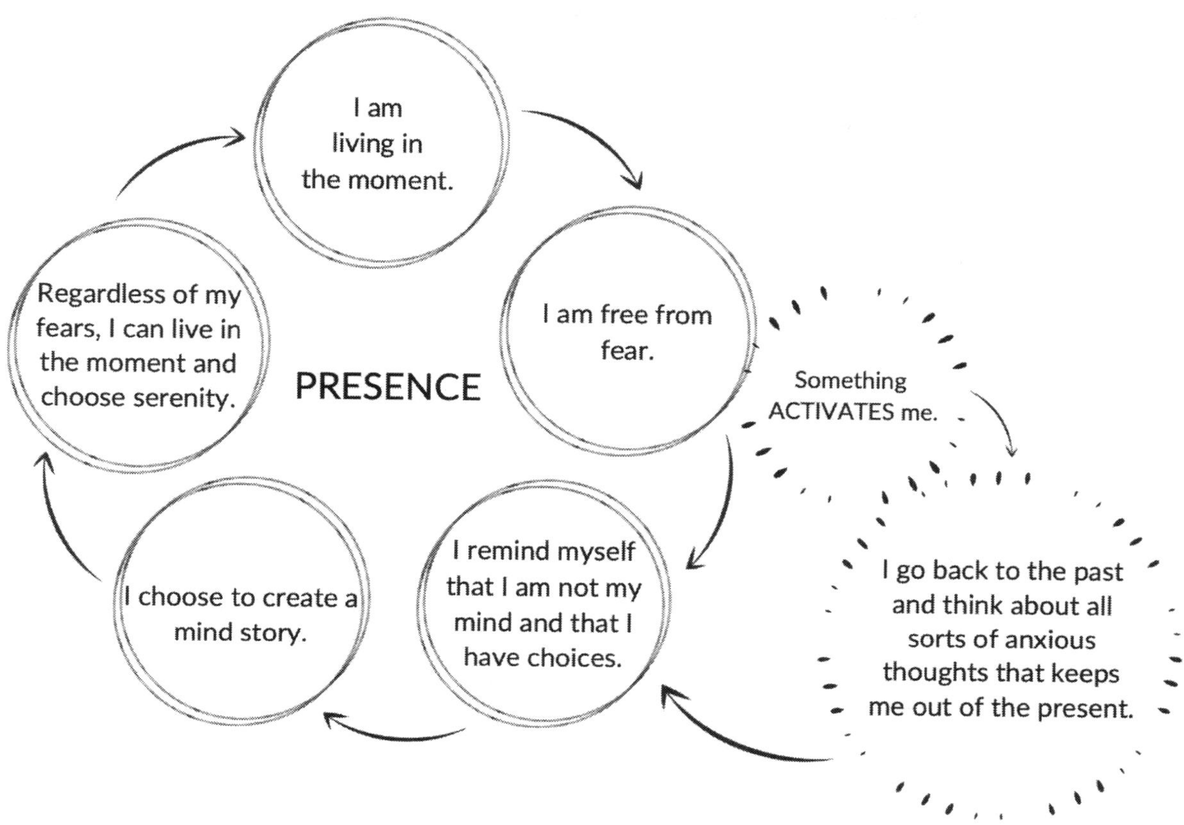

Changing your mind states and stories takes work but is worth the time to invest in your serenity. You deserve that and I so badly want you to have it.

I wish I could develop a "thought coach" who could sit on your shoulder, notice every time you start down the road of fear and uncertainty, and remind you to stay in the moment and look at your choices!

You both can do this for each other. Practice encouraging each other to acknowledge the fear, move it aside, create a thought to keep you in the present, and enjoy your new sense of awareness!

NOTICE AND FOCUS ON WHAT IS WORKING IN YOUR LIVES

The second factor that contributes to more happiness in both of your lives is having the attitude of gratitude.

The attitude of gratitude means that you look at "what is working in your life." You take on that mind state and notice everything around you that supports it. That may be that you got up 15 minutes early to read your devotional, and it was a beautiful warm day with plenty of sunshine. As you walked into work, you felt the cool breeze on your face and felt a sense of serenity. It may be that you are reading this book together and are thankful for the opportunity to rebuild the relationship.

To the Addict: You may be grateful that you have learned how to manage your addiction and that your individual recovery is strong. You feel a surge of gratitude because you are connecting with your wife better than ever. You feel very in sync with your life because you are operating on all cylinders. You are going to meetings, texting your sponsor daily, and doing 12-step work that you put off for years! Your life has changed now that you focused on the relational piece, and you couldn't be happier. Not only are you looking at what is working in your life, you are working it!

For the Partner: Perhaps you found that all-important support group and that perfect coach to help you get through this difficult time. I had a partner tell me that when she got into a healthy support group for partners, it moved her into PTG because she really started to focus on herself. She became an inspiration to the group, which motivated her to create her own sense of identity.

As you can imagine, it can be tough to be a partner and look at what is working because you're afraid to move away from the fear that feels oddly familiar and predictable.

However, you deserve to let go of the partner betrayal and work towards who you really want to be. There will be times in PTG that you revisit the first phase and find that you need more safety and stabilization, but you will not remain there. You have done so much work and will use these skills to move you right back in PTG.

In PTG, you are always aware of the choice to move away from pain and suffering and look for some normalcy in your life. You are always capable of noticing the small things, taking them in, and feeling gratitude for them. There are always things in your life that remain positive, hopeful, or uplifting. Even if it is petting your cat or your dog as you drink your coffee or tea and watch the sunrise. Now that being said, I do not want to minimize the impact of what you have been through, but I want to emphasize that you want to move out of this traumatized state, whether you are a partner or an addict. You will also need to accept that this fear can be a normal condition of the betrayal, and you can move through it.

Looking at what is working in your life helps to neutralize the impact of infidelity and deception. It does not alleviate it, but it allows your brain to take a break from the trauma.

So as a couple, review the day and list ten things that worked well or that you felt grateful for. Share them with each other.

1. ______________________________

2. ______________________________

3. ______________________________

4. ______________________________

5. ______________________________

6. ______________________________

7. ______________________________

8. ______________________________

9. ______________________________

10. ______________________________

As I review my last 24 hours, I might list the following: I am grateful for my birthday today. The warmth of my puppy who loves me unconditionally. My delicious cup of coffee. My friends who celebrated with me last night. My family who reunited for my aunt's funeral. My husband's kindness for cleaning up as I went to bed. The sunrise. The fall foliage. You for reading this book!

Now it is your turn. Get good at sharing it with each other!

REFRAMING

The third indicator of happiness is when you can begin to reframe. Reframing is when you take a picture of your life and decide to put another frame around it. When you put that other frame around your life, you create a different picture. This picture is one of empowerment and personal choice, and there are two ways that you can access it. One is by asking yourself, "How am I growing stronger?"

When you ask yourself this question, you take yourself out of the victim state and view life from an empowered state. Now, I know that you would not have ever asked for this horrible ordeal (and addicts, you never asked to be addicted either), yet you can take yourself out of the victim state by asking yourself two questions: "How am I stronger?" and "What have I learned from this crisis?"

You Both Are Stronger!

You both have put a lot of time into this book, and I promise you that this work changes lives. I can assure you both that addicts are learning skills they never had before, and if they did seem to have them, the addiction robbed them of those skills early on.

For the Partner: You are learning about your needs, boundaries, and feelings, and you are putting yourself on the front burner. You are no longer willing to take a back seat and let life pass you by.

You have been through a devastating experience, but you are choosing to "grow yourself stronger."

I remember a doctor reassuring me after I broke my back that I would heal even stronger than before. He explained that when bones break, it obviously takes a certain amount of time to allow for healing and for the bone to grow back. When it does, the point where it broke is stronger than any other part of the bone.

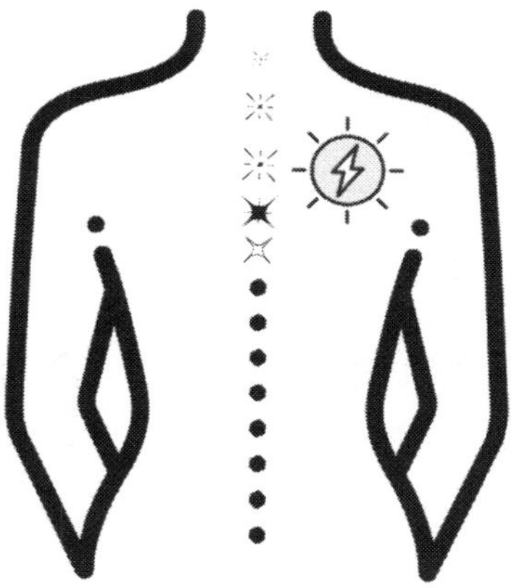

If you remain in your fear, sadness, and anger, it would stall your personal growth and the development of what you want your relationship to be.

You are making a choice to be stronger for you!

You obviously want to restore the relationship, and you understand that his addiction had nothing to do with you. It affected you greatly and impacted your life, but there was nothing about his addiction that was because of you. He had an uncontrollable compulsivity that got worse and worse until you became involved. You are the key to why he is working so hard on getting healthy. I know you may say, "I do not want that responsibility" or "I do not want to be the key," but he is working harder for this because he wants to be a better man for you.

These three happiness fundamentals are easy tools you can use anytime to remind yourself that you do have control of your life. You can shift your energy and find the happiness that you deserve to move you both in the desired direction.

It will never erase the damage that the addiction has caused, but it will begin to create a new foundation for both of you and will remind you that you did this together.

MINDFULNESS

Mindfulness is single-handedly the best tool to use to recalibrate your brain. Men who suffer from Compulsive Sexual Behavior Disorder also benefit from this new paradigm which always begins with mindfulness. You have dedicated yourself to repairing the relationship by using relational skills that always involve empathy.

Even though you are both in PTG, there will be challenging moments. You will need lots of support as you look for ways to find your purpose. The work is slow and laborious. Because you have both been through so much together, it is not uncommon for either or both of you to develop an indifference to the relationship and feel like this experience has "worn you out." This indifference and feeling of emotional exhaustion is called compassion fatigue.

For the Addict: Darrin Ford says that this can lead to a diminished ability to empathize or feel compassion for her, so it is very important to have LOTS of resources available to offset that fatigue. Mindfulness and other tools help remedy the natural fatigue that you might feel helping her work through the three phases of partner betrayal.

For the Partner: You could be experiencing compassion fatigue due to the exhausting nature of watching and assessing whether you are safe. Many partners describe the phenomena of wanting to believe his changes but being afraid to, therefore continuing to be on guard despite the respite you could be feeling. You can offset this natural phenomenon by using mindfulness.

Many mindfulness experts say that five minutes of meditation a day exponentially increases focus and awareness. But mindfulness is more than meditation—it is also self-compassion and intentional self-care. Self-care is the antidote to addiction recovery and partner betrayal, so together you must find things that feed your soul.

REALISTIC AND AFFIRMING POSITIVE SELF-TALK

It is imperative that both of you practice being gentle with yourselves, which includes how you speak to yourself and the language you use to get you through the day. We have 60,000 thoughts per day, and many of them are negative. They may be as ordinary as "I am going to be late," "I am not going to be able to do it," "Life works against me," or "I can never do anything right." Or they may be more critical and involve your life, situation, and shame. They might look like: "Can I really trust this?" "I just want a normal life." "I am a screw-up." "I am disgusting." "Is he really going to change?" "I am unlovable." "Will she really forgive me forever?"

Do not let these negative thoughts overwhelm you. It is possible for you to be in Post-Traumatic Growth and have some negative self-talk. Positive self-talk is a practice, and it takes time and effort. Do not get discouraged if you fall back into old patterns of thought and communication.

If you want to invest in yourself and your relationship, you will need to alter the way you talk to yourself to keep it more proactive and realistic. This means that you will have to consciously try to speak more gently and with more self-compassion.

POSITIVE SELF-TALK EXERCISE

I would like each one of you to spend 15 minutes in quiet contemplation in the same room. Ask yourself to think of three fears that continue to show up in your life. Write them out.

FOR THE ADDICT:

1. One thing that I fear is that she will never be able to trust me again.
2. I fear that we will never be able to have fun together.
3. I fear that I will not be able to do recovery perfectly, and it will interfere with her ability to regain confidence in me.

Now restate your fear and concern with a more realistic, kinder thought:

1. Even though I fear that she will never be able to trust me again, I can remind myself that when I was late the other night, she commented that she was angry with me but DID tell me that she knew I was not acting out.
2. Even though I fear that we will never have fun together, she did smile at me and laughed about our son's antics during the baseball game.
3. Even though I am not perfect in my recovery, she does keep assuring me that she is more interested in me being honest about my imperfections.

FEARS:

1. I fear that ____

____

2. I fear that ______________________________

____

3. I fear that ______________________________

____

Now attach a realistic, kinder, more compassionate thought at the end.

1. Even though I ______________________________

____

2. Even though I ______________________________

____

3. Even though I ______________________________

____

FOR THE PARTNER:

1. I fear that these triggers will never go away.
2. I fear that I will never be able to fully trust him.
3. I fear that I will never stop comparing myself to other women and images.

Now restate your fear and concern with a more realistic, kinder thought:

1. Even though I continue to struggle with triggers, they are less frequent and less haunting.

2. Even though I have recurring thoughts about not being able to trust him, I need to keep reminding myself that "this is a process" and that it is normal to be afraid periodically.

3. Even though I find myself comparing myself to other women and images, I keep reminding myself when Tom told me that now that he is out of active addiction, he loves me more than he ever thought he could love anyone.

FEARS:

1. I fear that ____

____

2. I fear that ____

____

3. I fear that ____

____

Now attach a realistic, kinder, more compassionate thought at the end.

1. Even though I ______________________________________

____

2. Even though I ______________________________________

____

3. Even though I ______________________________________

____

It is paradoxical that treating yourself with more compassion and kindness requires awareness and a sincere desire to want to nurture yourself and your relationship. It seems ironic because upon hearing the old negative tapes you must acknowledge your awareness and then reword the thoughts in your head. This requires discipline to acknowledge the negative thoughts and redirect your thoughts and feelings in a way that recognizes your effort, vulnerability, and progress in this process.

When you create an intention that you will speak to yourself with compassion, you have committed to the self-love and nurturance you deserve. It is a type of self-parenting that you likely never received and therefore never learned to give to yourself.

When you are in Post-Traumatic Growth, you know that you must be gentle with yourself and that you do not need to do anything perfectly.

I have decided to help you identify things you can say to yourself to offset the 60,000 negative thoughts you hear daily in your own head.

I have compiled two lists of statements that may be applicable to you when you want to diffuse some emotional reactivity.

Read the statements and circle the self-talk that you might use to dim down the negative thinking.

PRACTICAL COPING STATEMENTS

Try using some of these "practical" statements the next time you feel yourself becoming overwhelmed by your feelings. It is important to own your feelings but not let them overtake you. When you are in PTG, you notice the feelings and make the choice to acknowledge them and move on.

Many people have benefitted from these statements as they encourage people to change their focus. As you read the following statements, feel free to create your own.

Can you choose five of these statements that would support you as you walk through life together? Please number your top five with number one being your favorite practical statement that would reassure you as you walk through life together.

1. Stay calm. Just relax.
2. As long as I keep my cool, I am in control.
3. Just roll with the punches and do not get bent out of shape.
4. Think of what you want to get out of this.
5. You do not need to prove yourself to anyone.
6. There is no point in getting mad.
7. Look for the positives.
8. I am not going to let this get to me.
9. If my intentions are true, what they think of me is none of my business.
10. He is probably really unhappy if he's acting that irritable.
11. What she says about me does not need to define me.
12. I cannot expect people to act the way I want them to all the time.
13. My muscles feel tight. Time to relax.
14. I will look for a solution that is a win-win opportunity for both of us.
15. Let's work this problem out. Maybe he has a point.
16. I am not going to be pushed around, but I am not going to lose it either.

17. I am under control. I can handle this.

18. I have a right to be annoyed, but let's try to reason this out.

19. Slow down. Take a few deep breaths.

20. I can breathe through this.

These next statements are more philosophical in nature and are coping statements to remind you not to be hijacked by your situation or emotions. Which statements resonate with you? How might you apply them to your relationship so that you take things less personally and trust that the universe has your back? Being in Post-Traumatic Growth does not mean you do not have challenges, but it does mean that you are less affected by the challenges and are more willing to believe and know that you will get through them.

In a check-in, share with your spouse which philosophical statements brought comfort to you as you think about struggles in your life.

PHILOSOPHICAL COPING STATEMENTS

1. It is time to take care of you.

2. Create a family of choice.

3. Spray yourself with Teflon and let go.

4. Fake it until you make it, act as if.

5. One day at a time.

6. Face your fears head-on.

7. There will only be one of you at all times—fearlessly have the courage to be yourself.

8. You can do it.
9. Keep it simple.
10. Happiness is a choice.
11. You own the power.
12. Trust your head, your heart, and your gut.
13. Nurture yourself.
14. Replenish your energy—slow down.
15. Focus on the positives.
16. Appreciate your strengths.
17. Do not be so hard on yourself.

Lastly, I thought I would include some statements that come directly from the recovery world. There is a lot of wisdom in this community, so I thought I would include some slogans here. Hopefully, it will help you both in your coping, and as you strengthen your mental agility in the third phase of Post-Traumatic Growth, you will find these coping skills help you stay focused on the mindset you need to move forward in new possibilities.

Which of these slogans have helped you in your own personal recovery or with your relationship? Check all that apply.

RECOVERY SLOGANS

1. One day at a time.
2. Let go and let God
3. Act as if.
4. This too shall pass.
5. Expect miracles.
6. I cannot, He can, I think I'll let Him.
7. Sobriety is a journey, not a destination.
8. Faith without works is dead.
9. To thine own self be true.
10. Live in the NOW.
11. If God seems far away, who moved?
12. Turn it over.
13. Willingness is the key.
14. More will be revealed.
15. Before you say I can't, say I will try.
16. The price for serenity and sanity is self-sacrifice.
17. E.G.O. = Edging God Out
18. Serenity is not freedom from the storm, but peace amid the storm.
19. Remember nothing is going to happen today that you and God cannot handle.

20. Pain is the touchstone of spiritual growth.

21. Have an Attitude of Gratitude.

22. You will intuitively know.

23. We have a choice.

24. F.E.A.R. = False Evidence Appearing Real

25. This too shall pass.

THE PROCESS OF FORGIVENESS

As partner-sensitive professionals, we will tell partners that they never *need* to forgive their spouse. And although I endorse that wholeheartedly, I also believe that for you both to heal the relationship, you will need to work on forgiveness as a goal.

For the Partner: You have likely heard that forgiveness is for the person who feels the anger and resentment. Letting go of the resentment that has fueled your anger will set you free.

If you think about all the feelings attached to the betrayal, you will feel hijacked by them, which keeps you locked into a mind state of terror and control. Releasing your feelings will liberate you and allow you to experience a new possibility for your life.

Forgiving does not mean that you condone the behavior, but it is a process that allows you to emotionally detach from the betrayal.

TRAUMA-BASED MODEL OF FORGIVENESS

In this model, forgiveness is an ongoing process that takes time, rather than a distinct event. Gordon and Baucom (1998) presented a three-stage forgiveness model that conceptualized recovery from affairs as essentially the same as the process of recovery from any interpersonal trauma.

I have not been able to find any research that talks about forgiveness after sexual addiction and partner betrayal, but these stages fit the PTG research.

The stages in this model are:

- I. Dealing with the impact
- II. Search for meaning
- III. Recovery or moving forward

Individuals who are in Stage I report the least amount of forgiveness, and individuals in Stage III report the highest levels of forgiveness. That fits the integration of the three phases of partner betrayal and the research about Post-Traumatic Growth. It also endorses why it can take three to five years to work through Phases 1 and 2—so that you get through your own search for meaning as a couple and then begin to move forward as a couple and give back.*

The tough questions involve finding meaning from this ordeal. The toughest questions that I will ask you are:

What has this excruciating pain taught you? ________________________________

____

____

____

____

*Heintzelman, Ashley & Murdock, Nancy & Krycak, Romana & Seay, Larissa (2014).

What meaning have you applied to this ordeal?____________________________

____

____

____

____

Has it given you a new sense of purpose?_______________________________

____

____

____

____

Are you helping others as a result of it?_______________________________

____

____

____

____

In PTG, many couples find that trusting in the following beliefs is crucial to their healing:

- God can bring purpose
- God can give purpose to your pain
- Love is a Choice
- Forgiveness is a Choice
- Happiness is a Choice

You can choose to let go of your suffering and allow it to transform you into something that gives YOU purpose as a couple. When you do, you have rounded the corner of Post-Traumatic Growth!

YOUR NEEDS AS A COUPLE

As you strengthen PTG, you will find opportunities to bond and co-create together. This requires that you pay attention to what each of you need and make a note to brainstorm activities that you implement in your outer circle. This is the fun part of the relationship. You are working hard on making new memories, and you are also furthering your trust.

Start working on your couple's healthy circle behaviors and make plans that you can do together.

Ask yourselves, "What can we change to fine tune our marriage?"

1. More appreciation?
2. More teamwork?
3. More intentional self-care?
4. More time to myself?
5. More check-ins?
6. More family time?
7. More family meetings?
8. More volunteering?

Working on strengthening and building a solid marriage takes good communication. Do not be afraid of asking the hard questions that will move you both towards a happier life.

Ask yourselves the following questions:

1. What can we use from this experience? ____

2. How can we give back to our friends, our family, the community, etc.?

These are great questions to ask each other and talk about in a check-in.

Other additional questions for check-ins that increase your satisfaction in the relationship as you move forward are:

1. What do I want most from you?

2. What can we do to practice mindfulness together?

____

____

____

____

3. What can I do to show you how much I want us to be together forever?

____

____

____

____

4. What can I do to reinforce my love for you?

____

____

____

____

Create new dreams and realities that fortify how you want to live out the rest of your life. Journal about what you might want to focus on to create a more loving relationship and discuss it in your check-ins. This helps you follow my most important coaching rule: "I am 100% responsible for my behavior, no matter what has happened in my life and who has wronged me." When you ask yourself, "What do I need to do to create a more loving relationship?" you are accepting that you have the power to contribute in an important way to this relationship.

DECLARATION STATEMENTS

It is important for you to be intentional in declaring what you want for this relationship. We talked about the need for you to put into practice the belief system of: "When you conceive it and believe it, you will achieve it!"

The same thing works for the conceptualization of your marriage. What do you want to achieve as a couple? How would you like to feel as you enter into your new marriage? Create some declarations that honor your marriage and your growth. Repeat them to yourself, as a mantra for what you want in your life.

They might look like:

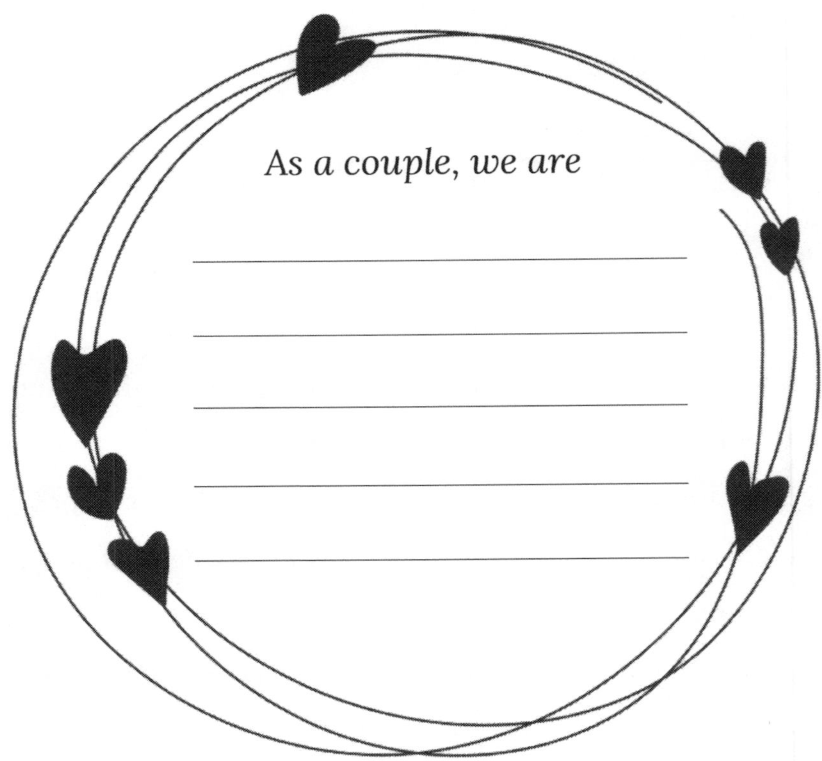

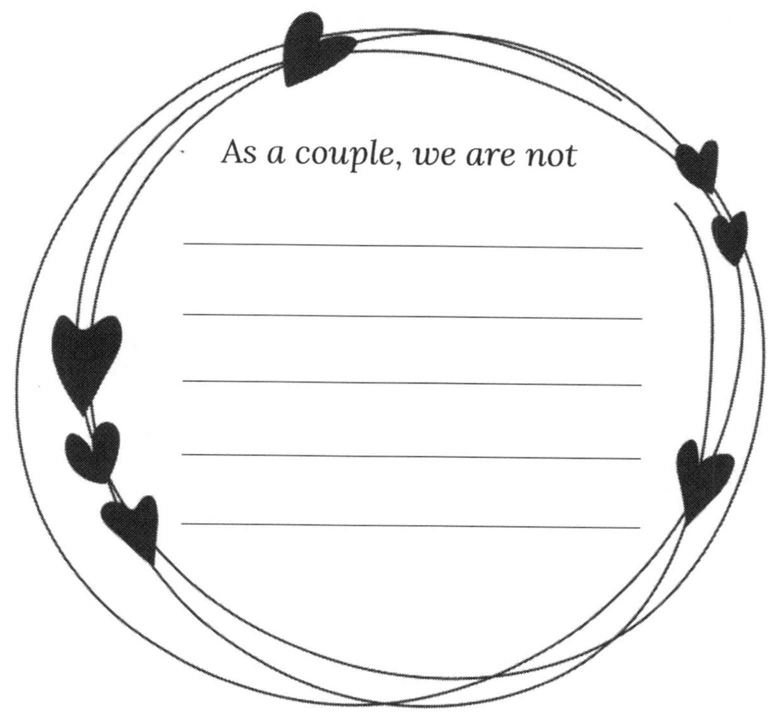
As a couple, we are not

As a couple, we want to

PHILOSOPHIES TO LIVE BY

PTG does not just happen—you must embrace it. That means you need to ascribe to the mindset that supports both of you being happy. There are some coaching principles that can reinforce these PTG philosophies. Look and decide which attitudes or mindsets that you would like to adopt. Which ones feel like the "best fit" for you?

- What You Conceive and Believe You Will Achieve
- Your Energy Flows Where Your Focus Goes
- Good Things Come from Change
- Does This Move Us Towards Each Other or Away from Each Other?
- I Create My Own Happiness
- Nothing That Is Ever Meant for Me Will Be Missed by Me
- As You Change Your View, You Will Change Your World
- The Universe Has My Back
- "You Are Never Given a Dream without also Being Given the Power to Make it Come True" ~ Richard Bach

It is so important for you to find inspiration from others. Some of you may have abandoned the guidance you acquired growing up. Others may have put inspiration on the back burner as you focused on the survival skills you needed to take the next step through partner betrayal. Now that you are in PTG, it will be important to revisit those tools that brought you comfort and clarity in your past. You may even decide to adopt some new strategies that come from inspirational teachings or guides. Be on the lookout for spirit-filled messages to take you forward on your journey.

Ask yourself the following:

- Are there Coaching Strategies that I believe have guided me/us through this process?
- Are there Spiritual Principles that have helped me/us get to the other side?
- Are there Biblical Scriptures that have comforted me/us on this journey?
- Are there Eastern Religious Spiritual Principles that have supported us as we walked this journey together?

This phase is all about changing your mind state and your mind story. Would you be willing to focus on gratitude so that you practice feeling grateful for your life, your spouse and your family? Is there a mind state that reinforces the changes that you have both made to strengthen you so that you will contribute to this world in a different way. When I was training to be a CSAT-Certified Sex Addiction Therapist, we spent one entire module learning how to reinforce the concept that recovery is the gateway for you to do great things. ERCEM is the model that reinforces the brilliance in you both as a thriving couple.

The recovery community needs more couples who won't hide from their own brilliance. In her book, Return to Love, Marianne Williamson says, "Your playing small doesn't serve the world." Ask yourself, *now that we have grown from this ordeal, how might we serve others, our community, and the world?*

Chapter 19

Review

I wrote this book for both of you! I created it so you could imagine that you were in my office every week doing the hard work of healing together. I took you through the three phases of partner betrayal and combined it with the couple's version of *Help. Her. Heal.* You may have finished the course, but you have not finished the journey. You will have many opportunities to strengthen your relationship, and for that I am so grateful.

I believe in my heart that couples who have experienced the trauma of sex addiction can heal if they work individually and together on developing the relational skills and tools to get through partner betrayal together. Your marriage can be stronger than 85% of the other relationships out there if you continue to build your identity as a couple and find purpose together in your lives.

This book has outlined how to do that together. Although a couple never has to stay together and must assess what is in their best interest, most of my couples choose to stay for a variety of reasons. The mental health therapist and the coach in me wants to help you do this because you deserve to learn how to create a new marriage with empathy, vulnerability, and trust.

You have learned what it takes to get through the three phases of partner betrayal, and the beauty of this book is that you can alter the exercises to customize what you both need.

I have developed ERCEM, which is a certification program for clinicians and coaches to assist you in doing this work. They have specialized skills to get you through all three phases of partner betrayal with the use of empathy.

I am also honored and humbled to walk beside you on this journey. It is the hardest thing you have ever done, but it has taught you so many skills that you can both use for the rest of your life and pass on to your families, children, and grandchildren.

My wish for you is that you stop talking about the past, continue to work on your future, and live your life in happiness. I have seen couples do this and know that you can too.

Thank you for believing in me enough to practice the principles in this book. Just know that my voice can go with you as you create the life you both deserve.

And as I say in every podcast, presentation, and teaching, "There will only be one of you at all times, fearlessly have the courage to work together to create the happiness that life intended you to have!"

My intention for you both is to grow stronger together everyday and make a difference in this world!

Blessings to you both!

~ *Carol Juergensen Sheets* LCSW, CCPS-S, CPC-S, CSAT, EMDR Certified

Addendum

THE ERCEM WAY

Professionals who have learned The ERCEM Way can walk you through safety and stabilization, grief, and mourning and take you into Post-Traumatic Growth.

ERCEM is the only training format that addresses the three phases of partner betrayal as defined by APSATS.

I created a curriculum, certification program, and this book to further explore the work necessary to get through Phases 2 and 3 effectively. This had not been formally developed because this is such a new field.

ERCEM is a structured, organized, systematic approach to teaching you both how to work through this together. I have been honored to take the skills and exercises from The ERCEM Way and give them to you in book format.

However, you may find it more efficient to rely on an ERCEM Specialist to get you through this work. You may have spent time and money working with professionals who did not seem to understand the dynamics of partner betrayal, so I want you to get the Gold Standard of Care when it comes to your relationship.

I am going to list some professionals that have been trained in ERCEM. For a complete list, go to my website (sexhelpwithcarolthecoach.com) and look for an ERCEM Specialist in your area who can guide you through this process. If there is no one in your state who can provide telehealth, look for a professional coach who has the designation of Certified ERCEM Specialist. They are able to work anywhere in the world to help you heal.

ERCEM CERTIFIED SPECIALISTS

(As of 4/1/2022. For an updated list, visit www.sexhelpwithcarolthecoach.com)

- Aarti Chidambaram, CCPS, CCES-S, Sr. Clinical Psychologist
  Master Practitioner Neuro-Linguistic Programming, Brainspotting Professional
  41 C, Joon Hiang Road, Singapore 548364
  +65 972-880-44 | Aarti28@hotmail.com

- Cindy Bajema, ACC, CPC, CES
  Colleyville, TX
  Cindy@corahaven.com | Cindy@visbleministries.com
  www.corahaven.com | www.nakedtruthrecovery.com

- Tiffany Comiskey, ACC, CPC, CES
  HOPE CFL 12505 Upper Harden Ave, Orlando, FL 32827
  (407) 815-3456 | Tiffany@hopecfl.com
  www.Hopecfl.com

- Cheryl McDonald, CPC
  2800 E. Enterprise Ste 333. Appleton, WI 54913
  (920) 383-1205 | Cheryl@RelationshipsMadeWhole.com
  www.RelationshipsMadeWhole.com

- Kim Hansen Petroni, MA- Counseling, BCC, CPC, CES
  Brainspotting Practitioner
  Springboro, OH
  Coachinghope4u@gmail.com
  www.Coachinghope4u.com

- Jake Porter, LPC, NCC, CSAT, CMAT, CCPS, CPC, CCTP, CCES-S
  3100 Edloe Street, Suite 210. Houston, TX 77027
  (855) 602-2554
  www.DaringVentures.com

- Donna Rennard, LCPC, CCPS, SRT, CAADC, CODP 2, CCES
  45 South Park Blvd. Glen Ellyn, IL 60137
  (708) 769-1547 | Donna@aspencounseling.org
  www.Aspencounseling.org

- Carol Sheets LCSW, CSAT, CCPC-S, CPC-S, PCC, CCES-S
  ERCEM Consultant
  Strategic Coaching and Therapies LLC
  8872 Crystal River Dr. Indianapolis, IN 46240
  (317) 847-2244 | carol@carolthecoach.com
  www.sexhelpwithcarolthecoach.com

- Susie Wilson, MA, LPC, LMHC, CCPS, CCES
  Wellsprings Counseling Center
  22-08 Rte 208, Fairlawn, NJ 07410
  (201) 956-6363 ext. 10
  Additional location: Nyack, NY 10960
  Susiew@wellsprings.org
  www.Wellsprings.org

ERCEM CANDIDATES IN PROCESS OF OBTAINING CERTIFICATION

(As of 4/1/2022. For an updated list, visit www.sexhelpwithcarolthecoach.com)

- James Annear, LMHC, CCPS-S, CSAT-S, CCPT
  CORE Relationship Recovery
  200 Butler St., Ste 303. West Palm Beach, FL 33407
  (561) 345-3510 | Info@HopeForUs.com
  www.HopeForUs.com

- Beth Denison, CLC, PRC, CPC
  3810 42nd Ave W. Bradenton, FL 34205
  (941) 526-4694 | Beth@TheresStillHope.org
  www.theresstillhope.org

- Debbie Ferree, CPLC, CPC
  Certified Peer Facilitator, C-SASI
  Winter Garden, FL
  (407) 797-1397 | Coachdebbieferree@gmail.com
  www.Livinginthelight.info

- Teri Matthews, CPC, CRC, ACC, CPC
  242 South Orange Avenue, #107. Brea, CA 92821
  (714) 386-9003
  teri@voiceoftruth.com
  www.voiceoftruth.com

- Susan Rankin, CPC-C
  Restoring Hearts Coaching, LLC
  Puyallup, WA
  (253) 225-8860 | susan@restoringheartscoaching.com

- Linda Wajda CPC-C,
  One Braver Life LLC
  Florida, NY
  (845) 200-5737
  www.onebraverlife.com

- Rachelle Weger, MA, PLPC, CCPS-C
  11104 Veterans Memorial Parkway. Lake St. Louis, MO 63367
  (636) 344-8401 | Info@BetrayalTraumaMO.com
  BetrayalTraumaMO.com

ERCEM TRAINEES

(As of 4/1/2022. For an updated list, visit www.sexhelpwithcarolthecoach.com)

- Jennie Bacon, MS, LPC
  Refuge Counseling Center
  Meridian ID
  Jennie@regugecounseling.com

- Stephanie Baker MS, LCPC, NCC
  EMDR Certified Therapist, CCPS-Candidate
  Warrior Programs
  1565 E. Leighfield Dr. Suite #100. Meridian, ID. 83646
  www.warriorprograms.com
  stephanie@refugecounseling.com

- Thom Bianco, MA, CPC
  Fourth Dimension Counseling
  Thom Bianco Counseling and Coaching
  Redmond, WA 98052
  (206) 755-0196

- Laura Blundo, ACC, CPC, DARTC, RLT, SEP-C
  Relationship & Betrayal Trauma Coach
  Moultonborough, NH
  (603) 986-2782 | LauraB@relationshipawakenings.com
  www.RelationshipAwakenings.com

- MaryAnn Bodnar, LMHC, CAP, CSAT, CPTT, TEP
  MAB Counseling LLC
  611 W Bay Street. Suite 1G. Tampa, FL 33606
  (515) 708-5570 | Maryann.bodnar@gmail.com
  mabcounseling.com
  MaryannBodnar.com

- Theresa Bonesteel, M.A., NCC, LPC-S, LMFT-SC
  EMDR, Brain Spotting, CSAT-C, APSATS-C,
  3039 Leaphart Rd. West Columbia, SC 29169
  (803) 465-5576 | hopeinthejourney1312@gmail.com
  www.theresabonesteel.com

- Mary Ellen Brown, CPC, BSP
  Passionate Hearts Coaching
  16 Michaelis Street. New Tecumseth ON L0L 1L0, CANADA
  www.passionatehearts.coach
  (289) 926-1010 | maryellen@passionatehearts.coach

- Bonny A Burns
  Strong Wives LLC
  186 Lake Crest Dr. Lenoir City, TN 37772
  (910) 612-7353
  www.strongwives.com

- Richard Butler, CPC, ASSAT
  UK
  +447778349071 | richardbutler2051@gmail.com
  www.holding-hope.com

- Anne Cannon, MA, MCLC
  ICF Certified Coach, CPC-C, BTRL and EFT
  Redondo Beach, CA
  (310) 909-6481

- Janice Caudill, PhD, CSAT-S, CCPS-S, CPTT-S, PBTT, IAT, SEP
  250 Adriatic Pkwy. McKinney, TX 75072
  (972) 540-9996 | Janice@intensivehope.com
  www.Intensivehope.com

- Jackie Chambers CPLC, CPSAS, PSAP, CPC-C
  Dallas, TX
  (469) 290-4322 | Jackie@redemptivejourney.com
  RedemptiveJourney.com

- Laura Childers, MA, LPC, BCN, QEEG-D
  5757 Woodway Dr., Suite 201. Houston, TX 77057
  (713) 702-2977 | Laurachilderslpc@gmail.com

- Andrew Connolly M.Ed. (Hons) Counselling, B.Min., ACSD, NZCEFT, ACC, CCSAS, CCPSCounsellor Registered with NZCCA , EFT level 2, BSP level 1.
  Counselling Creatively Ltd
  116 Fordyce Rd. Helensville 0874. New Zealand
  www.counsellingcreatively.co.nz
  Ph. 0272826305

- Karen Cooper
  Fourth Dimension Counseling
  cooperka0612@gmail.com

- MJ Denis, LPC, LMFT, CST, CCPS
  Healing From The Inside Out Counseling
  Crossroads Counseling Associates
  4131 Spicewood Springs Rd. Suite K1. Austin, TX 78759
  (512) 346-9299

- Patricia G. Doane, LCPC, CSAT-S
  9807 Veirs Drive, #301. Rockville, MD 20850
  (240) 464-8294 | (301) 983-1953
  patdoane@gmail.com

- Ellen Drews M.A., CLC, CPC-C, PSAP
  Ellen Drews Coaching and Consulting
  (941) 538-7705 | Ellen@ellendrews.com
  www.ellendrews.com

- Carin Dussé BA. Hon. Psych., ACC, CCPS, CPTM13
  Brainspotting Practitioner
  13 Seals Craig View. Burntisland, Scotland. KY3 0AX
  +44 (0)783625262 | carin@shatteredheartsrevived.com
  https://www.shatteredheartsrevived.com

- Michelle Dyett-Welcome MSEd., PCC, TICC, CPC
  Far Rockaway, NY 11691
  (718) 415-5919 | michelle@bectspsa.com
  http://bectspsa.com

- Jacki Elsom
  Jacki Grace Coaching
  14612 NE 50th Street. Vancouver, WA 98682
  (503) 481-5438

- Cat Etherington, CPC
  Glenn House, Houston Park, Salford, M50 2RP
  0161 637 0240 | cat@visibleministries.com
  www.nakedtruthrecovery.com

- Heather Fritch, PhD, LPC
  Foundations Counseling Center
  (757) 354-4306
  www.drheatherfritch.com

- Sibylle Georgianna, Ph.D., CST, CSAT, CCPS, C-EMDR
  The Leadership Practice, Psychology Consultations Inc., and its affiliates
  Sexual Health of Orange County, CA, and Tools for Sustainable Vitality Inc.
  25411 Cabot Road Suite 102, Laguna Hills, CA 92653
  (917) 620-0481 | toolsforvitality@gmx.de
  https://sexualhealthoc.com

- Patricia Goulbourne, BA, CPCC
  UR-Essence, Patricia Goulbourne Coaching
  Calgary, Alberta, Canada
  patricia@ur-essence.com
  www.patriciagoulbourne.com

- Cherie' Hammer, MA, LPC, EMDR, CCPS
  CMH Counseling Services, LLC
  5650 Greenwood Plaza Blvd. #202. Greenwood Village, CO 80111
  (303) 903-0278
  www.cmhcounseling.com

- Dr. Crystal Hollenbeck, CST, CSAT, CCPS, CCTP
  H3 Counseling
  7345 W. Sand Lake Road, Suite 303, Orlando, FL 32819
  (407) 408-6521
  www.CrystalHollenbeck.com

- Fran Hopwood CPC, Bravehearts Professional
  Naked Truth Recovery
  Glenn House, Houston Park, Media City, SALFORD, M50 2RP, UK
  fran@visibleministries.com
  www.nakedtruthrecovery.com

- Julianne Jackson MEd, MS, LPC, CCPS
  Arise Counseling Services LLC
  Mobile, AL
  (251) 216-9653 | jjackson@arisecounselingservices.org
  www.arisecounselingservices.org

- Aviva Kohl LCSW-R, CSAT, CCPS-C
  Connections Well-being Center
  16 Wits End. Spring Valley, NY 10977
  Avivakohl@connectionswellbeingcenter.com

- Christina Lin, MS, CPC, ACC
  Redlands, CA
  (909) 553-8776 | Jointhemiddlespace@gmail.com
  www.Jointhemiddlespace.com

- Rebecca Maestas, LMSW, CCPS
  Christian Counseling & Coaching
  845 Sullivan Ave. Farmington NM 87401
  (505) 609-8686 | rebecca@becomingyou.coach
  www.becomingyou.coach

- Rachel Middleton BA Counselling
  Adv Dip Counselling & Family Therapy
  Dip of Counselling (Christian)
  Hav-a-chat Services WA
  Mt Helena, Western Australia, 6082
  +61 400 593 331 | info@hav-a-chat.com.a
  www.hav-a-chat.com.au

- Karina Mueller, LSW, MPA, CCPS
  Firefly Transformations
  Denver, CO
  (347) 221-3347

- Brian Mulder BCMMHC
  Living Truth
  474 Lake Shore CT. Franklin, IN 46131
  (847) 651-8600 | briankmulder@gmail.com
  living-truth.org/mulder

- Sue Nazar, MA, LPC, CCPS
  Resilience Mental Health, PLLC
  (512) 375-3360 | sue@resiliencementalhealth.net

- Rebecca Orms, CPLC, CPC-c, CFSAS
  Broken & Beloved Coaching, PLLC
  526 E Commerce St, Ste A. Fairfield, TX 75840
  (903) 390-0068
  www.brokenandbelovedcoaching.org

- Kirsi Paulin
  Turku, Finland, Europe.
  kirsi.paulin@addicare.fi
  www.addicare.fi

- Brenda Petruska
  Coach ACC, APSATS-CPC-C
  Indianapolis, IN
  (317) 797-8045 | brenda@brendapetruska.com
  brendapetruska.com

- Tal Prince, LPC, NCC, CSAT, CPTT, Director
  Insights Counseling Center
  200 Cahaba Park Circle, Suite 214. Birmingham, AL 35242
  (205) 903.6282 | Tal@insightscc.com
  www.insightscc.com

- Teresa Prince, MA, NCC, ALC, ASAT, CCPS-C
  Insights Counseling Center
  200 Cahaba Park Circle Suite 214. Birmingham AL 35242
  205-903-6282 | teresa@insightscc.com
  www.insightscc.com

- Heather L Putney
  Untethered Therapy
  570 Lincoln Avenue. Bellevue PA 15202
  (412) 213-8633

- Shawna Schumacher, LMFT, CCPS
  608 College Ave. Santa Rosa, CA 95404
  (707) 207-8230 | shawna@shawnaschumacher.com
  www.shawnaschumacher.com

- Rosemary Smith LCSW, CSAT, CCPS-c, EMDR Certified
  859 S. Yellowstone Hwy, Suite 304
  Rexburg, ID 83440
  (208) 313-1203 | Smithr58@gmail.com
  www.cornerstonecounselingrexburg.com

- Dara M. Stockton, M.A., LMFT, LPC, CSAT, CPTT
  Renewed Hope Counseling LLC
  2230 Towne Lake Parkway. Building 200, Suite 120. Woodstock, GA 30189
  (770) 617-5145 | dara.stockton@comcast.net
  www.newhope-counselingcenter.com

- Karla Summey, BN, ACC, CPC
  Karla Summey Coaching
  Richardson TX
  (214) 842-7333 | karlasummey@gmail.com
  www.karlasummey.com,

- Sandi Timmer, MA, APCC 7006, CCPS
  7403 La Tijera Blvd. #003. Los Angeles, CA 90045
  Sandi.timr@gmail.com
  Sandi@centerforintegrativechange.com

- Eric Tooley, MA, LPC, NCC, CSAT, IAT, CCPS, CPSAS
  250 Adriatic Parkway, McKinney, TX 75072
  (972) 439-5731 | Eric@intensivehope.com
  www.intensivehope.com

- Angela Tooley CPC-C
  Noble Choices
  Allen, TX
  (214) 415-4555
  www.Noblechoices.org

- Tanya Uribes
  Tanya Uribes Coaching
  223 Greenbriar CT. Redlands, CA 92374
  (909) 477-0269
  www.tanyauribes.com

- Jennifer Utech, LPC, CCPS-C
  8859 Cincinnati Dayton Rd, #203
  West Chester, OH 45069
  (513) 443-6494 | Jenn@bytherivercounseling.com
  www.Bytherivercounseling.com

- Jo Vanatta, CHC, CFSAS, BTRL, PSAP
  Betrayal Undone
  208 W Broadway St. Unit B
  Kennedale, TX 76060
  (214) 984-4332
  www.betrayalundone.com

- Cheryl Vance, MA, LMFT
  Indy Psych
  9465 Counselors Row, Suite 200. Indianapolis, IN 46240
  (317) 514-0491 | cherylvance.lmft@gmail.com
  indypsych.com

- Jeanne Vattuone, LCSW, CCPS-S, CSAT-S, CPTT-S
  Willow Tree Counseling
  608 College Ave, Santa Rosa CA 95404
  707-200-2332 | Jeanne@WillowTreeSantaRosa.com

- Charlene Young
  Houston's First Julianna Poor Memorial Counseling Center
  7401 Katy Fwy, Houston, TX 77024
  (713) 335-6462

INTENSIVES FOR COUPLES

Heidi Kinsella, LMHC, SUDP, CSAT, CPTT, CMAT, EMDR trained. Equine Assisted Mental Health Practitioner-in training. Licensed in the states of Washington, Alaska, Hawaii, Idaho, Montana and Arizona. Office locations in Issaquah, Washington, Kirkland, Washington and Maple Valley, Washington. Offering 3-4 day intensives over long weekends for Sex Addiction, Betrayed Partners, using the partner sensitive Help. Her. Heal and ERCEM models.

Resources

- Training Organization for Certified Partner-Sensitive Specialists: The Association of Partners of Sex Addicts Trauma Specialists (APSATS.org)
- Training Organization for Certified Empathy Specialists: The Early Recovery Couples Empathy Model (sexhelpwithcarolthecoach.com)
- Training Organization for Certified Sex Addictions Therapist CSATS: The International Institute for Trauma and Addiction Professionals (IITAP.com)
- A Twelve-Step Program of Recovery from Sex Addiction: Sex Addicts Anonymous (ssa-recovery.org)
- A Twelve-Step Program of Recovery from Lust, Sex, and Pornography Addiction: Sexaholics Anonymous (sa.org)
- Groups for Men Wanting to Heal from Unwanted Sexual Behavior and Betrayal Trauma: Pure Desire Ministries (puredesire.org)
- Groups for Men Wanting to Heal from Unwanted Sexual Behavior and Betrayal Trauma: Men in the Battle (wild@heart.org)

References

CHAPTER 1

Brown, B. (2013). *Daring Greatly: How the Courage to Be Vulnerable Transforms the Way We Live, Love, Parent and Lead*. London, England: Penguin.

Juergensen, K., Sheets, C., & Katz, A. J. (2019). *Help. Her. Heal: An Empathy Workbook for Sex Addicts to Help Their Partners Heal*. Long Beach, CA: Sano Press.

CHAPTER 3

Alcoholics Anonymous Big Book. (2002). 4th ed. New York, NY: Alcoholics Anonymous World Services.

CHAPTER 4

Carnes, P. (2001) *Facing the Shadows Starting Sexual and Relationship Recovery*. Gentle Path Press.

Herman, J. (2015). *Trauma and Recovery*. New York, NY: Basic Books.

Steffens, B. and Means, M. (2009) *Your Sexually Addicted Spouse: How Partners Can Cope and Heal*. New Horizon Press Books.

CHAPTER 6

Brown, B. (2021) *Atlas of the Heart: Mapping Meaningful Connection and the Language of Human Experience*. Random House Publishing Group.

Carnes, P. (2009) *Recovery Zone, Vol. 1: Making Changes that Last—The Internal Tasks*. Gentle Path Press.

Corley, M. & Schneider, Jennifer. (2002). *Disclosing Secrets: Guidelines for Therapists Working with Sex Addicts and Co-addicts. Sexual Addiction & Compulsivity.* 9. 43-67. 10.1080/107201602317346638.

Caudill, J. & Drake, D. Full *Disclosure: How to Share the Truth After Sexual Betrayal, Volume 1.*

Caudill, J. & Drake, D. Full *Disclosure: Seeking Truth After Sexual Betrayal, Volume 1: How Disclosure Can Help You Heal.*

Caudill, J. & Drake, D. Full *Disclosure: Seeking Truth After Sexual Betrayal, Volume 2: Preparing for Disclosure on Your Terms.*

CHAPTER 7

Juergensen Sheets, C., & Katz, A. J. (2019). *Help. Her. Heal: An Empathy Workbook for Sex Addicts to Help Their Partners Heal.* Long Beach, CA: Sano Press.

Juergensen Sheets, C., & Turo-Shields, C. (2020) *Unleashing Your Power Moving Through the Trauma of Partner Betrayal.* Long Beach, CA: Sano Press.

CHAPTER 8

Brown, B. (2013). *Daring Greatly: How the Courage to Be Vulnerable Transforms the Way We Live, Love, Parent and Lead.* London, England: Penguin.

Caudill, J. & Drake, D. Full *Disclosure: How to Share the Truth After Sexual Betrayal, Volume 1.*

Caudill, J. & Drake, D. Full *Disclosure: Seeking Truth After Sexual Betrayal, Volume 1: How Disclosure Can Help You Heal.*

Caudill, J. & Drake, D. *Full Disclosure: Seeking Truth After Sexual Betrayal, Volume 2: Preparing for Disclosure on Your Terms.*

CHAPTER 9

Gottman, J. (2000). *The Seven Principles for Making Marriage Work.* London, England: Orion.

CHAPTER 10

Juergensen Sheets, C., & Katz, A. J. (2019). *Help. Her. Heal: An Empathy Workbook for Sex Addicts to Help Their Partners Heal.* Long Beach, CA: Sano Press.

CHAPTER 11

Carnes, P. (2001) *Facing the Shadows Starting Sexual and Relationship Recovery.* Gentle Path Press.

Ford, Darrin (2018). *Awakening from the Sexually Addicted Mind: A Guide to Compassionate Recovery.* Claremont, CA: Sano Press.

Gottman, J. (2000). *The Seven Principles for Making Marriage Work.* London, England: Orion.

CHAPTER 12

Freyd, J.J. (1997). "Violations of power, adaptive blindness, and betrayal trauma theory." Feminism & Psychology, 7, 22-32.

Henderson, W. (2002). *The Science of Soulmates.* Booksurge LLC Edition.

International Service Organization of SAA. (2000). “The Three Circles Redefining Sexual Sobriety in SAA.”

Juergensen Sheets, C., & Katz, A. J. (2019). *Help. Her. Heal: An Empathy Workbook for Sex Addicts to Help Their Partners Heal*. Long Beach, CA: Sano Press.

CHAPTER 13

Juergensen Sheets, C., & Katz, A. J. (2019). *Help. Her. Heal: An Empathy Workbook for Sex Addicts to Help Their Partners Heal*. Long Beach, CA: Sano Press.

Ruiz, D.M. (2001). *The Four Agreements*. San Rafael, CA: Amber-Allen Publishing.

CHAPTER 15

Bercaw, B., & Bercaw, G. (2010). *The Couple's Guide to Intimacy: How Sexual Reintegration Therapy Can Help Your Relationship*. California Center for Healing, CA.

Chapman, G. D. (2010). *The Five Love Languages*. Farmington Hills, MI: Walker.

Juergensen Sheets, C., & Katz, A. J. (2019). *Help. Her. Heal: An Empathy Workbook for Sex Addicts to Help Their Partners Heal*. Long Beach, CA: Sano Press.

Lewis, L.D. (1998) *The Eight Levels of Intimacy*. Couples Company, Inc.

Schnarch, D. (1991) *Constructing the Sexual Crucible An Integration of Sexual and Marital Therapy*. Norton and Company, Incorporated.

CHAPTER 16

Van der Kolk, B.A. (2014) *The Body Keeps the Score: Brain, Mind, and Body in the Healing of Trauma*. New York, New York: Penguin Books

CHAPTER 18

Alcoholics Anonymous World Services.

Dyer, W. W. (2007). *Change Your Thoughts-Change Your Life: Living the Wisdom of the Tao*, Hayhouse Carlos Bad, CA.

Calhoun, L. G., Cann, A., & Tedeschi, R. G. (2010). “The posttraumatic growth model: sociocultural considerations.” In T. Weiss & R. Berger (Eds.), *Posttraumatic Growth and Culturally Competent Practice: Lessons Learned From Around the Globe* (pp. 1–14). John Wiley & Sons, Inc.

Ford, Darrin (2018). *Awakening from the Sexually Addicted Mind: A Guide to Compassionate Recovery*. Claremont, CA: Sano Press.

Gordon, K. C., & Baucom, D. H. (1998). “Understanding betrayals in marriage: A synthesized model of forgiveness.” *Family Process*, 37(4), 425–449. https://doi.org/10.1111/j.1545-5300.1998.00425.x

Juergensen Sheets, C., & Turo-Shields, C. (2020) *Unleashing Your Power Moving Through the Trauma of Partner Betrayal*. Long Beach, CA: Sano Press.

Shimoff, M., Kline, C., & Canfield, J. (2009). *Happy For No Reason: 7 Steps to Being Happy From the Inside Out*. Simon and Schuster. New York, NY.

Made in the USA
Las Vegas, NV
13 May 2024